Designing with

Designing with Roses
Tony Lord
Trafalgar Square Publishing

HALF TITLE PAGE *Rose 'Magenta', a vigorous Hybrid Tea capable of being grown as a shrub, underplanted with pinks.*

TITLE PAGE *Rambler rose 'Goldfinch' trained as pillars in a Monmouthshire garden.*

RIGHT *The shrub rose 'Cerise Bouquet' with its wildly exuberant growth allied to sophisticated flower shape and colour, is well suited to areas where highly cultivated gardening gives way to wildness.*

First published in the United States of America in 1999 by
Trafalgar Square Publishing,
North Pomfret, Vermont 05053

Printed in Hong Kong by Kwong Fat Offset Printing Co.

Library of Congress Catalog Card Number: 98-89785

ISBN 1-57076-148-5

Set in 11/15.2 Bembo by Frances Lincoln Limited

9 8 7 6 5 4 3 2 1

Contents

I have loved roses for as long as I have gardened: all roses – yes, even modern Hybrid Teas and Floribundas. I am passionate about their versatility for almost every garden and will not accept one jot of criticism of them from people who have habitually misused them or, worse still, never used them at all. Few genera have such floral beauty and diversity, from the simple charm of the single species such as *Rosa mulliganii* to the complex formality of historic doubles like 'Charles de Mills' and the sculptural perfection of the finest Hybrid Teas. Their petals may be as thin and translucent as tissue paper, the sunlight reflected or transmitted through them creating a shimmering kaleidoscope of delicate and harmonious hues, or they may have the opulent bloom of the richest velour. There are roses of almost every tint except blue, to flower – in temperate zones – in every season but winter. Their variety of habits, from tiniest Miniatures to large shrubs and the most rampant Ramblers, fits them to innumerable garden uses, made even more various by the efforts of breeders in recent decades. Yet although some classes of rose, for instance shrubs and Ramblers, are well understood and imaginatively used by gardeners, the potential of others has yet to be exploited to the full. Here the use of each class of rose will be analysed and suggestions given for how each can be used to maximum effect.

This then is a book not about varieties but rather about how roses can be used in the garden. There is no room for the complete story of the development and genealogy of garden roses, nor is it relevant here. However, each phase in the development of the rose has brought in new elements of garden design, made possible by the ever-increasing versatility of the rose. Thus, looking at the ways roses have been used and have changed our gardens reveals to us ways they can be used to enhance our gardens today. It should also help us to assess the possibilities of the newer classes of rose that have yet to find widespread and imaginative use. Never before have gardeners had so many distinct sorts of rose, suited to so many different roles; and never before have gardeners so wilfully failed to exploit the potential of this, the most valuable of garden plants.

I care little for gardens that depend on the beauty of flowers alone, without any consideration for the beauty of the whole. Most rose gardens would be vastly improved by digging up three-quarters of the roses and replacing them with other plants to flatter or contrast with the roses and draw attention away from their normally unappealing habit and leaves. Yet even roses of the often uncompromisingly stiff and ugly-leaved groups such as Hybrid Teas and Floribundas are not uniformly bad: many have mitigating characteristics of deportment and foliage that can make a great difference to the beauty of the garden, though such traits are seldom mentioned in flower-based descriptive books.

Photographers see the rose's faults all too readily, knowing that a rigid habit and lumpish, stiffly borne, harshly glittery leaves can render their pictures useless; so can a single withered bloom, a yellow or blackspotted leaf. Varieties that demand spraying to stop disease disfiguring them are at a disadvantage – and are simply not an option for the organic gardener – although much can be done to minimize disease by good culture and pruning (two aspects that will be discussed here only so far as is necessary to optimize garden effect). Rosarians have the ability of the florists of old to ignore all the rose's faults, including the imperfections of most blooms, being able to see only those flowers that are flawless. As a photographer and as a gardener, I cannot afford this luxury: the reason why a grouping of roses does not make a pleasing picture also suggests why that grouping is not effective and how it might be improved.

The value of roses must be judged by the beauty of the entire plant and of its contribution to the garden as a whole. Scale – both of the group and of its individual blooms – is crucial, and single plants of bush roses seldom work. The rose bloom is often the largest individual flower in the whole garden and can look disproportionately large, particularly if it is of a day-glo color or perched on a solitary small bush. It is for this reason that Peace looks so odd when we see it in a tiny suburban front garden. Conversely, Miniatures can look impossibly precious unless their scale is related to that of the surrounding planting; gardeners should reflect carefully on this unless they want to introduce a *Honey, I Shrunk the Kids* comic pathos to their gardens.

It must be owned that not everyone loves the old roses. All too often, for each perfect bloom there are three or four in a state of ugliness, their blooms withered or balled with grey mould. Their foliage is undistinguished, their habit ungainly or at best amorphous; unless their pruning is exemplary, their blooms can be few and fleeting. Rosarians, and romantics like Vita Sackville-West, are oblivious to these faults and see only the flawless blooms. But with perfect cultural conditions, pruning and training, the defects of the old roses can be substantially overcome.

Nor are bedding roses universally loved. Recent years have undeniably seen a decline in their popularity: in Britain this is witnessed by a drop of two-thirds in the number of rootstocks imported since the 1960s and a sharp drop in the yearly number of new Hybrid Teas submitted to the trials of the Royal National Rose Society. The unimaginative use of bedding roses, which generally entails filling each bed with one rose variety and no other plants, has rightly attracted criticism, for example from Stephen Lacey who has likened the practice to "Las Vegas all summer, and the Somme all winter." The Rose Society has countered such opinions by suggesting that this decline in popularity is due mainly to the perversely complex mystique surrounding the pruning and culture of bedding roses, now no longer regarded as necessary: these roses need nothing more difficult than a yearly trim with hedge-cutters and the sort of good husbandry and soil conditioning we would give to any other garden plant.

Such blandishments have failed to address the most serious complaints of the critics. Pre-eminent among these has been Christopher Lloyd, who in the early 1990s removed most (but not all) of the roses from his Lutyens-designed rose garden at Great Dixter to replace them with tropical-looking exotics. Few can doubt that the new planting has been a stunning success, far more colorful and exciting from high summer until autumn, an imaginative replacement for a universal but inadequate style of gardening that should have disappeared, or at least been refined to minimize its faults, decades ago. Rosarians now cross themselves and curse darkly at the very mention of the infidel Lloyd. But I have yet to hear any of them provide convincing arguments to counter Christopher Lloyd's criticisms, nor do we see from them many examples of the use of modern roses that are beautiful by absolute standards, the strongest possible justification for the continued supremacy of the rose in the summer garden.

Christopher Lloyd's complaints about roses are perhaps most clearly set out in his *The Adventurous Gardener* (1983). Although he fairly provides some of the rosarians' counters to his criticisms, he does not give them all, nor do rosarians themselves seem to have published a balanced response. I hope he will forgive my attempt to weigh the arguments on both sides near the start of my book, so that readers can assess for themselves whether to read further or simply dig out their roses and plant cannas and dahlias.

Firstly, roses are "much overplanted." I agree with this: any bad or ineffective use of a plant is one planting too many; it is not surprising that a genus that is more often used than any other is also more frequently poorly used; roses are placed with more recklessness than we would accord, say, the precious blue of a ceanothus. But I am not so sure that roses still "feature too prominently in our gardens," as Mr Lloyd asserts: provided they are sympathetically used, I would like to see even more of them. Roses are so versatile that many more opportunities to use them to spectacular effect could be seized.

I agree with him that we too often see roses arranged in "a horrible jarring jumble of strong colors." This is not the roses' fault, nor does it diminish their value; it indicates that we use them with too little consideration of color combinations and often as single specimens when groups might look more harmonious. Nor can I disagree that, when out of flower, rose bushes are "singularly unlovely" and that they need to be mixed with other plants if they are to be successfully absorbed into the garden. However, this is equally true of many other popular plants whose floral qualities make them indispensable – narcissi, penstemons, chrysanthemums, daylilies, fuchsias and Mr Lloyd's beloved dahlias, to name a few.

Then there is the "notion that roses are labor-saving:" "Complete fallacy," says Mr Lloyd, nor do they offer the opportunity for change and different seasons of display, spring as well as summer and autumn, given by bedding. True, deadheading and pruning are essential for maximum effect but this amounts to little more effort per unit area per year than for most herbaceous planting and a good deal less than for bedding. If a rose monoculture and disease-prone varieties are avoided, the need for spraying is almost eliminated. Those wanting to ring the changes can space their roses widely enough to admit planting between and beneath, giving the opportunity for variations from year to year.

Christopher Lloyd suggests that those who value bush roses for cutting would be better advised to use something less stiff. This is a sweeping statement: there are plenty of bush roses with enough grace to be used in this way, admittedly including some of the older varieties such as the sisters 'Ophelia', 'Madame Butterfly' and 'Lady Sylvia' as well as Iceberg and 'Michèle Meilland'. Even rather more rigid varieties, such as Margaret Merril, can happily be assimilated in arrangements if other flowers are used to hide their stiffness. The bunch of stocks or pinks that Christopher Lloyd suggests in their place are not direct equivalents, having less subtlety of flower shading, texture, form (including sculptural shape) and line quality, nor are stocks and pinks as evocative as the old roses of a romantic past. But the qualities of individual blooms do not figure largely in the thoughts or writings of a gardener who strives constantly, heroically and successfully for bold effect of foliage against flower or of one plant group against the next. Not all gardeners have the same priorities: there are many who derive great pleasure from the bloom itself.

Some gardeners eschew bush roses but get "bogged down" with old shrub roses. Christopher Lloyd considers that these are exacting, demand careful management and look dull unless complemented by companion plants. I agree: though they have a subtlety and romance lacking in some of the newer varieties, these qualities must be offset against the wretchedness of an old rose covered from top to toe in dead and dying blooms. I cannot ignore such nastiness and, though I love old shrub roses, couldn't tolerate them unless they were deadheaded regularly, not an easy task if bushes are large and thorny. To be fair to the roses, they are not alone in this: other shrubs such as rhododendrons, buddlejas, lilacs and many camellias look equally hideous as their blooms fade.

Mr Lloyd summarizes by suggesting that the rose should be "considered as a companion for other plants rather than as an isolate." I cannot fault this. With the possible exceptions of two French gardens, Bagatelle in the Bois de Boulogne in Paris and the Roseraie Départementale du Val-de-Marne at L'Haÿ-les-Roses, gardens that rely on roses alone rarely give as much pleasure as those with a harmonious combination of plants.

For all Christopher Lloyd's criticisms, however, I am still convinced that the rose is the queen of flowers, the most useful of all genera of hardy garden plants. There is no other that produces abundant blooms of so many excellent qualities for so long, nor can any other match it for versatility or garden usefulness.

From the 1950s onwards I have experienced roses at first hand and watched their development, using them and working with them at home and in other people's gardens, including those of the National Trust of England, Wales and Northern Ireland. When I was five, my parents bought an Edwardian house in north Leeds with a long, narrow and overgrown garden. A few roses survived, weaving themselves through untidy borders and brambles, their gorgeous and sophisticated flowers contrasting with surrounding dereliction. Here were the luscious pink Bourbon 'Mrs Paul', voluptuous 'Climbing Mme Caroline Testout' plus an old and velvety Hybrid Perpetual, still unidentified but perhaps 'Louis van Houtte', its scent of extraordinary richness and complexity. Some, such as tousled 'De la Grifferaie', its blooms an unpredictable mix of crimson, pink and near white, were rootstocks for some long-lost treasure. Gawky Rugosa 'Hollandica' was another such, prized for its few crumpled flowers of deep rose satin. Here bumble bees bustled, the half-open blooms reverberating with their buzzing, a sound I always associate with balmy summer days.

We cleared the borders and added Hybrid Teas. To a child, as I was then, the appeal of Hybrid Teas was simple and direct: they had a sculptural shape, bold lines and often bright colors; their unfolding from a tiny bud seemed miraculous. That era, the 1950s, was a time of excitement for rose lovers: the efforts of the previous fifty years, using *Rosa foetida* to create rich yellows and its sport the Austrian copper briar for vibrant geranium reds and bicolors, were approaching perfection. It is easy for the snob to dismiss such qualities for their lack of subtlety but they remain positive attributes that enrich the garden, although as we grow older we learn to use them with discretion, where they are appropriate.

Among those we planted in our garden were 'Opéra', more Offenbach than Mozart in gaudy carmine-red suffused with peach; 'Shot Silk', paler and more appealing; 'Madame Dieudonné', quite shockingly bicolored and not a good "doer"; 'Serenade', with petals of salmon pink reversing to rose-red, the opposite of the dark top and light underside of the Austrian copper and an interesting effect, though marred by stiff deportment; the Wagnerian soprano 'Helen Traubel', with apricot blooms of rather poor shape, though the color was then so unusual that she was welcomed; 'Josephine Bruce', with wide, blood-red velour blooms that were, and still are, remarkable; Peace (1945) had to be there, though then as now it was so astonishingly large and vigorous that it seemed quite out of scale with the other roses, indeed with the rest of the garden. None of these prodigies pleased me half as much as the radiantly beautiful and elegant 'Michèle Meilland' (1945): borne on long stems with silk-sheened, not harshly glossy, foliage, the long flesh-pink buds unfurl gently, without ever recurving too much. Even when fully open and a little untidily informal, this is always a paragon of elegance, subtly colored and charming. Though she suffers from a little more blackspot now, Michèle still seems to me to be one of the classic roses of the mid-twentieth century.

My teenage years in the 1960s brought a perverse desire to rip up the garden and remake it. I uprooted the roses and made a new border where I could plant favorite Hybrid Teas with one or two of the choicest new Floribundas, plus some furnishing plants to hide their bare ankles and provide a contrast in leaf texture and color. The sixties was a golden age for rose lovers, with many first-rate new varieties, often in rich, vibrant and sometimes rather garish colors; they had their own typical shape, buxom, full, usually high-centered, the petals scrolled back rather too much to be considered classically elegant. I tried to study every new rose as it appeared, examining them at Roundhay Flower Show and the Great Yorkshire Show in the magnificent displays of McGredy's, Mattock's, Wheatcroft's and the other leading rose nurseries. Like it or loathe it, the shining vermilion of Tropicana (1960) was a turning point, though it proved a difficult color to blend. I couldn't love 'Masquerade', its chameleon yellow, orange and red, its untidy flowers and ungainly habit just too hard to combine with the other contents of our garden, though Vita Sackville-West used it to great effect at Sissinghurst; Graham Stuart Thomas values it for its second flush when its autumnal tones seem more natural and blend happily with the hot colors common in late flowers. 'Rumba' has a similar color scheme, though it is more tidy in flower and habit and less prone to blotchy blooms; it was still too difficult to combine and also had to go.

Those who liked rich coral had plenty of choice: Mischief, Fragrant Cloud and 'Irish Mist', all excellent, gave me quite enough of this color; I could manage without 'City of Leeds', grown in quantity by partisan locals but seeming to me too stiffly upright and lacking in flower quality. I liked salmon-pink Blessings® not just for its flowers, which were good enough, but also for its bright red young foliage; if pruned early, this could be used to splendid effect, harmonizing with red Cowichan polyanthus and contrasting with narcissi and tulips planted beneath its feet. Iceberg (1958) was not at all typical of Floribundas of its day, its slender flower stems, long-pointed leaflets and ability to produce flowers from the most spindly shoots showing characteristics more commonly found in the China roses. I grew one bush, pruned lightly, as a large and spectacularly floriferous shrub.

I grew another Iceberg as a standard with steeply banked perennials beneath in a narrow border that had become a wall of flowers. I have to confess that I loathe standards of most Hybrid Teas and Floribundas. Usually planted among other roses of identically coarse foliage and ungainly habit, they do little to alleviate the monotony of form and texture of their shorter bedfellows and hold aloft the ugly base of the plant for all to see. But this was a use of standards that seemed to work; some others will be covered in future chapters. In spite of a little tendency to blackspot and mildew, Iceberg remains one of the most valued and beautiful roses; I feel sure that Gertrude Jekyll would have loved it and included it in the very select canon of varieties she favored.

As a teenager I spent most pocket money and money earned from jobbing gardening on plants. There was little left for books, though I regularly scoured the local library for the latest gardening titles. New books by Margery Fish or Alan Bloom always proved stimulating but in the rose world the appearance of books praising the old roses were equally inspiring: Constance Spry, the collected *Observer* articles of Vita Sackville-West and Graham Stuart Thomas's *Old Shrub Roses* (1955) all proved that old roses had characteristics of flower shape, fragrance and texture that were deliciously different from the modern roses, plus a powerful air of the romance of a bygone age. Nancy Steen's *The Charm of Old*

Roses (1966) was an inspiring account of how varieties of the last century were rediscovered in the churchyards and old homestead gardens of New Zealand, their names often lost but mostly found again through diligent research, an unusual and welcome book to find in a provincial English library.

Membership of the Royal National Rose Society brought with it the Society's excellent *Rose Annual*. This was my first introduction to an invaluable resource. I voraciously devoured each scrap of information and every picture then, and in writing this book, thirty years on, I have found no source more informative. I now have copies running from 1910 to the last issue in 1984. The best sorts of roses were considered each year and drew criticisms, comments and comparisons with newer varieties from the most expert British and a few overseas rosarians. Perhaps more importantly, each of these topics was from time to time the subject of an exhaustive review in which leading experts gave opinions on techniques, culture and varieties in the greatest detail. They did not always agree with each other, but a clear consensus was usually reached on most of the aspects of growing roses that remains as relevant today as the day it was written, and for the most part applies worldwide. Many of the varieties recommended are still the best for these uses today. For all its great merits, the *American Rose Annual* does not seem to be so exhaustive in its coverage of major topics, consisting mainly of a much greater number of shorter articles. The breadth and depth of knowledge displayed in the *Rose Annual* could hardly be acquired by any individual in a lifetime; no other publication provides anything like so much detailed information on roses. Hence my merciless plundering of this treasure house in the pages that follow.

We despatched orders to Murrell's and Mattock's and within a few years the garden contained several dozen varieties of roses ranged across most of the classes. Several became firm favorites, among them sumptuous 'Gloire de Ducher' and 'Tuscany Superb', and 'Reine Victoria', usually one of the first to flower in a warm spot near the house. *Rosa* × *centifolia* and its sport 'Muscosa' were disappointing in the cool northern climate, frequently balling up into a globe of unappealing brown mush. The Hybrid Musks were a revelation, providing some flower throughout the summer and a strong second flush in autumn.

We also included several Rugosas in the garden. Although these were excellent, vigorous and healthy, I had my doubts about them: the vividness of their shiny, deep parsley-green leaves still looks alien to me and I am not sure I like them mixed with other old roses; perhaps it is just that they are too new (mostly raised early in the twentieth century); I know if I lived in a Z4 climate where few other roses thrive, I would welcome them with open arms.

After finishing at school, I went to work in Roundhay Park near my home. Here were two rose gardens: the older one, in a walled garden with a deliciously scented phlox border along the shady side, contained mainly roses of the first half of the century, with few Victorian or post-war varieties. Here were 'Etoile de Hollande' and the excellent threesome 'Ophelia', its sport 'Madame Butterfly' and in turn its sport 'Lady Sylvia'. The new rose garden was based by L.G. Knight on one in Brighton and featured the best modern roses in a wedge-shaped central parterre with shrub rose borders around the outside. Pruning these was an immensely satisfying job, especially as it paid an extra (old) penny farthing an hour; I counted myself lucky to be allowed to do it, being untrained and not a member of the trade union.

After six years at college, gardening only at weekends and in holidays, I decided to take up gardening as a career and went to work at Hyde Park in London. One job here was the resoiling and replanting of the rose beds: it was then held that roses are best replanted every twelve years and resoiling is necessary to prevent rose replant disease; sterilizing would have been easier but was not then commonly used on such a small scale. Professional gardeners would now generally sterilize in such cases.

Three years training at Kew followed where I scarcely touched a single rose, nor did I at Bressingham Gardens where I worked subsequently for Alan Bloom. It was only on joining the National Trust and working, latterly as Gardens Adviser, in a widely varied range of gardens that I was again able to indulge my love of roses. For whatever other plants they did or did not contain, almost all had roses. Working with Graham Stuart Thomas was a particular privilege and it was especially interesting to help him in the assessment of the newly introduced roses from Sangerhausen in then Communist East Germany. In the years since, photography has been perhaps my strongest influence, making me look with a critical eye at roses in gardens.

This, then, is the personal history that has led to the pages that follow: an analysis of the potential and the problems of roses, and a paean to their beauty.

The Naming of Roses

Readers might be puzzled by the varied styling of rose names in the following pages. Is this a sign that the author has gone mad, or merely evidence of sloppy editing? It is neither: merely a strict application of the Codes of Nomenclature and as such a rare occurrence in rose literature. Readers who find such topics dull and pedantic might wish to skip the next paragraphs and merely be reassured that the varied presentations of names are there for a purpose. For those who are amused by such arcana, there follows an explanation of how the rules of nomenclature apply to roses and require different styles to be used for different sorts of name.

With so many thousands of varieties, some of them hundreds of years old and some known by a host of synonyms, the naming of roses is perhaps more complex than that of any other genus of garden plant. There are basically five sorts of name used for roses: botanical epithets, usually in Latin, are governed by the *International Code of Botanical Nomenclature 1994* (*ICBN*) and are given in italics; cultivar (cultivated variety) names are styled in Roman within single inverted commas and must follow the *International Code of Nomenclature of Cultivated Plants 1995* (*ICNCP*); classifications are effectively Group names, also covered by *ICNCP* and spelled with initial capital letters; trade designations or selling names, used for most modern roses, are styled in a different font, as recommended by *ICNCP*, here sans serif, without any inverted commas; lastly, there are common names, not governed by any rules and obviously differing from country to country, here styled without capitals.

The botanical epithets, which most gardeners would probably call Latin names, are made up of several parts. The most important are the genus, *Rosa*, and species, e.g., *sericea*. Other parts of the name may follow: the subspecies, varietas (botanical variety) or forma, here shown as subsp., var. and f. Each of these ranks indicates a successively less significant change in the characteristics of the plant from the original type on which the species was based. Generally a subspecies, such as *Rosa sericea* subsp. *omeiensis*, may be expected to be more markedly different from the type of a species than a varietas such as *Rosa sericea* var. *morrisonensis*, while a forma may differ in only one characteristic such as flower color, hairiness of leaf or habit.

Occasionally, when the same botanical name has been used by different botanists for different plants, the name's original author has to be appended. Thus *Rosa glauca* is a name used by five authors for five different species. Under the *ICBN*'s rule of priority, the oldest of these, *R. glauca* Pourret, published in 1788 and thus predating *R. rubrifolia* Villars (1789) for the same species, is correct, though there is still some debate about whether it is identical with *R. ferruginea* Villars (1779). It is not the same as *R. glauca* Villars, now correctly *R. caesia* subsp. *glauca* though sometimes seen in rose catalogues as *R. vosagiaca*.

Hybrid species, indicated by a multiplication sign, may occur in the wild, as does *Rosa* × *hibernica*, or have been created by hybridists, as was *R.* × *harisonii*. *ICBN* also insists that names such as this last that commemorate a person must always be based on the correct spelling of their name and that the ending of the name conforms to its rules. This requires corrections to some spellings, such as × *fortuniana* to × *fortuneana*, × *hardii* to × *hardyi*, × *mariae-graebneriae* to × *mariae-graebnerae* and *wichuraiana* to *wichurana*.

Some of the most important garden roses derive from hybrid species that might or might not have arisen in the wild such as *Rosa* × *alba* and *R.* × *centifolia*. Garden roses like each of these should only be included within these species if they are derived solely from that species, for instance sports such as *R.* × *alba* 'Alba Maxima' or *R.* × *centifolia* 'Muscosa'. Roses that show predominantly the characteristics of these two species but might involve other roses in their parentage can in these two cases be listed within the classes that bear the same names, the Albas and Centifolias.

Cultivars are distinctly different plants that may have arisen by breeding, mutation or by selection from a naturally occurring species. Their names, if published since 1958, must not be in Latin: 'Variegata' or 'Superba' would not be allowed for new plants. Cultivar names from before 1959 may validly be in Latin but must conform to the rules of spelling set out in *ICBN*. Generic names, whether in Latin (e.g., 'Corylus') or a modern language, common names (such as 'Cabbage Rose') and trademarks are not allowed as cultivar epithets. Many rose books of the late eighteenth and early nineteenth centuries, such as Redouté and Thory's *Les Roses* (1817–24) give usually two names for each variety, one in Latin, the other either a translation of the Latin or a common name. In such cases, the Latin varietal name was intended to be the rose's 'proper' name and should be used as the cultivar epithet. For example, 'Cymbifolia', corrected according to *ICBN* from Thory's *Cimbaefolia*, must be used rather than 'A Feuilles de Chanvre'

Thory's alternative name, which is in effect a common name. According to *ICNCP*, translations of Latin names or of names in any other language are not allowed as cultivar names and should be styled as trade designations (here in sans serif). Thus 'Green Rose' is not permissible for what was originally 'Viridiflora', though green rose could be a common name or Green Rose a selling name.

It is often very difficult to establish the correct cultivar epithet of an old rose found without a name; numerous muddles have resulted from tentative identifications that have later been proved to be wrong. The task is not made any easier by the fact that the same name has often been used for a handful of different varieties. The usual process is to work out the class of the rose, guess at its date of introduction and examine descriptions of all the roses of that class from an encyclopedic rose dictionary of a few years after the guessed date. Often there are about ten descriptions that fit, usually very sketchy, such as "pink, double, medium height." Some of the ten will be other cultivars that still exist and so can be eliminated; some will have been of limited popularity, seldom mentioned in rose literature and unlikely to have made their way to the country where the rose was found; these too can with tolerable certainty be eliminated. The remainder can be checked in other rose books of the time and particularly in the catalogues of the raiser, in collections such as that of the Royal Horticultural Society at Vincent Square, London. A more detailed description can often give an 80 per cent certainty that the right name has been found but one 100 per cent is almost never possible.

Many of the old roses we grow today have come to us as unnamed plants that have been reidentified in such a way. Inevitably, such identifications have seldom been proved with absolute certainty and mistakes have been made. The same rose might have been identified as being one cultivar by British gardeners and quite another in the United States or Australia. In some cases, the identity of the rose has never been lost in one of the rose's homes but a wrong identification has been supplied elsewhere and has gained widespread currency. Gardeners cannot assume that identities are correct in their own country and wrong elsewhere in the world. For instance, the superlative rose grown as 'Louise Odier' in the British Isles is called 'L'Ouche' in Germany. The 'Louise Odier' shown in the admirably encyclopedic *Botanica's Roses* is not the British one, which appears as 'L'Ouche'. Who is right? At this stage, without further research, it is impossible to say.

When identity has been proved, we should not hang on to old wrong names, however beloved and familiar they may be. The correct original name provides rose lovers with a link to a wealth of information about the variety, from old catalogues and rose books, that enriches our knowledge and understanding about its history and parentage immeasurably. Professor Arthur Tucker has proved by vapor profile analysis of its essential oils that the Damask rose grown by British gardeners for generations as 'Kazanlik' (syn. 'Trigintipetala') is not that variety at all but another Damask, 'Professeur Emile Perrot'. The true 'Kazanlik' is still found in European gardens and both cultivars are widely grown in Bulgaria for the production of attar of roses. Mystery still surrounds 'Charles de Mills' and 'Fantin-Latour', both of them varieties that seem to be much older than the names attached to them.

Classifications such as Gallica or Hybrid Musk are Group names and should relate to some recognizable morphological characteristic such as growth habit (Rambler, Climbing or Miniature) or to parentage (Centifolia or Alba), which itself visibly and predictably determines morphology. Classifications such as Old or Modern cannot be consistently applied and should not be used; admirable though they are, the English roses of David Austin do not count as a class or Group because they have no characteristic to differentiate them from other roses. However, many roses are hybrids between two classes and may with some justification be considered to belong to either of their parent classes or to both.

Throughout the book, three very general terms that should not be considered as classes will be found that describe the main sorts of rose: bush roses are generally shorter than about 4ft/1.2m and include Hybrid Teas, Floribundas, Patio roses and Miniatures, plus all but the tallest Polyanthas; shrub roses are non-climbing roses that are taller than this; climbing roses account for most of the rest, though the class of Ground Cover roses includes individual varieties that may be considered to belong to one or other of each of the three main sorts. Two "catch-all" classes of rose can cause confusion unless readers remember that the use of an initial capital letter differentiates them from the more general term, which has a lower case initial: Shrub roses include all shrub roses that do not belong to another class such as Gallica, Hybrid Musk or Rugosa; Climbing roses include all climbing roses that do not belong to another Group such as Rambler, Noisette or Climbing Hybrid Tea.

I have chosen to keep Hybrid Tea as the classification here for what the World Federation of Rose Societies now classes as Large-flowered roses, and to stick to Floribunda in preference to Cluster-flowered roses. I have sympathy with the view that, as far as the new varieties are concerned, the old names have little to do with the parentage or appearance of modern roses. However, they apply perfectly well to many of the older roses still grown, and Cluster-flowered is impossibly imprecise, describing the majority of all roses, including most species and Groups such as Ramblers and Polyanthas. There is something to be said for keeping plant names, whether for Groups or cultivars, as stable as possible and retaining names such as Hybrid Tea and Floribunda that remain the most familiar around the world. However, I have been cowardly in following the crowd by using Patio roses as the Group name for what are otherwise called Dwarf Cluster-flowered roses, a much more exact and meaningful name.

Increasingly over the last fifty years, new roses are first mentioned in print under a code name, a system that came about partly as a requirement of plant patent law, particularly in the United States. Usually the first three (sometimes two or four) letters of this derive from the breeder's name. Thus the rose sold as Tropicana in the United States and Super Star® in the British Isles was first published as 'Tanorstar' by the breeder Tantau in 1960; the rose called Iceberg in the English-speaking world, Schneewittchen in Germany and Fée des Neiges® in France first appeared in 1958 as 'Korbin' from the breeder Kordes; Meilland's 'Meban' (1955) is sold as Message in the British Isles and White Knight in the United States. The code name is the cultivar name of the rose and should appear alongside the selling name in catalogues and on labels. Many catalogues and lists print those letters derived from the breeder's name in capitals (e.g. 'KORbin', 'MEban') but this convention is not sanctioned by *ICNCP*. Those who wish to propagate roses that have code names, particularly if they intend to sell them, should check that there are no legal bars such as plant breeder's rights.

The cumbersome and irritating system of code names and selling names has advantages for the breeder: roses can be bulked up and trialled, marketing can begin and information can be published about them before selling names for each country have been decided. The complex business of determining the most commercial trade designation for each country, establishing that this is not already trademarked and, in many cases, registering it as a trademark can proceed in tandem with the bulking up of stock of the new rose prior to release.

Breeders can use whatever names they wish as selling names, provided they do not breach trademark laws, and can have a different one for each country in which a single variety is sold. For instance, they may reuse a name of an existing cultivar: 'Schneewittchen' is also the name of a Polyantha raised in 1901 and still available from nurseries. They can also transfer their own name from an old variety to a newer, better one, as in the case of Bonica® and Cherry Brandy®. They can sell the right to attach the name of a commercial product to their rose for a fixed term, to lend that product the notional fragrance of a rose. Thus Dickson's 'Dicjana' was sold as Peaudouce, the name of a leading brand of diapers, in the British Isles for some years until the commercial arrangement ran out and this name was dropped in favor of the rose's other selling name, Elina®. And they can trademark a name first published as a cultivar name. According to *ICNCP*, this invalidates the name as a cultivar epithet, leaving it without one unless a code name is provided at this stage.

How does this nightmarish confusion help the amateur? The answer is, it doesn't. One regrets also the use of selling names that can cause confusion with common names, such as The McCartney Rose®/the Macartney rose (*Rosa bracteata*) and Eglantyne/eglantine (*R. rubiginosa*). In fact, all this seems to be directly contrary to the intention of *ICNCP*, which was devised to simplify naming, to avoid any possibility of duplication and to keep names as unchanging and international as possible, with a single acceptable name for each plant throughout the world. However, provided the code or cultivar name is always given with the selling name, amateurs have a means of tracking down the rose and information about it, even if the selling name does not appear in the rose literature of their own country. An American gardener, seeing and admiring The Times Rose in England, would be able to track it down under its code name 'Korpeahn' at home, where it is sold as Mariandel®. One wishes that all rose catalogues and books would include and adequately cross-reference code names as well as cultivar names, to make it as easy as possible to correlate selling names used in one country and those used elsewhere via the code name that unites them. Accordingly, though code names and major synonyms are not given on every occasion throughout the text, they will be found cross-referred in the index.

The Heritage of the Rose

The genus Rosa *consists of over a hundred species, all from temperate regions of the northern hemisphere and about forty-five of them from Europe.*

The exact number of species is almost impossible to quantify: many are a result of chance hybridization in the wild and owe their survival to cultivation by gardeners; as such they are discounted by some botanists from the tally of species. The oldest garden roses are hybrids or sports of species roses from Europe and the Middle East. Legends, perhaps holding a grain of truth, cluster around them. It is said, for instance, that *Rosa gallica* var. *officinalis* was brought from Palestine in 1240 by the crusader and troubadour Thibaut IV, Count of Champagne, later King Theobald I of Navarre, and cultivated around his home in Provins, south-east of Paris. Blanche, widow of Thibaut's son Henri I of Navarre, may have been responsible for the adoption of the red rose as the badge of the House of Lancaster on her marriage to Edmund Crouchback, Earl of Lancaster, second son of Henry III, in 1275.

Until it has been unravelled by the wonders of genetic fingerprinting, the true parentage of these old roses must remain to some extent a matter of conjecture. However, perhaps the most convincing scheme proposed so far is that by Gordon D. Rowley, based on the work of the geneticist Dr C.C. Hurst and shown in the charts on page 182. A full discussion of Dr Hurst's ideas on the evolution of garden roses is outside the purpose of my book: those who want to read about it can find it included in *The Graham Stuart Thomas Rose Book* (1994). The discussion here on the evolution of garden roses is restricted to the most general principles of how they came to be introduced or raised, plus a couple of comments that might shed new light on Dr Hurst's account.

Particularly since the beginning of the nineteenth century, when controlled hybridization began, nurserymen's breeding programmes and the roses they selected have been determined by the taste of the day and gradually shifting perceptions of rose beauty. Thus the flat, quartered blooms of the early nineteenth century gave way to the spherical Bourbons and Hybrid Perpetuals of the late century and ultimately to the high-centered twentieth-century Hybrid Teas with their scrolled petals. The *Rose Annual* gives insights into such changing opinions and their application. For example, in the 1922 issue we are told of faults that were not acceptable in the exhibition rose, such as quartering ("Gloire de Dijon is addicted to this") and over-doubleness, as in the cabbage roses. Today we regard these as virtues, to be enthusiastically welcomed in the English roses of David Austin and the Romantica® series from Meilland.

The evolution of the forerunners of the garden roses of today is complex. Today these old roses are classified in groups that are wildly simplistic, hiding their true parentage and the skill of their creators. Gardeners glibly call their roses Gallicas, Damasks or Centifolias without stopping to notice that many have the characteristics of two or more groups. We recognize that a Centifolia rose is one in which the attributes of *Rosa × centifolia* predominate but apparently choose to ignore the source of the rest of its traits that derive from other roses in its parentage. It seems that, particularly during the first fifty years of controlled hybridization, breeders deliberately and frequently tried to produce hybrids between two classes. Graham Thomas is one of very few rose authors to acknowledge this in his description of varieties as being "Gallica with Damask affinities" or some such. ⋆

New varieties usually arise by one of three means: chance mutation (sporting) and chance hybridization as well as deliberate hybridization. Before deliberate hybridization came into play, in about 1800, any change that occurred was fairly haphazard. Sports usually show a change in one characteristic, such as flower color, growth habit or number of petals. Thus a pink rose might mutate to a white or deeper pink variety, a bush rose might produce a climbing variant or a single rose give rise to a double. Propagating from the mutant shoot would perpetuate the new variety and, once the principles of plant breeding became known, the characteristics of the sport could be passed on to a new generation of roses. Occasionally a seedling of a wild rose might also exhibit a similar change in a single characteristic that made it more appealing to gardeners and caused it to be brought into cultivation.

Some of the ancient progenitors of garden roses, such as the Summer and Autumn Damask roses, *Rosa* × *alba* and *R.* × *centifolia*, might well be chance hybrids that had their origin in the wild, in regions where their respective parents grew together. Such accidental hybrids would occasionally have been recognized as different and, especially if they were more appealing because of, for instance, a powerful fragrance or striped or double flowers, might have been taken into cultivation. It was only with the appearance in the mid-sixteenth century of botanic gardens that more sophisticated hybrid garden roses started to appear. Here all the representatives of a single genus were grown side by side; seedlings raised from these occasionally included chance hybrids of garden merit. It is possible that some of the oldest of surviving Centifolia roses arose in Holland in this way. Dr Hurst has suggested that 'De Meaux' may have been a chance sport from the garden of Doménique Séguier, Bishop of Meaux in 1637 and one of the leading rose growers of his time, but it might equally have been a chance hybrid.

The apothecary's rose, Rosa gallica *var.* officinalis

PAGES 14–15 Rosa gallica *'Versicolor'*

An indication of the high esteem in which roses were already held at this time in continental Europe is given by the Dutch flower painters. The likes of the Bosschaert family (active in the early seventeenth century) and Jan "Velvet" Brueghel (1568–1625), followed by Rachel Ruysch (1664–1750) and Jan van Huysum (1682–1749) in the early eighteenth, showed a rich appreciation of the beauty of roses, their complexity, their delicate shading, the subtlety of their texture and the play of light on and through their petals. Indeed, the works of the old masters sometimes appear to depict new roses before they are mentioned in print: for example, a number of eighteenth-century paintings seem to show white cabbage roses some time before the first documented appearance of one, 'Unique Blanche', in 1775.

*It is sometimes assumed, for example, that all Mosses are derived from *Rosa* × *centifolia* 'Muscosa', the common Moss, though many Damask Portland Mosses are more probably the offspring of 'Quatre Saisons Blanche Mousseuse', a sport from the Autumn Damask. The richly colored Mosses such as those raised by Laffay ('Lanei', 1845, 'William Lobb', 1855 and 'Henri Martin', 1863) could have originated from self-pollinating a hybrid of a dark Gallica with a Moss or from crossing two such hybrids rather than from the original old red Moss. As Graham Thomas has pointed out, roses derived purely from *R. gallica* tend to have a sturdily upright habit, harsh-textured leaves and flowers borne aloft, erect. Many so-called Gallica roses of today also seem to be hybrids between two classes and tend to have a laxer habit.

The early rose authors knew this: they had first-hand knowledge of which varieties were being used by contemporary raisers to create the magnificent so-called Gallicas we still treasure today and they were aware that their parentage was often complex. De Pronville grouped together the cultivars of *Rosa provincialis* as defined by the botanist Willdenow, saying that they were intermediate between *R. gallica* and *R.* × *centifolia*. These and crosses between Gallicas and Damasks he called Agates (Agathes). Among them he included 'Duchesse d'Angoulême', perhaps or perhaps not the same variety we grow today which also clearly shows hybridity. English rose expert Charles Quest-Ritson has shown that seedlings from self-pollinated 'Tuscany Superb' (possibly the same as 'Rivers's Superb Tuscan') contain a proportion of repeat-blooming offspring, a sign that an autumn Damask might have been involved in their parentage.

I suspect the rich color of 'The Bishop' to be the product of a dark Gallica crossed with a Centifolia. The so-called Gallicas with a multitude of petals in a flat bloom, such as 'Charles de Mills', could derive their number of petals and flower shape from historic Centifolias such as 'De Meaux'. All these fascinating and contentious uncertainties may well be resolved through DNA fingerprinting, a technique that has the potential to give us a far clearer picture of the development of garden roses in all its complexity than Rowley and Hurst's schematic model.

The popularity of the rose in England is indicated by the prominent position roses were given among the other esteemed florists' flowers in Robert Furber's colored engravings in *The Flower Garden Display'd* of 1730–32, the first illustrated nursery catalogue. In his plate for June, the most bountiful of all months for flowers, more than a fifth of those shown are roses. Other leading English depictors of flowers included Mary Delany (1700–88), a close friend of Queen Charlotte and of many leading botanists of the day, whose cut paper representations of flowers include fourteen of roses, all showing minute botanical detail. The paintings of Mary Moser (d.1819), a founder member of the Royal Academy, also show roses, perhaps most famously in the Mary Moser Room created at Frogmore House, Windsor, for Queen Charlotte in 1792.

Rosa × centifolia *'Cristata', the crested Moss rose, commonly known as 'Chapeau de Napoléon'*

Nevertheless, for most of the eighteenth century the range of varieties was still very limited. The same few Gallicas, Albas, Damasks and Centifolias appear again and again and only the Autumn Damask and *Rosa moschata* were available for late display. Van Huysum once wrote to a client that he could not finish a painting because he could not get a yellow rose to depict from life to complete the composition; *R. hemisphaerica* was then the only fully double yellow, and was then as now uncommon and difficult to grow.

In the 1743 edition of his *Gardeners Dictionary* Philip Miller (1691–1771), Curator of Chelsea Physic Garden and a respected botanist, listed only forty-nine different rose varieties, most of them single-flowered species. However, three years earlier, in the 1740 edition, he had already reported that "of late years, since some curious persons have sowed the Seeds of Roses, there have been many new Varieties obtained, some of which are very double, and of beautiful Colours; which success should encourage others to practice this Method, since there is not a more beautiful Genus of Plants in nature, than that of the Rose." Miller was not discussing controlled hybridization, whose day had yet to come. And he did not include these novelties in his forty-nine varieties: presumably they were not widely distributed and had yet to be fully evaluated. Nevertheless, his testimony clearly indicates that gardeners had become aware that the seedlings of garden roses were different from and occasionally better than their parents, and were beginning to exploit this discovery.

As the century progressed, nurserymen as well as farmers came to understand that by crossing individuals with desirable characteristics, whether cattle or Centifolia roses, there was a chance that good traits could be combined and less satisfactory ones eliminated in the offspring. Among nurserymen, much of the credit for this new knowledge goes to Thomas Fairchild (1667–1729), a gardener with a keen interest in science, who raised the first deliberate plant hybrid by crossing a carnation with a sweet William to produce what was known as "Fairchild's mule". However, it was probably breeders of livestock such as Robert Bakewell (1725–95) who were more influential in spreading the principles and possibilities of breeding plants, as well as animals, throughout western Europe.

André Dupont, the foremost rosarian of the day and designer of Josephine's rose garden at Malmaison, is credited with being the first rose breeder to make controlled rose crosses by hand pollination, in about 1800. Others followed him, and the number

A typical example of what Vita Sackville-West called "the Dutchman's canvas, crammed to absurdity," this painting of 1736 (?) by Jan van Huysum shows a representative selection of garden plants of the day including the cabbage rose Rosa × centifolia *(bottom right), double yellow* R. hemisphaerica *(center right, against the vase) and the Jacobite rose* R. × alba *'Alba Maxima'.*

1 Perennial dwarf Sun flower.
2 Ultamarine & Prusian blew-Iris Major.
3 Blew Nigella, or Fennel flower.
4 Moon Trefoile.
5 Upright Sweet William.
6 Saxifrage.
7 Cinquefoile.
8 Pansies, or Hearts-ease.
9 Maidens blush Rose.
10 Yellow Jasmine.
11 Blew Corn flower.
12 Blush Belgick Rose.
13 The Franceford Rose.
14 Double Martagon.
15 Orchis or Bee flower.
16 Scarlet Colutea.
JUNE
17 Fraxinella.
18 Moss province Rose.
19 Double Virginian Silk-grass.
20 White Rose.
21 Dutch Hundred Leav'd Rose.
22 White Batchelors Button.
23 Rosa Mundi.
24 Mountain Lychnis.
25 Dwarf Iris Strip'd.
26 White Jasmine.
27 Scarlet Geranium.
28 Yellow Martagon.
29 Red Martagon.
30 Teucrium or Germander.
31 Mountain dwarf Pink.
32 Yellow Corn Marygold.
33 Purple sweet Pea.
34 Greek Valerian.
From the Collection of Robt. Furber, Gardiner at Kensington. 1730.
Engrav'd by H. Fletcher

of varieties began to rise exponentially. In George Don's *General History of Dichlamydeous Plants* (1832) some 1600 varieties are listed, allotted to 205 species; and Don admitted that he was only scratching the surface of the total number of available roses and that breeders in France and Italy were then introducing innumerable varieties each year.

The date when the first China roses arrived in European gardens is not known with certainty. Dr Hurst identified the roses thrown at Venus by Cupid in Bronzino's painting *An Allegory of Love and Time* (1529) as being pink China roses not significantly different from Parsons's pink China. If this is so, the China rose must have reached southern Europe via the silk route, its distribution to gardens in the colder north presumably being hindered by its slight tenderness. Though Dr Hurst may well be right about this early introduction, the identification must remain speculative. However, we can be certain that at least two China roses had reached Europe by 1752, because they are recorded as being grown in the Botanic Garden at Uppsala, Sweden, in that year.

Gallica rose 'Charles de Mills'

One of these, a blush-flowered clone of *Rosa* × *odorata* (*R. chinensis* × *R. gigantea*), was taken by Linnaeus as the type for his species *Rosa indica* (no longer an acceptable name because Linnaeus included roses belonging to at least three different species within it). The other China rose growing at Uppsala was sent by Linnaeus to Philip Miller at Chelsea Physic Garden, where it was growing in 1759. This rose, also pink-flowered, and probably another clone of *R.* × *odorata*, is likely to have been the same clone that was grown at Kew in 1769 and was listed as a hothouse plant in Richard Weston's *English Flora* in 1775 under Jacquin's name *Rosa chinensis*. Jacquin had based his name on a dried herbarium specimen of 1733, presumably collected in China, of a non-hybrid red-flowered plant. A similar clone was reported to be growing in England by 1782. However, none of these first-cultivated China roses seems to have been given a varietal name or to have played a part in the further development of garden roses.

That role fell to a further four arrivals from China, the so-called stud Chinas. The first two of these, Slater's crimson China (*Rosa chinensis* 'Semperflorens', introduced

The plate for June from Robert Furber's The Flower Garden Display'd *of 1730–32 shows a representative selection of varieties popular at the time. No 9, Maidens blush Rose, is a rather irregular Alba rose, probably not the 'Maiden's Blush' of today. No 12, Blush Belgick Rose, is a rose described by Lindley as a Damask but probably a Damask × Gallica hybrid. No 13, The Francford Rose, is 'Agatha',* Rosa francofurtensis *of various botanists from 1640 (Parkinson's* Theatrum Botanicum*) onwards. This loosely double-flowered plant was described by Miller as 'of little Value . . . for the Flowers seldom open fair', though he recommended it for grafting. De Pronville called it 'Agate de Francfort', saying that it had flowers that seldom took on a regular form or opened completely because of the bush's very vigorous growth. It is not clear whether this belongs to the same hybrid species as* R. × francofurtana *of Otto von Münchhausen (syn.* R. turbinata *of Aiton =* R. gallica × R. majalis*), de Pronville and Thory's 'Rosier de Francfort', represented now in gardens by the shorter and clearly different clone 'Empress Josephine'. No 18, Moss province Rose, is our common Moss rose,* R. × centifolia *'Muscosa'. No 20, White Rose, is* R. *'Alba Semiplena'. No 21, Dutch Hundred Leav'd Rose, is the common cabbage rose,* R. × centifolia. *No 23, Rosa Mundi, is the plant we know by the same name today,* R. gallica *'Versicolor'. Several roses are also shown in the plate for May, a few others in later months. These include Strip'd Monthly Rose (a repeat-flowering striped Damask, not our York and Lancaster rose and perhaps now extinct), White Monthly Rose (*R. × damascena *var.* semperflorens *'Quatre Saisons Blanche', now extremely rare, though available in South Africa) and Double White Musk Rose (*R. moschata *'Plena').*

1792) and Parsons's pink China (*R.* × *odorata* 'Pallida' or old blush China, 1793), were perhaps most widely used in breeding, though the original Tea roses (so-called because of their tea-like fragrance), Hume's blush tea-scented China (*R.* × *o.* 'Odorata', 1809) and Parks's yellow tea-scented China (*R.* × *o.* 'Ochroleuca', 1824), also played a part. *R.* × *odorata* and *R. chinensis* itself are suited to Mediterranean or hotter climates, where their garden selections and their hybrids such as Teas and Chinas will flower incessantly and profusely. Thus they are perhaps the most important of all parents of roses for areas such as the southern United States, India, South Africa and Australia. They have also contributed to the parentage of roses for less hot climates such as the Bourbons, Hybrid Perpetuals, Hybrid Teas, Floribundas and all the modern classes of rose derived from these.

So it was that by about 1800 the precursors of most modern roses had been brought into cultivation. The Gallicas, among the most ancient groups of garden roses and including dark-colored cultivars such as 'Violacea' and 'Tuscany', were exploited at about that time to raise richly hued new varieties. Some of these were described by early authors such as August de Pronville in his *Nomenclature Raisonnée des Espèces, Variétés et Sous-variétés du Genre Rosier* (1818). They predated the introduction of equally dark and sumptuous Chinas and themselves gave way to another generation of Gallicas, the superlative creations of the great French rose breeders such as Jean Laffay (1794–1878) and Jean-Pierre Vibert (1777–1866), including 'Cardinal de Richelieu'. This period also saw a proliferation of varieties bred from other ancient garden roses such as the cabbage rose, *Rosa* × *centifolia*, the first Moss rose, *R.* × *centifolia* 'Muscosa' (named for the mossy outgrowth on its flowerbuds) and the oldest Damasks.

Throughout the nineteenth century many thousands of new roses were raised or introduced and several important new groups of roses were developed. The influx of myriad new varieties had a profound effect on garden design. It became aesthetically and practically convenient to provide roses with their own gardens: they all needed similar culture, they usually flowered at the same time and they were not always easy to mix attractively with other plants. A host of architectural solutions was devised to show off the finest Ramblers and Climbing roses, beginning early in the nineteenth century but becoming something of a frenzy as the twentieth century approached and multitudes of new Wichurana and Multiflora Ramblers were introduced.

Noisette rose 'Maréchal Niel'

The Bourbons were among the most important of the new classes of rose to be raised in the nineteenth century. The first was found on the French island of that name (otherwise known as Ile de Réunion) in 1817, a chance hybrid between a China rose and an Autumn Damask. It was sent to Paris and thereafter used to create many sweet-scented varieties flowering well in the autumn, most of them hardy to Z6. Capable of being grown as large free-standing shrubs, some of them have long flexible stems that suit them to pillars or training on walls, though in the drier, stiller, warmer air here they may be more susceptible to blackspot and mildew.

The first Noisette, 'Noisette Carnée' (Blush Noisette), was a repeat-flowering seedling of the once-flowering 'Champneys' Pink Cluster' (*Rosa* × *odorata* 'Pallida' × *R. moschata*). Raised by Philippe Noisette in Charleston and sent to his brother Louis in Paris, it was first offered for sale in 1819 called *R.* × *noisettiana*, a name that came to be applied to all Noisettes. Though the original 'Noisette Carnée' may be grown as a shrub and pruned as for the Bourbons, other Noisettes of later raising were produced by hybridizing with *R. multiflora* or *R. sempervirens* to give roses more akin to Ramblers or Climbing roses in their uses and pruning requirements. 'Noisette Carnée' is hardy to Z6, but crossing with Parks's yellow tea-scented China (*R.* × *odorata* 'Ochroleuca') to introduce yellow colorings produced a number of less hardy varieties, many with soft yellow blooms, including the lovely 'Maréchal Niel'.

Ramblers are distinguished from Climbing roses by producing stems that flower in their second year and may then usually be pruned away; Climbing rose stems will produce blooms for several years and are not usually pruned immediately after flowering. The early years of the nineteenth century saw the development of Ayrshire Ramblers from *Rosa arvensis* and probably *R. sempervirens*. Capable of blooming in shade, the most famous survivor of this class is the myrrh-scented rose, 'Splendens'. Soon after, in the 1820s, came Sempervirens Ramblers, most of them raised by M. Jacques, gardener to the Duc d'Orléans. Also richly scented, the most famous of these are 'Félicité Perpétue' (named after Jacques's two daughters) and 'Adélaïde d'Orléans', its nodding bunches of blooms, like those of a double cherry, making it particularly suitable for arches and pergolas.

A many-petalled variant of Rambler rose 'Albertine'

The development of two important races of Ramblers in the late nineteenth and early twentieth centuries had an enormous impact on the way roses were used in gardens. Multiflora Ramblers were raised from *Rosa multiflora* or its very double cultivar 'Carnea' (in cultivation by 1804) to create many vigorous, often sweetly scented cultivars, most of them hardy to Z5. *R. multiflora* was also crossed with China roses to produce Polyanthas. Although some of these, such as 'Perle d'Or' (1884) and 'Cécile Brünner' (1881) make quite large plants, it is the dwarf Polyanthas derived from crosses with a dwarf China rose that have played the more important role in rose history, bringing the many-headed flower stems of *R. multiflora* into a short-growing bedding rose and paving the way for the creation of the Floribundas.

The introduction of glossy-leaved Japanese *Rosa wichurana* in 1891 allowed the creation of two distinct races of Wichurana Ramblers: those with fairly large flowers borne singly or a few together, a speciality of Barbier's nursery and including 'Albertine' and 'Albéric Barbier', and those with clusters of smaller flowers such as 'Dorothy Perkins'. (The spelling *wichuraiana* is common but banned by the *International Code of Botanical Nomenclature*.) Such was their popularity that almost every rose garden had to include them and to devise a means of supporting them; thus pillars, arcades, catenaries, treillage and pergolas proliferated. Many Multiflora and Wichurana varieties make superlative weeping standards, another increasingly common feature in early-twentieth-century rose gardens, especially in France.

In the middle years of the nineteenth century there were few roses suited to bedding other than Hybrid Perpetuals that could usually only be adapted by Procrustean and labor-intensive pegging. The Hybrid Perpetuals were derived from 'Rose du Roi', a Portland × China hybrid dating from 1816. Crossed with China and Bourbon varieties, this ultimately gave rise to thousands of repeat-flowering, generally quite vigorous varieties. Production of new Hybrid Perpetuals declined towards the end of the century with only a few raised since 1900.

The last of the major nineteenth-century groups to be evolved was to dramatically increase the importance of roses for bedding and remains of key importance today. Hybrid Teas, otherwise classed as Large-flowered roses, were not recognized as a distinct class until 1884, though the first member of the class, 'La France', was raised by J.-B. Guillot in 1867 from a cross between a Hybrid Perpetual, 'Madame Victor Verdier', and a Tea rose, 'Madame Bravy'. The first representatives of the class were triploid and were thus relatively sterile, and so it was not until some fertile tetraploid Hybrid Teas such as 'Lady Mary Fitzwilliam' (1882) and 'Madame Caroline Testout' (1890) appeared that the breeding of many new varieties became possible.

An important development from the 1880s onwards was the raising by Joseph Pernet-Ducher (1859–1928) of crosses between almost sterile *Rosa foetida* 'Persiana' and Hybrid Teas and Hybrid Perpetuals. In 1900, 'Soleil d'Or' was released, considered by some to be the first truly yellow Hybrid Tea, although it is sometimes also classed as a Hybrid Foetida. It was this work that led to a race of yellow- or orange-flowered Pernetiana roses (usually inheriting *R. foetida*'s susceptibility to blackspot), and ultimately to many of today's Hybrid Teas and Climbing roses in this same color range. Further twentieth-century breeding along the same lines used the Austrian copper briar, *R. foetida* 'Bicolor', to produce bicolor roses and roses in brilliant scarlet or vermilion. Perhaps the first true bicolor was 'Juliet', a Pernetiana introduced in 1910. It rapidly became prone to blackspot, so most rosarians turned to its successor 'The Queen Alexandra Rose', in vermilion with gold reverse, soon after its introduction in 1917.

The first half of the twentieth century saw further progress in the development of Hybrid Teas, widening their color range, improving their health and refining their flower shape. Meanwhile the Danish breeder Poulsen crossed hardy dwarf Polyanthas with Hybrid Teas to produce Hybrid Polyanthas or Poulsen roses, which through further crosses with Hybrid Teas gave rise to the Floribundas. British attempts along similar lines by the Revd Joseph Pemberton and by Messrs Paul & Son to produce more or less dwarf perpetual-flowering roses were hailed in the 1921 *Rose Annual* but have had less long-term significance. However, Pemberton's Hybrid Musks, raised from 'Trier', a seedling of 'Aglaia' (*Rosa multiflora* × 'Rêve d'Or'), remain treasured today, their scent deriving principally from *R. multiflora* rather than from the musk rose, *R. moschata*.

Polyantha rose 'Perle d'Or'

Experimentation in color and form continued. The vermilion color due to pelargonidin pigment had appeared in Polyantha roses raised by Dutch rose breeder de Ruiter, such as 'Gloria Mundi' (1929). Single roses, like 'Irish Elegance', were a new development, and although yellow Pernetiana Hybrid Teas were much improved, none yet combined perfect flower shape, scent and disease resistance. Although rose breeders had known about Mendelian genetics for some thirty years, cytologists had failed to give them any more useful information than the importance of chromosome numbers; most breeders still relied largely on trial and error in selecting parents for new roses.

The development of so many exciting bedding roses caused a lack of interest in older roses, though fortunately there were a few devotees left to carry the torch. In England, Mrs Maud Messel and Edward Ashdown Bunyard were among those to inspire the next generation of old-rose lovers, including Constance Spry, Graham Thomas, Vita Sackville-West, James Russell and Bobbie James. After World War II it was this generation who showed gardeners, through both their publications and their gardens, just what they had lost by abandoning the old roses.

In the decades since World War II there have been many advances in rose breeding that will doubtless change the way we use roses in future years. Many Miniatures have been derived from 'Rouletii' (which may or may not be the same as 'Pompon de Paris' and/or *Rosa chinensis* 'Minima') and its offspring such as 'Oakington Ruby' (found by Charles Bloom in 1933). Immensely speedy to raise from cuttings as a glasshouse crop, these have become popular potted plants. Larger-flowered than these are the Patio roses derived from them, a popular and promising group for beds, parterres and containers. Many Ground Cover varieties of diverse parentage have also appeared. The more recent of these have the great virtue of being reliable for continuous blooming during the summer months; however, they can be difficult to use sympathetically, their brightness and in some cases sophistication of shape looking out of place in some rural or semi-industrial sites.

The most dramatic and useful advances in the range of rose varieties have come when enterprising breeders have considered what sort of roses gardeners lack and how recombination of existing classes and species could produce them. Thus the Wichurana Ramblers and Hybrid Musks greatly extended the versatility of the rose. David Austin's English roses, combining the form of old roses with the colors, perpetual flowering and bush habit of modern sorts, have become popular worldwide. Meilland's new Romantica® series, similar in their floral shape and range of habit, will doubtless also prove to contain exceptionally useful and beautiful roses. For cold climates, the Explorer series, Rugosa hybrids raised by the Canadian Department of Agriculture, are proving immensely useful additions to the range of hardy varieties.

For all this admirable activity, one feels that only a small part of the potential of the genus *Rosa* has been tapped by breeders. Relatively few species have been used. Those species that were crossed with bush roses by breeders such as Pemberton and Barbier eighty or a hundred years ago might provide even more useful and attractive new varieties if hybridized with modern bush roses. *Rosa multibracteata* has produced one very good rose, 'Cerise Bouquet', but could surely yield many more. Little use has been made of foliage color, employing the likes of glaucous *R. soulieana*, *R. brunonii* 'La Mortola' or red-flushed pewter *R. glauca*, nor of the ferny foliage of *R. multiflora* 'Watsoniana'. There must surely be more potential for using hitherto untried species to introduce other desirable characteristics such as disease resistance, perpetual flowering or hardiness. Modern breeding techniques would surely extend the range of possibilities and also improve the success rate.

Hybrid Tea rose 'Gail Borden'

A less desirable recent trend is that familiarity with roses seems rather to have bred contempt. A similar effect can be detected with other popular flowers, notably those that are grown year-round for cutting. Pinks, chic in the late sixties through the advocacy of the likes of Mrs Desmond Underwood and Lanning Roper and widely used in schemes of silver, white and pink, have lost most of their popularity through their omnipresence on every flower stall and most restaurant tables. Chrysanthemums have suffered a similar fate, though they are indispensable for the autumn border. We must not let such prejudices blind us to the usefulness of roses. There are still plenty of possibilities for enterprising designers and gardeners to show us how to use them to the best effect and for breeders to create yet more new and exciting classes of rose. I hope the coming chapters will prove their potential.

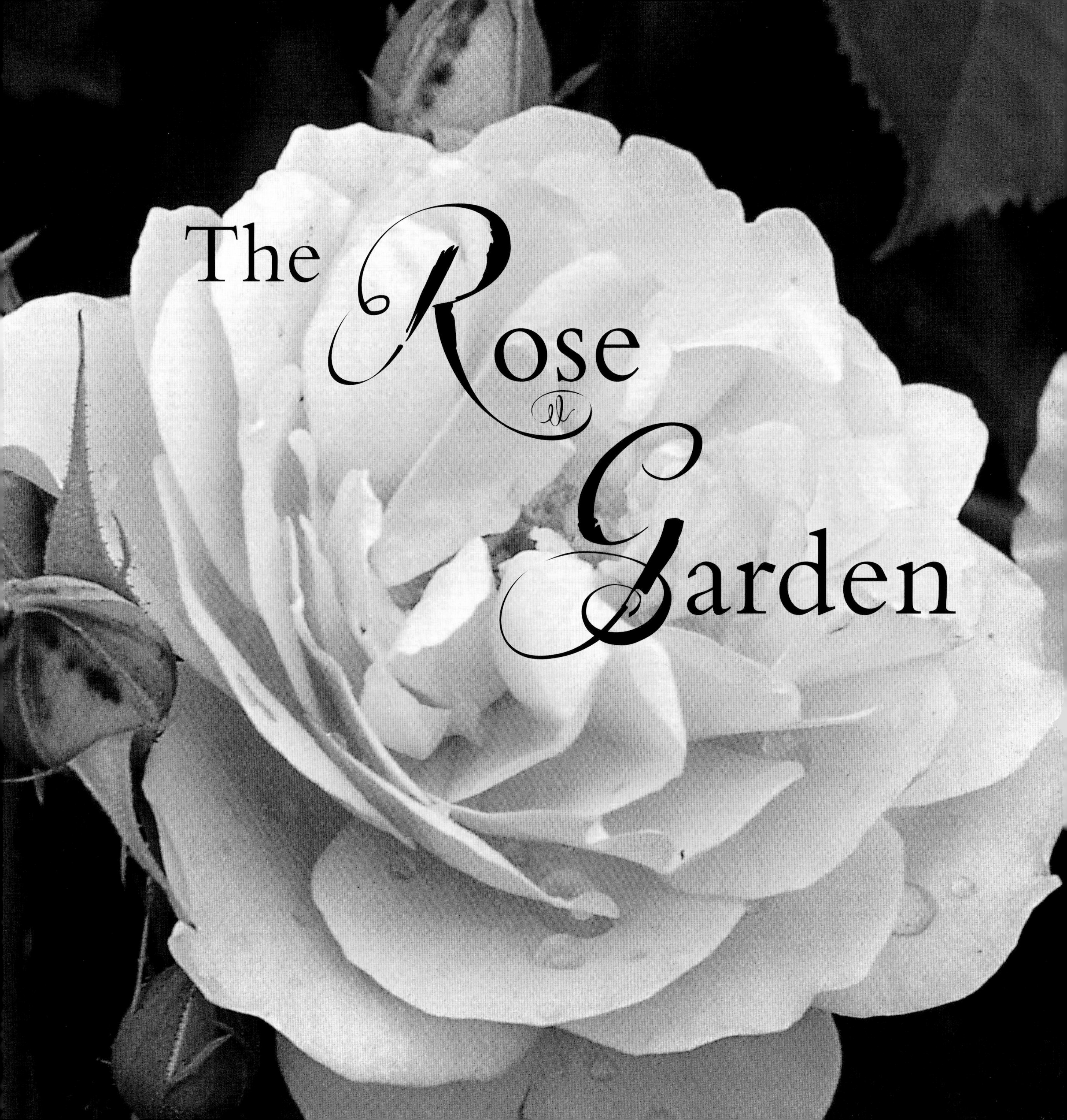
The Rose Garden

"The value of the rose is in the glory of its individual flowers . . . The idea is not the rose for the garden but the garden for the rose."

REVD ANDREW FOSTER-MELLIAR, *The Book of the Rose* (1894)

Writing thus, in the last decade of the nineteenth century, the Revd Andrew Foster-Melliar (d.1904) was merely restating a widely held notion. Throughout his lifetime roses had been grown exclusively for the beauty of their blooms and been singled out in separate gardens or at least beds of their own. In 1869 the rosarian Dean of Rochester, Samuel Reynolds Hole (1819–1904), had pronounced the rose "that queen who brooks no rival near, much less upon her throne." The trend, reflected in many books and treatises on the genus, was to gather roses together in collections, or to raise them apart for cutting or for show purposes. There was little attempt to integrate them into the garden as a whole. This was to change.

There was no Damascene conversion that instantly altered the ways rosarians used their favorite plants, but a distinct shift of emphasis became apparent at the end of the nineteenth century. It was articulated by the giant of horticultural publishing, and the most influential voice in gardening of his day, William Robinson (1838–1935), who poured vitriol on the prevailing view. An unfailingly self-assured and opinionated man, his scorn for gardens with isolated roses was undisguised: "Since the time when people went in for patterned colour, many flowers were set aside, like the Rose, the Carnation, and the Lily, that did not lend themselves to flat colour; and thus we see ugly, bare, and at the same time costly gardens round country houses," he wrote in *The English Flower Garden* (1883). He continued:

> There is great loss to the flower-garden from the usual way of growing the Rose as a thing apart . . . It is surprising to see how poor and hard many places are to which the beauty of the Rose might add delight, and the only compensation for all this blank is what is called the rosery, which in places is often an ugly thing with plants that usually only blossom for a few weeks in summer . . .

Robinson saw Foster-Melliar as a prime proponent of rosarian beliefs and in later editions of *The English Flower Garden* he directly addressed what he saw as the typically misguided opinions put forward in *The Book of the Rose*. Foster-Melliar had proclaimed:

> I look upon the plant in most cases only as a means whereby I may obtain glorious Roses. I do not consider the Rose pre-eminent as a decorative plant; several simpler flowers, much less beautiful in themselves, have, to my mind, greater value for general effect in the garden. . . . It must be remembered that the Rose is not like a bedding plant, which will keep up continual masses of colour throughout the summer, but that the flush of flowers is not for more than a month at most, after which many sorts, even of the Teas, will be off bloom for a while, and the general effect will be spoiled.

Robinson dismissed his opponents' reasoning as outdated, arguing that there were now many roses that bloomed almost continually from early summer through to the frosts, and scoffing at the idea that the rose was not "a decorative plant." "The Rose," he declared, "must go back to the flower-garden – its true place, not only for its own sake, but to save the garden from ugliness and hardness, and give it fragrance and dignity of leaf and flower."

Thus the battle lines were drawn. The war of the rose for the garden versus the garden for the rose continued for almost fifty years before Robinson's views became accepted by even hard-line rosarians. By that time, a century and a half of concentrated attention had set the rose on the path to the eminent position it holds in the flower garden today.

In gardens from medieval times to the eighteenth century, roses would be planted in beds and borders, sometimes trained against fences or walls, mixed with other plants and never predominating. Seldom do they seem to have played a significant part in the design of the whole garden and there are no references from these times to rose gardens in which their floral beauty was the *raison d'être* of the garden as a whole. However, occasional rare examples foreshadow twentieth-century taste: it is interesting to see in Robert Smythson's 1609 plan of Wimbledon House roses planted through the orchards in what must have been a formally regular version of the orchard at Sissinghurst Castle, Kent, over three hundred years later.

One of the earliest, and certainly the most famous, of gardens actually planned for the rose was Malmaison, created in 1799 by Napoleon's wife, later the Empress Josephine, near Paris. Designed in the then popular English landscape style, but with many beds, shrubberies and specimens designed to show off the plants to their best advantage, it is probably the first of its kind for which plans and plant lists survive. The main garden design was by Louis Berthault but the distinguished rosarian André Dupont designed the rose garden itself.

Near the house the design kept an element of formality, with straight axes edged with narrow rose beds, while further away from the chateau the paths took on more flowing lines, a scheme later echoed at Paxton's Birkenhead Park, designed in 1843, and in Edouard André's Sefton Park plan of 1867. From the plans it is apparent that the Malmaison design was elegant and agreeable, its narrow beds allowing every bloom to be examined at close quarters and with paths running on both sides of the beds. The large number of Ramblers necessitated structures such as arches, pagodas and pillars to support them, design elements that were widely copied. Thus the characteristics of the Rambler rose had already had an impact on garden design.

At that time, the flood of new hybrids created by the early plant breeders had yet to appear. The species and ancient garden hybrids discussed in the previous chapter formed the backbone of Josephine's collection, along with a number of species of lesser importance in breeding. At her death in 1814, the collection contained some 250 different roses – including 167 Gallicas, 27 Centifolias, 3 Mosses, 9 Damasks, 8 Albas and 22 Chinas. The significance of the collection was not just that it was large but that it was well researched by the botanist Claude Antoine Thory (1759–1827) and that the roses were painted with astonishing accuracy and delicacy by Pierre Joseph Redouté (1759–1840). Their publication *Les Roses*, which appeared in thirty fascicles from 1817 to 1824, is a cornerstone of rose literature. Because of its superlative colored plates, it remains an important source of information today. De Pronville's *Nomenclature Raisonnée* of 1818 was also based on the Malmaison collection and provides some subtly different and interesting new insights. In the early nineteenth century the ever-increasing number of garden plants made it possible, indeed almost essential, to specialize by creating gardens devoted to a restricted range of plants. Josephine's Malmaison rose garden was one of the first examples of this trend but it can also be seen in the work of Humphry Repton (1752–1818). Repton, the first designer to call himself a landscape gardener, worked at Ashridge in Hertfordshire from 1813 and created a rose garden (or rosary) there, illustrated in his *Fragments* of 1816. These paintings are especially interesting in

Centifolia rose 'De Meaux'

PAGES 26–27 *Shrub rose* Graham Thomas

that they show beds of short varieties, probably true dwarfs such as 'De Meaux', not the standards and half-standards that were to become the norm for rose gardens until the 1880s.

Repton also popularized a return to formality in the garden: for Ashridge he designed a circular garden with beds of short roses radiating out from a central fountain and pond like the petals of a flower. The whole was surrounded by an arcade of Ramblers on round-topped arches, with a trellis fence at its foot. The beds appear in the plans to have an edging, perhaps of box. In creating this plan, Repton recognized that roses lack the necessary structure to make a garden by themselves: a strong design enhanced by architecture and topiary or hedging is essential and provides a pleasing framework even when the roses are out of bloom. Some later garden architects have ignored this lesson to their cost.

In his more informal designs such as those for the Royal Pavilion at Brighton, Repton used *corbeilles* or basket beds scattered liberally across lawns, their outward-curving perimeters providing the structure and neatness that the plants, often including the shorter roses, could not supply. The original baskets were made of wicker or heavy wire work; Repton's son John Adey Repton devised a cast-iron version, the Hardenberg basket, in 1823.

Gardens such as these signalled the growing popularity of the rose and a series of books began to appear on the subject. *A Collection of Roses from Nature* (1796–99) by Mary Lawrance was one of the first books devoted to roses; its importance was recognized across the English Channel, where de Pronville, writing of the roses grown in England, made reference to it. John Lindley's *Rosarum Monographia or A Botanical History of Roses* (1820) is also evidence that an interest in roses was growing apace, though he gives no discussion of their use in gardens.

By the time John Claudius Loudon published his *Encyclopaedia of Gardening* in 1822, the rose garden was a well-established feature of many gardens. Loudon's comments show clearly how roses were used at that time:

> Roses are generally planted in the front of shrubberies, and in borders; they are also planted by themselves in rose-gardens or roseries, in groups on lawn or gravel, either with common box or other edgings, or with edgings of wire in imitation of basketwork. These last are called baskets of roses; the ground enclosed in the basket-margin is made convex, so as to present a greater surface to the eye, and increase the illusion; the shoots of the stronger sorts are layered or kept down by pegs till they strike roots into the ground, so that the points of the shoots furnished with buds appear only above the soil . . . Under this treatment, the whole surface of the basket becomes, in two or three years, covered with rosebuds and leaves of one or of various sorts.

Rose lovers in large numbers began buying books on their favorite genus. The *Rose Amateur's Guide* of 1837 by Thomas Rivers (1798–1877) proved such a great success that it was enlarged twice by 1843. Catherine Frances Gore (1799–1861), who found contemporary fame and fortune as a novelist, is perhaps more remembered for her *Book of Roses or the Rose Fancier's Manual* (1838). This followed too soon upon Rivers' work to draw principally from it, though she admits to having derived most of her material from the slightly earlier *Manuel Complet de l'Amateur de Roses* by Paul Boitard. Mrs Gore writes that "it is now about twenty years since standards, or tree-roses, were introduced into our gardens from France, having been originally created by the Dutch." John Kennedy, who was the supplier of plants to the Empress Josephine at Malmaison, is credited with being the introducer of standards in England.

Loudon considered they were often used badly: "Standard roses . . . have certainly the best effect in flower-borders, or when completely detached on a lawn; their sameness of form, and that form being compact and lumpish, prevents them from grouping well, either among themselves or with other subjects." Non-weeping standards were then the usual way of growing roses (bottom-worked bushes did not overtake them in popularity until late in the century), though Loudon does show an illustration of a support for a weeping standard rose. It is believed now that the older hybrid Ramblers such as 'Félicité Perpétue' and 'Adélaïde d'Orléans' would have been used. Mrs Gore reports that the royal rosary at Versailles contained standards 18ft/5.5m high worked with twenty different varieties, a style of culture also then practised at Düsseldorf and Brussels. She describes too a "balloon" of Multiflora or Boursault varieties, formed by planting several near to each other and training the stems together.

Loudon's encyclopedia shows two designs for rose gardens, both of them dull: one is based on curved beds making up a flattened quatrefoil; the other is of concentric flattened octagons. However, he does mention other possible features that might relieve the inevitable boredom such gardens would engender. One is the training of roses to a trellis fence around the perimeter of the garden, with standards planted against the fence at intervals, an effect noted by Mrs Gore, who also suggests training them against walls in garlands. Another feature Loudon mentions is the training of roses to narrow cones of poles, for which he suggests using varieties capable of growing to 30–40ft/9–12m. These must have been very large: the sort of iron or treillage obelisks we find cowering in beds and borders today scarcely holding their heads above the surrounding planting would be far too small for such vigorous varieties and a height of 15–20ft/4.5–6m would seem more likely. We seem to be afraid of such exhibitionism and panache today: I would love to see such structures, though I should not like the task of training Ramblers to them every year.

Standards of Iceberg *with* Lychnis coronaria *'Alba' and 'Climbing Iceberg', at the Cellars Hotel in South Africa*

Mrs Gore comments that the French were then pre-eminent in the culture of roses, though the blooms themselves reached greater perfection in England. Certainly, the most imaginative garden uses of roses are seldom recorded by English authors and most of the designs they show seem dull, little more than vast collections devoted solely to the production of perfect blooms and not to the beauty of the whole garden. Mrs Gore, who had emigrated to France in 1832 to write her book, suggests that one reason for the limited success of rose gardening in England then was that almost all the gentry were in London away from their country gardens at rose time, although she also mentioned that since her departure from England she had heard "by report" of "the daily multiplying rosaries of England; of which the finest are said to be that of the Horticultural Society, formed by Professor Lindley, and the Duke of Devonshire, formed by Mr Paxton . . . and one of the earliest and most interesting made in England, was that of the illustrious Charles James Fox, at St Anne's Hill [Chertsey, Surrey]."

Charles Hamilton, principal creator of the famous garden at Painshill near by, provided the landscape design for Fox's garden. I have found no other mention of the rose garden but as Hamilton died in 1786 it probably predated Malmaison. Fox was still actively gardening in 1796 and it is interesting to speculate whether Josephine's enormous purchases of plants from John Kennedy had any connection with her meeting in 1802 with Fox, the leading francophile among English politicians; perhaps Fox also bought his plants from Lee and Kennedy's Hammersmith nursery in London. It is also possible that Fox, Foreign Minister for some months until his death in 1806, had a hand in securing the safe passage of the Empress's roses found on any captured French ships. Fox's great friend Georgiana, Duchess of Devonshire, is believed to have planted a rose garden at Chiswick House, near London, perhaps with the help of John Kennedy's father, Lewis, who is thought to have been the designer of several English rose gardens.

Mrs Gore also mentions in 1838 that another English nursery, Loddiges of Hackney, offered 2,500

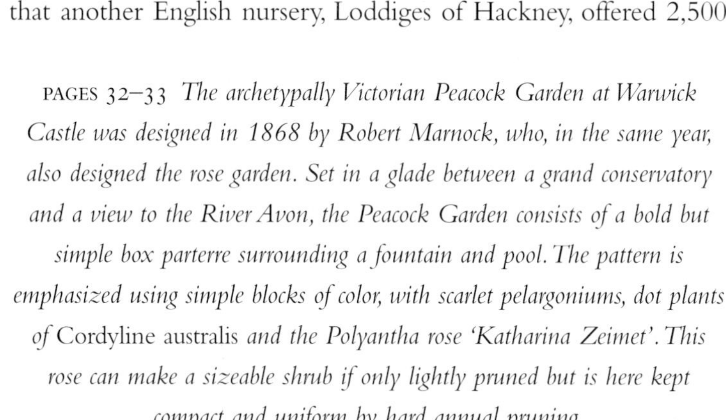

PAGES 32–33 *The archetypally Victorian Peacock Garden at Warwick Castle was designed in 1868 by Robert Marnock, who, in the same year, also designed the rose garden. Set in a glade between a grand conservatory and a view to the River Avon, the Peacock Garden consists of a bold but simple box parterre surrounding a fountain and pool. The pattern is emphasized using simple blocks of color, with scarlet pelargoniums, dot plants of* Cordyline australis *and the Polyantha rose 'Katharina Zeimet'. This rose can make a sizeable shrub if only lightly pruned but is here kept compact and uniform by hard annual pruning.*

varieties of rose and that the Jardins du Luxembourg in Paris contained some 1,800; however, she considered that only about 1,200 were worth growing.

Across the Atlantic, Robert Buist's *Rose Manual* (1844), loosely modelled on Rivers' book but nevertheless containing original elements, is evidence that roses were also popular in North America and that many of the best English and French varieties were then well established in cultivation here. His near neighbor and rival William Robert Prince (1795–1869), owner of the largest collection of roses in North America, some 1,600 in all, was spurred by Buist's book into producing his own work, *Prince's Manual of Roses* (1846), which draws more directly on Rivers' work, only one quarter of the content being Prince's own, though that portion is perceptive and informative. Some comments on the design of rose gardens are included but on the whole these are too vague to be of use.

The most celebrated of English mid-nineteenth-century rosarians, William Paul (1822–1905), produced his masterpiece *The Rose Garden* in 1848. It contained descriptions of over a thousand varieties. The book ranges over many aspects of roses and rose growing. Paul writes of the leading French growers Vibert and Laffay, then at the end of their careers, though Laffay hoped his last saving of seed of hybrid Moss roses would yield more treasures. He also mentions some of the first English rose gardens, such as Dane-end, Munden, Hertfordshire, home of Charles S. Chauncey, "one of the earliest and best collections; and to which this country is no doubt indebted in some degree for the celebrity she enjoys for Roses." He describes Mrs Gaussen's garden at Brookmans, Hertfordshire, as containing "a wide variety of beds formed and planted with much taste: in the center stood a temple covered with climbing Roses. The whole was blinded from distant view by a wide laurel bank; and the surprise created on suddenly entering was most agreeable, and the effect magical." Paul singled out the garden of George J. Bosanquet at Broxbournebury, also in Hertfordshire, as being the best in the country; but a rectangle 85 x 27yds/78 x 25m divided into three walks, two straight and one serpentine, designed to accommodate a collection of 2,200 roses of which 1,000 were repeat-flowering, sounds dull to me.

For all the apparent failure of rosarians at this date to produce or even envisage beautiful gardens, Paul does suggest some useful precepts: walks should be of grass, which sets off the flowers better than gravel; if gravel is necessary, an edging will be needed of box, slate or fancy tiles, or otherwise dwarf roses such as 'De Meaux' or Dwarf Chinas (today's 'Rouletii'); an elevated mound, preferably with a rose "temple" on top, provides a *coup d'œil*, though a raised walk is also an advantage; surrounding trees create shade and hinder the circulation of air, giving rise to disease; roses should be grouped with like sorts, not jumbled willy-nilly, and it is a particular sin to mix summer- and autumn-flowering varieties. He advises autumn pruning to cause early flowering, allowing hips sufficient time to ripen for the raising of new varieties. It seems that by this date Repton's example of using dwarf bottom-worked or own-root bushes had been forgotten, and standards and half-standards, as at the Jardins du Luxembourg, were the norm.

Paul recommends other ways of growing roses for effect that begin to insinuate them into the garden as a whole. He suggests Ayrshire, Sempervirens and Boursault Ramblers, Noisettes and the more lax of the Bourbons for weeping standards, with a specimen of 'Ruga' grafted at 8ft/2.5m with a seat beneath especially commended; "every Rosarium, and indeed every Flower Garden" should possess some pillar roses, drawn from the same classes,

> to form temples, avenues, singly on lawns, or in groups of three, five, or more. . . . Climbing Roses may be planted to cover arbors, rustic seats, or to form arcades or arches over covered walks. I have seen them trained on arches by the sides of walks, a line of arches on either side running their entire length, not stretching over them . . . although they are not always in harmony with surrounding objects, or in good taste . . . the effect may sometimes be heightened by running chains, in curved lines, from arch to arch. . . . The Evergreen and Ayrshire may also be planted in rough places in parks, to trail over waste ground, hillocks, or the like: they may also be made to climb old trees. . . . A bank of Roses produces a very agreeable effect, especially when seen from the windows of the house. . . . In some places, where the shrubbery-walks are extensive, we have seen groups of roses introduced with good effect.

A little more interesting than the average rose garden of the time are the designs for Knostrop (Knowsthorpe), near Leeds, by Joshua Major, then one of the most successful landscape gardeners in the north of England. Paul gives two examples of these; regularly punctuated with fastigiate trees (probably Irish yews) and scattered with round beds and others of more elaborate shape, both are surrounded by shrubberies with scrolled margins, also planted with roses. Major explained to Paul:

> we found it necessary to front the whole of the shrubbery enclosing the compartment both with Standards and Dwarfs; and during the blooming season it presented a scene truly splendid, surpassing the assemblage of any other family of plants we ever saw. . . . The arcades in both designs are for exhibiting Climbing Roses, which we need not say will produce a very imposing effect. Some of the round beds may be of basket-work, twelve or fifteen inches [30 or 38cm] deep. . . . In order to make the Rosarium as interesting as possible, the beds might be planted with patches of early flowering bulbs to precede the general bloom of roses; which bulbs, after flowering, might be lifted, and their places supplied by all the different kinds of Annuals, to succeed the general Rose bloom. So that there would first be a show of early bulbous flowers; then the grand display of Roses; and, lastly, the show of Annuals.

It is interesting to note that Major, the only non-rosarian to comment on the use of roses in our story so far, allows them to be mixed with other plants, albeit ones that bloomed at different times, in direct contradiction of almost every nineteenth-century rosarian. Except for Malmaison, all the rose gardens were kept away from the house and there is no mention of their use for terrace parterres in front of grand houses; perhaps there were too few varieties sufficiently neat and showy for a long time to allow such planting. Major comments in his own book, *The Theory and Practice of Landscape Gardening* (1852), that flower gardens visible through the windows were an interruption of the lawn and a decided fault.

Paul, then, described almost all the elements of the rose garden today, though they had not yet been seen executed with the skill, perseverance and taste needed to create a truly beautiful garden. Nothing mentioned by Miss Jekyll, none of the schemes employed at Sissinghurst or any garden created since the mid-nineteenth century has been new: Paul wrote of them all, though there was then no gardener-artist to use them to their full potential.

A collection of Paul's works, *Contributions to Horticultural Literature (1843–92)*, shows that his interest and influence in theories of rose gardening continued throughout his life. Here we find fuller accounts of the rose gardens of Hertfordshire, noting other interesting features such as Ramblers 'Madame d'Arblay' and 'Léopoldine d'Orléans' covering an immense apple tree at Dane-end and beds of three rows of roses edged with 'Red Fairy Rose' at Ponsbourne Park. He quotes a Scottish correspondent from 1857 who championed once-flowering "Summer Roses" because later flushes of bloom were generally not suited to the cool damp climate; Paul concurred, with "an emphatic 'No'," that the time had not yet come when such roses should be altogether displaced by perpetual-flowering varieties. However, we see in the closing decades of the century little production of new once-flowering varieties and a strong proliferation of Hybrid Perpetuals, Teas and Hybrid Teas so that by 1900 classes such as Gallicas, Centifolias and Albas are rarely mentioned. Mrs Gore's insight on the "London season" keeping owners of gardens in the capital while the old classes of rose were at their best might well have been a factor in their decline in popularity.

In *The Rose Book* (1864), the eminent gardening author Shirley Hibberd discussed his subject from the point of view of the non-rosarian. He pointedly remarked that he had twice written articles about the pegging of roses to make larger varieties suitable for beds, implying that the technique championed by Loudon had been largely forgotten and that Hibberd believed himself to be responsible for its revival. Hibberd used as his frontispiece an illustration of a garden surrounding a rose temple very similar to that shown by Paul sixteen years earlier, and he discussed the rose garden made at the Crystal Palace, Sydenham, south London in 1861, which was an exactly analogous design with a rose mount topped by a temple.

Robert Marnock (1800–89), Curator of the Royal Botanic Society's Garden, Regent's Park, from 1840 to 1869 and for some time before his retirement in 1879 the leading British landscaper of his day, came perhaps nearer than anyone to creating a rose garden that was aesthetically satisfying while also exploiting much of the potential of different sorts of roses. His Warwick Castle layout of 1868, set in a glade surrounded by shrubs and trees like the designs of Joshua Major, used climbing roses, bush and shrub varieties in a simple but pleasing geometrical plan. Recently restored, the rather fuzzy growth of the roses here might be variously considered to give to the formal design a charming informality or to make the whole a touch too amorphous for perfect beauty. The mainstream of the English rose-growing world failed to respond to the possibilities shown by Paul or the lead given by Marnock, and continued to plough the same tedious furrow until it became a deep, century-old rut.

The Revd Samuel Reynolds Hole was one influential rose grower who was by no means stuck in the conventional rut of rose use and who set down some very firm opinions about how rose gardens should be laid out. Dean Hole can be seen as a central figure in the history of rose gardening, heir to many of the great names of the mid-nineteenth century, not least his "Past-Master, Mr Rivers of Sawbridgeworth, who did more than any other man to evoke and to educate a love of the Rose." For his own garden, he called in some of the leading lights of the day: "With wise instructions from the best (in my opinion) of our landscape gardeners, Mr Marnock, and with very kindly help from my friends Mr William Robinson and Mr Ingram of Belvoir, I restored and reclothed the plot of ground about my home." Robinson had been Marnock's assistant at Regent's Park from 1861 to 1867 and as already noted came to play a major role in the development of rose gardens.

Hole's *A Book about Roses* (1869) is significantly subtitled "How to grow and show them," for it is less clear about how to use them. What advice he gives on arrangement and design is largely directed against the prevailing obsession with geometry, and seems seldom to have been followed. For all Hole's rantings, it was geometry, simple, tedious and often inappropriate, that continued to predominate in the rose garden well into the twentieth century. This may partly be due to the inadequacy of his illustrations, which, though charming, do not show his own garden, nor sufficiently endorse the sort of planting he recommends. Between this failure and the welter of verbiage obscuring the point of his arguments, it is not to be wondered at if his many readers derived only the vaguest impression of how their plants should be arranged: "In a Rose-garden . . . no formalism, no flatness, no monotonous repetition should prevail. . . . There should be beds of Roses, banks of Roses, bowers of Roses, hedges of Roses, edgings of Roses, pillars of Roses, arches of Roses, fountains of Roses, baskets of Roses, vistas and alleys of the Rose."

His specific advice on rose culture is more useful, as in the description of the pegging of Hybrid Perpetuals and the larger Hybrid Teas:

> the long, strong shoots, only shortened 4 or 5 inches [10 or 13cm] (all weakly produce being excised), must be very gently and gradually bent down to earth and secured with thick wooden hooks, cut from the trees and hedgerows, two or three to each lateral branch. These branches will not only flower early and late, but, if well treated, will make robust wood in the summer and autumn, which (the older branches being removed) will be pegged down in the following spring; and so we shall have annually a continuous renovation. . . . In two years these beds will be densely covered with flowers and foliage.

He is adamant that roses must be planted on their own. He suggests using twelve to twenty bushes per bed and, among varieties extant today, recommends particularly 'La France', 'Charles Lefèbvre', 'Merveille de Lyon', 'Louis van Houtte', 'Xavier Olibo', 'Duke of Wellington', 'Madame Gabriel Luizet' and, with some persuasion (she is relatively unbending), 'Baronne Adolph de Rothschild'. However, he admits that "this process is tedious, requiring a constant supervision; and, where there is not time for a watchful and frequent manipulation, it will be wiser to abstain from the system of pegging, and to grow dwarf roses." It seems that by this time pegging had caught on, allowing a substantial number of more vigorous roses to be used for beds. Pegging is seldom seen today, though one group of 'Ulrich Brünner Fils' is still pegged annually at Sissinghurst.

In 1874, Paul reported a display of six thousand roses "in stone bottles laid out as though in beds" that he had staged at the Royal Botanic Society's garden in Regent's Park and showed diagrams of the plans. These look very similar to the design of the Rose Garden at the back of the Palm House at Kew and indicate both that Paul believed in roses as plants for beds and that he felt this message still needed to be proved to a wider public. He boasted that his display was "the talk of the town the next day."

The 1885 edition of Hibberd's book, retitled *The Amateur's Rose Book*, is shrewdly refocused not on the landed classes but on the then new legions of middle-class hobby gardeners. He, like Loudon, Paul and Robinson before him, took up the battle against the misuse of standards, writing that "nine tenths of all the entrance courts to snug villas are disgraced with things called standard roses, that rise out of the green turf like so many mops, or scarecrows, or machines for sweeping chimneys, and proclaim to the passersby that 'roses are not grown here, and it is to be feared, never will be!' "

Recognizing that not all his readers would have the room and resources for a separate rose garden, he wrote that "the rosarium is not absolutely necessary for the ... tasteful enjoyment of roses" and allows their use throughout the garden, mixed if necessary with other plants, for instance standards planted with rhododendrons. Hibberd also commented on the use of "hedgerow and wilderness roses" to create "the *négligé* style" and "to clothe the stems of decrepit trees and associate with ivy on ruins." Having a catholic interest in garden plants of every sort, Hibberd was free of the rosarians' dogma: his proclamation that roses may be used throughout the garden and not just on their own is a sign of the increasing decorative value of the newer roses, a signal of the end of the age of the garden for the rose and the coming of the age of the rose for the garden.

Two main driving forces brought about this shift. First, in the course of the nineteenth century, the rose had become more decorative and showy, particularly towards the end of the century when more bush roses suited to bedding and many superb Ramblers were introduced; by 1900, rose gardens were planted not just to house the most beautiful flowers but because the overall effect was attractive, rivalling herbaceous planting and even bedding. Secondly, as Hibberd realized, gardening had ceased to be mainly the preserve of the wealthy, those who had space, money and staff for a separate rose garden.

Indeed, hardly had Foster-Melliar declared his support for the isolation of the rose, because of its unsuitability for garden ornament, when the weakness of his stance was made apparent by the creation of the great rose garden at L'Haÿ-les-Roses by Jules Gravereaux in 1898. Now the Roseraie Départementale du Val-de-Marne, this is a garden that is as ornamental as any of its age; though intended as a home for a collection of roses, it proves that by that date roses were capable of stunning decorative effect.

Gravereaux had acquired the property in 1892 and in 1894 began feverishly collecting every available rose. By 1898 he had so many he realized that a structured garden was needed to add form to plants which can, it must be owned, appear amorphous, and to provide opportunities to display each type of rose in a separate garden. The landscape architect Edouard André provided such a design with some six gardens divided by allées and arcades of Ramblers, Noisettes and Climbing roses and surrounding a grand central parterre, its lawns edged with *plates bandes* of bedding roses. The parterre is flanked by walks of pillar roses and surmounted by a spectacular *coup d'œil*, a treillage pavilion with arcades to either side, the whole completely covered with the deep pink Wichurana Rambler 'Alexandre Girault'. This is an object lesson in fitting the rose to the site: 'Alexandre Girault' is perhaps the only Wichurana Rambler capable of producing stems long enough to clothe such a large structure.

The range of Hybrid Perpetuals in the garden is remarkable and includes colors less common than the usual rose pink or light crimson, but of all the roses here, the Ramblers are the most impressive. Multiflora 'Mrs F.W. Flight' is superb grown here as a pillar rose. Although the individual pink florets are not as pretty close up as those of 'Dorothy Perkins', the effect *en masse* is stunning. There are other excellent Wichurana Ramblers, many of them raised by the French breeder Barbier, including varieties not widely grown outside France such as 'Source d'Or' in pale apricot shading to gold, 'Alexandre Tremouillet' (pale peach), 'René André' (delicate pale pink) and 'Edmond Proust' (a soft creamy pink shading to rich pink at the center). Roses such as these lay to rest once and for all the myth that historic roses are uncommercial and of academic interest only; I wish some enterprising nurseries would acquire them and make them available for us all to grow.

Another French garden at Bagatelle in the Bois de Boulogne, designed by J.C.N. Forestier in 1906, also makes triumphantly successful use of roses for decorative effect. It was created with the help of Jules Gravereaux, who provided several hundred of the original roses. As at the Roseraie, the garden is formal in the classic French tradition and makes use of the architecture of pillars (again clothed with 'Mrs F.W. Flight'), weeping standards and pergolas, with the extra addition of immaculately shaped yew cones. Many of the Hybrid Teas and Floribundas are grown through grass in narrow beds between dwarf box hedges – a charming effect, though doubtless giving a thorny problem to gardeners who have to clip the grass by hand. An informal area to one side of the main garden contains some of the shrubby species, plus some larger bush roses including Grandifloras; some of these are splendid and

A pergola forms the backbone of the garden of David Austin, breeder of English roses, at Albrighton in Shropshire. 'Alexandre Girault', a useful richly colored, large-flowered Wichurana Rambler, is easily vigorous enough to bridge the gap between adjacent piers, though Bourbon 'Zéphirine Drouhin' scarcely reaches to the top of the pergola.

could be worked into borders and shrubberies with good effect, providing rich color for summer and early autumn.

Of the two gardens, I feel that Bagatelle is the more masterly because the design is never subjugated to the need to cram in another dozen varieties; in some areas of the Roseraie there seem to be just too many roses, though of course the purpose of the garden is first and foremost to accommodate a vast collection. Nevertheless, both are stunningly successful, perhaps more so than any rose garden before or since, making full use of the diversity of the genus while providing a strong architectural framework to make up for the roses' deficiency of form. Both vindicate Robinson's views.

Robinson's contribution to rose gardening was not confined to his assault on the rosarian dogma of Foster-Melliar. His *The English Flower Garden* (1883) was a pivotal work. Though its plant catalog was written with the help of nearly ninety other contributors, including Gertrude Jekyll and the rosarian clergy-men Charles Wolley-Dod (1826–1904), Henry Honywood d'Ombrain (1818–1905), Henry Nicholson Ellacombe (1822– 1916) and Dean Hole, the first half of the book provided a mouthpiece for Robinson's radical opinions about taste and design in the garden. Robinson believed that "it is the spirit of natural beauty we should seek to win into the garden, and so to get away from the set patterns on the one hand and labelled 'dots' on the other." By this he meant the excessively geometrical formal gardens of the day and the botanic-garden approach: massive collections of plants dominated by labels and arranged without art.

His brand of fiery and opinionated dogmatism has given rise to a number of tales, most of them probably apocryphal. It is said that he maintained that there were "only ten minutes in the life of a pear when it is fit for eating" and accordingly would have the dish of pears in his dining room changed several times during the course of a meal. When, after a lifetime's smoking, he decided one day to give up, house guests who accepted the offer of a post-prandial cigar would be informed of the time of the next train to London. He approached his discussion of roses with customary certainty, railing not only against the isolation of the rose but also against florists, their dogmatic rules ("standards of ugliness"), the hideousness of standard roses ("few things have had a worse influence on gardening"), the frequent use of inappropriate rootstocks and the unnecessary habit of heavy annual mulching.

> The old standard Rose had something to do with this separate growth of Roses, it being laid down in the books that the standards did not "associate" with other shrubs, and so it came about that all the standards grafted were placed in the rosery and there held up their buds to the frost! . . . Shows, too, have had a bad effect on the Rose in the garden, where it is many times more important than as a show flower. The whole aim of the man who shows Roses, and who is too often followed as a leader, was to get a certain number of large flowers grown on the Dog Rose, Manetti, or any stock which enabled him to get this at the least cost; so, if we go to any Rose-showing friend [did he have any left after this?], we shall probably find his plants for show hidden in the kitchen garden with a bed of deep manure on the surface of the beds, and as pretty as so many broomsticks. This idea of the Rose as a show flower leads to the cultivation of roses that have not a high value as garden flowers, and Roses that do not open their flowers well in our country in the open air, and are not really worth growing, are grown because they happen to produce flowers now and then that look well on a show bench. So altogether the influence of the shows has been against the Rose as a garden flower, and a cause why large gardens are, in the flower garden, quite bare of the grace of the queen of flowers.

Robinson returned frequently to the themes of the iniquities of standard roses and of inappropriate rootstocks. The latter do not generally present a problem today. A hundred years on, most good rose nurseries have a thorough knowledge of the best rootstock for each class of rose; gone are the days of gathering briars from the hedgerows to use as stocks; many new clones of rootstock have been developed or selected. However, I remember my disappointment as a child when no less than a third of our old roses ordered from one nursery failed at the union. Another third persistently sent out forests of suckers; those that haven't yet been overwhelmed by the stock still do to this day. This should not happen nowadays so long as plants are bought from a reputable and experienced nursery.

In juxtaposition to his various diatribes, Robinson described how his own planting differed, and offered specific advice on how to attain his standards of excellence.

> It is very easy to add, in putting the soil in, all the manure which the Rose may want for some years, so that the surface of the bed might be planted with light-rooting rock and like plants, one of the prettiest ways being to surface it with Pansies and Violets. I have beds of Tea Roses over which the Irish mossy Rockfoil has been growing for years without the roses suffering. . . . The Rose can be nourished for six to eight years without adding any manure to the surface, and after six, eight, or ten years most beds will probably require some change, or we may change our view as regards them.

Robinson explained that his aim was

> to get the best of the Roses into the flower garden instead of bedding plants or coarse perennials, to show at the same time the error of the common way of growing Roses, and also the stupidity of the current idea that you cannot near the house (and in what in the needless verbiage of the day is called the "formal" garden) set flowers out in picturesque and beautiful ways. Another point was to help to get the flower garden more permanently planted instead of the eternal ups and downs of the beds in spring and autumn and the ugly bareness of the earth at these seasons, and to see if one could not make a step towards the beautiful permanent planting of beds near the house and always in view.

Robinson seems to have been a pioneer of bottom-working of bush roses, for he discusses this as though it was not then the norm:

> I had to follow the usual way of getting all the Tea Roses grafted on the common Dog Rose, but always getting the plants "worked" low either on the base of the stock or on the root, so that it is easy in planting to cover the union of the stock with the more precious thing which is grafted on to it, and so to protect the often somewhat delicate kind from intense cold. For ten years or so, of the many kinds we have planted we have had no losses from cold. The Tea Roses were often cut down by the frost, but they came up again . . .

This is a crucial development: not only did it give a degree of protection to more tender sorts of rose but it allowed Tea and the then fairly new class of Hybrid Tea roses to be used for relatively low beds. Previously, bedding with roses had only been possible for gardeners happy to use the few truly dwarf varieties or to engage in laborious pegging. With the advent of the Teas and Hybrid Teas the rose had become a bedding plant. Gone were the days of the forests of stalky bushes. These were shown by Paul but significantly seldom portrayed by contemporary artists: they must have been very ugly.

Evidence of the trend towards bedding and other large-scale effects is given by the adoption of the term "Decorative Rose" by the then National Rose Society in their tables of ratings in the 1910s. This term covered varieties with blooms not large or regular enough for exhibition, that is, roses grown primarily for garden effect rather than the quality of their individual flowers. T.S. Allison in the 1913 *Rose Annual* criticized breeders for concentrating on the cut flower's floral form, size and endurance, to the detriment of other admirable characteristics, such as fragrance and natural grace, and commented: "The Exhibition Rose is trembling in its seat of what has hitherto been secure authority. The Decorative Rose, with the powerful aid of the ladies behind it, is fighting for place and power."

Robinson's war against the formalists, whose case was put by John Dando Sedding (1838–91) in his *Gardencraft, Old and New* (1891) and Sir Reginald Blomfield (1856–1942) in *The Formal Garden in England* (1892), was famous and divided horticulturists into two camps: those who believed that gardens were essentially works of art and thus artifice, and those who believed they should strive towards an idealized version of nature. Both sides had valid points but Robinson made no attempt to balance the arguments: the publicity created by his dogmatism and pugnacity towards his opponents probably helped to sell his books.

It remained for Gertrude Jekyll to show through her planting designs and writing how an ideal balance could be achieved: that is, by using generous and informal planting to soften an architectural design and making the garden ever more natural and informal farther from the house. It is, perhaps, somewhat ironic that Robinson's own garden, at Gravetye, Sussex, had a formal garden near the house and also that some of his designs for clients were formal, such as the borders created in 1898 at Killerton, Devon, for the Acland family, for whom Sedding was working at the time of his death.

Did anyone take any notice of Robinson's intemperate ranting and one-sided arguments? It seems clear that the bottom-working of bush roses caught on quickly and was a significant change, altering altogether the appearance of the rose garden, though there were doubtless rosarians who had seen its sense independently. *The Rose Book* (1913) by Harry Higgott Thomas (1876–1956) shows numerous plates of gardens with bedded roses; some standards remain, though those that are not weeping standards are used solely as punctuation.

What of Robinson's instruction to use roses with other plants? Around the turn of the century his friend Miss Jekyll certainly used a limited range of edging plants with roses, including *Stachys byzantina*, catmint, lavender and santolina, though this was not to become the norm for some twenty or thirty years. H.H. Thomas wrote:

> There is a charm about the unexpected that is not to be denied, and to come across a big rose bush, lusty and abounding in blossom, rubbing shoulders with a clump of Larkspur or jostling the stout shoots of a Paeony, may perhaps not afford evidence of good gardening as standardized for us nowadays, but it is uncommonly delightful. . . . There is no reason why you should not smother the ground beneath and between the roses with those delightful and daintily varied tufted Pansies or Violas that begin to bloom in May and are scarcely without blossom onwards until November.

In addition, Thomas recommended lobelia, alyssum and pinks, although, perhaps tellingly, here there was no mention of the edging plants that Miss Jekyll favored and that were subsequently to become common.

In the 1916 *Rose Annual*, Robert Harris wrote of bedding roses bordered with violas (white roses with yellow violas, red with white, pink with mauve and blue nemophila with yellow roses). Norman Lambert, in the 1925 annual, repeated the recommendation, suggesting that violas could also be used as "groundwork" between the roses "for the 'Queen of Flowers' need not reign alone." Eleanour Sinclair Rohde mentioned in her *Gardens of Delight* (1934) "rose gardens where the roses grow surrounded with broad borders of violas; sunk rose gardens with paved walks gemmed with stonecrops and other lowly plants; diminutive plots surrounded with lavender hedges and where the central beds of pink and red China monthly roses are edged with Mrs Sinkins pinks in rich profusion."

The painting of Robinson's garden at Gravetye by Beatrice Parsons shows the sort of scheme he intended, with sparsely placed China or Hybrid Tea roses in shell pink underplanted to overflowing with annual pinks, border carnations and campanulas while in the background clematis in violet-blue and burgundy foam forward across banks of shrubs. Though charming, I feel this is something of a jumble with too little attention to the foliage of the underplanting, which also bears flowers too close in size to those of the roses so that the pure and elegant lines of the roses are lost in the mêlée.

Few gardeners have mixed their companion plants so fully with the roses as Robinson, nor have they used such an imaginative range of varieties. However, there has been a general acceptance that rose beds can be edged with other flowers. In 1971, novelist H.E. Bates commented:

> Remembering how William Robinson had . . . almost fanatically recommended the planting of various dwarf plants under roses to provide not only color but cool ground cover I proceeded to do the same, planting many scores [of auriculas] in a bed of that most excellent of floribunda roses, Europeana, of the rich burgundy flowers and about the same wine-colored leaves. No marriage was more stupendously and happily successful.

Within fifty years of the appearance of *The English Flower Garden*, Robinson's advice on mixed planting had become the accepted norm among gardeners. However, the garden historian should not attribute changes in practice and design entirely to prophets or critics like Robinson and Jekyll: to some extent the prophets reacted to irrationalities that gardeners would have rebelled against eventually without their intervention; they also reported the beginnings of trends that would have proceeded without them.

There were still exceptions to the new norm among hard-line rosarians: in T. Geoffrey W. Henslow's *The Rose Encyclopaedia* (1922), we read: "let me lay down the law that Rose-beds should contain only Rose trees." These opinions seem to have lingered in municipal rose gardens, though I did see *Viola* 'Maggie Mott' as an underplanting for roses in a Devon seaside park over twenty years ago, before the revival of interest in violas, in what I take to be a survival of an Edwardian, if not Robinsonian, scheme.

Violas are exceptionally pretty and co-exist happily with roses, provided the planting distance of the bushes is wide enough to allow a little light into the bed. Though 'Maggie Mott' is perhaps regarded as the traditional Edwardian variety for underplanting, I feel sorts with even smaller flowers such as the Cornuta hybrids are more attractive, and they are not so aggressively vigorous as their parent species. A wide range of colors is available, allowing contrasts of china blues or purples with clear light yellows or whites, or harmonies of dusky pinks or yellows with roses of similar tones. At Powis Castle in Wales, however, *Viola cornuta* proved a failure, being far too vigorous, growing up into the rose bushes and eventually suppressing them, though it would doubtless have been a success with the bigger shrub roses; diascias worked much better, especially *Diascia vigilis* and *D. barberae* 'Ruby Field', flowering agreeably wherever they were not entirely in the shade. The many new cultivars in shades of deep coral, apricot, magenta, lilac, rose pink and blush white will surely yield a good number that are suited to underplanting, though, as for pinks, it is preferable to choose a tone that harmonizes with the roses but is not so close to them in depth of tone that it prevents them from being seen distinctly.

Many primroses and polyanthus could also be used, both seed-raised and clonally propagated, though my favorites are the Cowichan sorts with sumptuous velvety flowers with almost no contrasting eye and dark leaves, available in shades of Venetian red, garnet, violet-blue, royal purple and old gold. It is advisable to grow at least several dozen of each required color from seed and to select only the very best to be increased over the years by division to complete the cover. Fairly frequent division, in at least every other year immediately after flowering, is advisable to keep them healthy and floriferous.

Heucheras, heucherellas and tiarellas have been receiving the attention of hybridists in recent years, resulting in many new sorts that are attractive both in leaf and flower. A couple of decades ago, *Heuchera micrantha* var. *diversifolia* 'Palace Purple' was the only commonly available bronze-leaved sort; now there are dozens more, some of them also having attractive pink flowers, others with leaves overlaid with a metallic pewter finish; some green-leaved varieties have a silver upper surface. Suitable for the front of beds and borders but also sufficiently tolerant of shade to be used as underplanting, provided roses are not too close, they benefit from fairly frequent replanting in early autumn, allowing them to make new roots while the ground is still warm.

Robinson recommended sedums for planting with roses, though their need for sun means that most of the clump-forming sorts are best at the front of beds and borders and not suitable for underplanting. Apart from the glaucous-leaved clumpers *Sedum spectabile*, *S. telephium* and the slightly tender *S. sieboldii*, all of them valued for their foliage as much as their flower, which is too tardy for all but the latest roses, there are many with foliage in tones of purple and bronze; eminent among these are *S. telephium* 'Arthur Branch' with upright habit, deep bronze leaves and rich red stems, and purple-leaved 'Vera Jameson', 'Ruby Glow' and 'Bertram Anderson'. Some of the sedums with in-between-colored flowers having tints of salmon or brick need careful placing and do not associate well with pure pinks; these include esculent-sounding 'Stewed Rhubarb Mountain' and 'Strawberries and Cream' as well as the better-known 'Herbstfreude' (Autumn Joy). *S. spurium* and its cultivars are more suited for underplanting, being low spreaders, rooting as they run; they include bronze- as well as green-leaved sorts.

Pinks are still a favorite plant for associating with roses and many of the more recent cultivars have the advantage that they bloom continuously. Nevertheless, the older cultivars are still highly popular, particularly those such as white *Dianthus* 'Mrs Sinkins', found in a workhouse garden in Slough, Buckinghamshire, in 1868 and commemorated in the town's armorial bearings; Graham Thomas prefers the similar 'White Ladies' because of its superlative blue-green foliage. 'Excelsior' is a similar pink variety and all three have the advantage that they are fairly persistent and do not need frequent repropagation. For years, before being tempted by some of the more recent sorts, I used to grow (raised from cuttings from an uncle's garden, along with several sorts of border carnations) 'Mrs Sinkins', 'Excelsior' and another popular old variety, 'Inchmery', in front of our roses. These three were all relatively easy, in spite of the heavy acid soil of Leeds, and their fragrance was captivating.

Other varieties I bought from Mrs Desmond Underwood in

the late 1960s included cherry-red 'Thomas', the still popular 'Doris' and its salmon-red sport 'Doreen', all of them first-rate though lacking the strong and persuasive fragrance of 'Mrs Sinkins'. 'Pink Bouquet' was another great success, though it flowered so freely it was hard to prevent its death after blooming; shoots for cuttings were sparingly produced, perhaps a reason why it seems to have disappeared from cultivation. I do not know why 'Doreen' should also have vanished for it was as persistent and as excellent as 'Doris'; I hope it might still lurk somewhere waiting to be reintroduced. Laced pinks from Mrs Underwood were also treasured, although they may have lacked the floriferousness of 'Pink Bouquet' and the persistence of the others so far mentioned. Other pinks, gifts from friends, included superlative green-eyed single white 'Musgrave's Pink' and slightly rangy but long-flowering salmon 'Old Square Eyes'.

In National Trust gardens most of these same varieties predominate in association with roses, notably 'White Ladies', 'Musgrave's Pink', 'Doris' and 'Thomas'; at Mottisfont Abbey in Hampshire, *Dianthus* Allwoodii Alpinus Group is a particular feature, especially as an underplanting throughout the bed of China roses. None of these is as tall as the majority of more recent varieties such as the Devon Series: bred for use as cut flowers, these are perhaps not so telling used with roses, for their stems can adopt untidily divergent angles and their flowers can lift themselves among those of the roses, making for a degree of visual confusion, particularly if colors and flower sizes of both pinks and roses approach equivalence. Perhaps for this reason, there is much to be said for using the smaller-flowered sorts, such as the Allwoodii Alpinus Group, and for avoiding planting pinks with roses of a similar hue.

A bed of China roses (this one is 'Hermosa', introduced in 1840) at Mottisfont Abbey, Hampshire, underplanted with Dianthus *Allwoodii Alpinus Group*

Robinson also used *Campanula carpatica* among his roses. Here I have to confess a reservation: campanula blue mixed with rose pink does nothing for me. I neither like nor dislike the combination, but it seems at best to be a missed opportunity, although I would be perfectly happy to see blue with white or yellow roses, and white campanulas with pink roses. Violet-blue *C. glomerata* would also make a very telling combination with rather earlier yellow shrub roses such as 'Agnes' or 'Frühlingsgold' and would tolerate whatever shade they cast.

I have the same reservations about campanula-blue-flowered geraniums such as 'Johnson's Blue' and 'Kashmir Blue' and would be reluctant to use pink *Geranium* × *oxonianum* cultivars with pink roses of similar hue. I would not let *G.* × *magnificum* anywhere near my roses: for ten days its flowers jostle in hideous congestion, squashed up against each other and unable to carry themselves distinctly or with poise, to produce a violent block of color that completely overwhelms any rose with the misfortune to be near by; thereafter there is nothing but fairly dull foliage. Most of the geraniums of middling size have a role to play, usually combined with shrub roses rather than bush varieties; the latter can be planted with the likes of *G.* × *riversleaianum* cultivars to the front or *G.* × *cantabrigiense* varieties in the shade beneath to create some charming associations.

Hostas also have their uses as underplantings or edgings for rose beds. Unfortunately, they are not problem-free. The variegated sorts can look frantic and yellow foliage does not always flatter roses. Then there is the added complication that in climates with hot and sunny summers, hostas will scorch. Nevertheless, where conditions allow, it is well worth trying some of the glaucous-leaved varieties such as the Tardiana Group. There is a particularly successful use of *Hosta* (Tardiana Group) 'Halcyon' to edge a bed of 'Rosemary Rose' at Arley Hall in Cheshire. Of course there are other plants with a similar leaf color that might have been used, for instance 'Jackman's Blue' rue, but it is doubtful whether any of them has the same bold and appealing line quality, a strong element lacking from the roses themselves.

Bugles also make first-rate ground cover beneath and in front of roses, tolerating shade and providing late spring flowers as well as foliage in a range of different colors. They also have the immense advantage that they are low enough to underplant even relatively short spring or autumn bulbs such as scillas, chionodoxas or crocuses, including autumn-flowering sorts and, perhaps more importantly, colchicums; these must have their spatterdashes if they are not to become besmirched by mud and bugles are as good as any. There can be few more telling combinations than *Ajuga reptans* 'Atropurpurea' with the classic white goblets of *Colchicum speciosum* 'Album' appearing above; there is no reason why such a display should not be backed and overtopped by late-flowering roses, perhaps Chinas or Hybrid Musks, and a succession of colchicums could be used to flower continually from late summer to mid-autumn.

Although Joshua Major had suggested using bulbs in rose beds, no rosarian seems to have done so until 1924. In that year, H.R. Darlington committed the heresy of recommending bulbs for rose beds and made some helpful suggestions, though he considered most bulbs best around shrub roses and not appropriate for use with bedders. He tells us that chionodoxas are especially useful throughout beds, but the likes of snowdrops, winter aconites and muscari are better as edgings. Early daffodils are best used with roses pruned in early spring so that rose stems do not interfere with the display, and the latest-flowering sorts, such as Poeticus varieties, are to be used with the last roses to be pruned, the Teas. Tulips have the advantage of foliage that dies off less messily than daffodils, though they harbor greenfly that Darlington thought could infest the roses. (The aphid in question, *Dysaphis tulipae*, attacks only monocots and does not move on to broad-leaved plants once the tulips die back.) Mulching must be done in autumn or before the bulbs appear. This is not easy if the mulch consists of large mats of strawy manure and rose stems are in the way. However, autumn thinning of the roses would help and many modern mulches are fine and friable enough to find their way through the stems. Bulbs should be deep enough to hoe over throughout the summer, though with reasonably good mulching and weed control this should not be necessary. The bulbs are generally vigorous and persistent enough to stand some losses from occasional digging in of manure or other cultivation.

Floribunda Mariandel®, an excellent bedding rose with bronze-red young foliage

I feel that bulbs can be used even more widely than Darlington suggested, though to incorporate them through bedding roses requires a slightly wider spacing of the roses than usual. However, such a spacing also allows the sort of interplanting Robinson suggested, using herbaceous plants to take over the display after the bulbs have died back. The young foliage of roses often has a copper or red flush, particularly marked in, for example, Blessings® and Mariandel® (syn. The Times Rose), that can play a part in the color scheme. Such foliage can contribute to combinations with richly colored tulips, narcissi with deep orange or scarlet trumpets and an underplanting of velvety Venetian red Cowichan polyanthus.

Many good new Rambler roses raised around the turn of the century necessitated gardens with structures suitable for supporting and displaying them. British gardeners did not excel in this respect. The French were supreme, as

PAGES 46–47 *At Arley Hall in Cheshire, a formal sitting area flanked by two grand vases is surrounded by the Floribunda 'Rosemary Rose', introduced by the Dutch breeder de Ruiter in 1954. With its rich raspberry-cerise many-petalled flowers, bronze foliage and compact growth, this is still a useful bedding variety, though it is now more prone to mildew than when it was introduced and must be sprayed with fungicide if it is to remain healthy. Catmint and* Hosta *(Tardiana Group) 'Halcyon' provide attractive edgings.*

demonstrated by their prodigious rose gardens at Bagatelle and L'Haÿ-les-Roses. On a less grand scale, Monet's garden at Giverny, made between 1883 and his death in 1926, shows an amateur, well connected with his country's horticultural élite, using roses in a free and exuberant mixture with other plants. His use of roses was ahead of its time in France and perhaps a couple of decades ahead of similar planting in the British Isles. As the designer of Bagatelle's rose garden, Monet's friend J.C.N. Forestier, remarked in 1920: "Barely twenty years ago the much-disdained roses were barely admitted to our gardens; they were rejected from our public gardens. Often, in the parks of large country houses, they were exiled to the potager, along with the multitude of perennials grown solely for their cut flowers." At Giverny Ramblers tumble across the spacious central arcade as well as on the climbing frames of the east half of the garden and weeping standard roses are used throughout as telling and graceful accents.

The excellent new Ramblers that originated mostly from France in the years around 1900 were usually trained in British gardens on to unworthy and ramshackle structures of larch poles. However, the extra brilliance and versatility of such plants and of their frequent companions, the clematis hybrids, meant that architectural features such as pergolas could look more exuberant than ever, and drip and foam with spectacular blossom throughout the summer months. Several British garden architects made a speciality of pergolas, notably Edwin Lutyens, Thomas Mawson and Harold Peto. In the United States, it was perhaps Peto's structures that most influenced the leading garden designer Beatrix Farrand, though here too there was hardly a hotbed of revolutionary ideas on the design and planting of rose gardens.

Gertrude Jekyll's planting plans for Lutyens' designs, and her many publications, assisted substantially by her friendship with Robinson, the leading publisher, made her perhaps the foremost influence in planting style in the decades before her death in 1932. Made for clients who lacked plant knowledge and who employed gardeners without the skills to arrange plants attractively, her designs were static: no advice was given on parameters for changing them from year to year to keep them fresh and alive. Their lack of change and the shortage of skills of those who controlled them ensured that they were doomed to last but a few years. World War II hastened the demise of the planting in all but a couple of Miss Jekyll's gardens. It was not until a revival of interest in her work in the 1970s that gardeners came to look again at her books and planting plans and found in them a wealth of insight, inspiration and sound common sense.

Miss Jekyll was not interested in growing vast numbers of different plants for their individual beauty but concerned herself with a couple of hundred that she valued for their ability to combine with other plants, bearing in mind not just their flowers but the color, texture and architecture of their foliage. Every page of *Colour Schemes for the Flower Garden* (1914), her most influential work, is packed with useful analysis and advice, but I have to admit that I find her *Roses for English Gardens*, written with Edward Mawley, published in 1902, disappointing. Although she gives good advice on the use of some classes, such as Scotch briars for banks and near the house, Ramblers for pergolas and more informal shrubs for wilder areas, her advice for rose gardens themselves is a little thin.

However, she did show that she was influenced by the likes of Paul, Marnock and Robinson. She begins her discussion on rose gardens with a Robinsonian attack on the excessive and inappropriate use of geometric designs. After discussing the use of the wilder Ramblers to grow into trees (as William Paul had done) and such roses as *Rosa virginiana* and *R. wichurana* to tumble over a retaining wall or down a bank, she continues by extolling the virtues of setting the rose garden in encircling woods (like Paul, Major and Marnock), as in so many of the great Italian gardens. Then follows a description of the

> English Rose garden that I dream of . . . embowered in native woodland, that shall approach it nearly enough to afford a passing shade in some of the sunny hours, though not so closely as to rob the Roses at the root. My Rose garden follows the declivities of a tiny, shallow valley, or is formed in such a shape. It is approached through a short piece of near home woodland of dark-foliaged trees, for the most part evergreens; Yew, Holly and Scotch Fir. . . . As it belongs to a house of some importance, it will be treated, as to its midmost spaces, with the wrought stone steps and balustraded terraces, and such other accessories as will agree with those of the house itself. . . . The balustrade is not covered up or smothered with flowery growths, but here and there a Rose from above comes foaming up over its edge and falls over, folding it in a glorious mantle of flower and foliage.

Thus her ideal rose garden differed little from those of Paul or Marnock save that it depended on more stonework, and roses of looser and more informal growth could be more widely used around the perimeter. Indeed, the second of the two examples she showed in plan adopted the same outline as Marnock's Warwick Castle rose garden with a square superimposed on a quatrefoil; the outer edge is shown hedged with yew within the surrounding woodland, while the inner beds have a catenary of Rambler roses trained on posts and chains around their circumference.

Miss Jekyll's further comments on the nature of the rose garden are interesting: "the Rose garden can never be called gorgeous; the term is quite unfitting. Even in high Rose tide, when fullest of bloom, what is most clearly felt is the lovable charm of Rose beauty. . . . The gorgeousness of brilliant bloom, fitly arranged, is for other plants and other portions of the garden; here we do not want the mind to be distracted from the beauty and delightfulness of the Rose." In this she was almost paraphrasing the words of Foster-Melliar eight years earlier.

We might quibble with this assessment today: surely some of our favorite rose gardens, depending substantially on the varieties of Miss Jekyll's time, are truly gorgeous; I would rate among these Bagatelle, the Roseraie at L'Haÿ-les-Roses, Sudeley Castle and Sissinghurst. It may perhaps be that, with the benefit of another hundred years, we have found the means of wresting every last ounce of brilliant effect from our roses, and we are no longer content with rose gardens that serve as a setting for the display of the beauty of individual blooms. But in any event, Miss Jekyll's criticism of rose gardens must surely have been made with their main denizens the bush roses in mind, for her photographs show Ramblers looking distinctly gorgeous. Her prose is much too understated to allow the extravagant turn of phrase we find in texts by some of her contemporaries. Here is Sir George Sitwell (1860–1943), a client of Miss Jekyll's in 1910, writing in his book *On the Making of Gardens* (1909):

> if it is to be a rose-garden, do not choose those stunted, unnatural, earth-loving strains, which have nothing of vigour and wildness in them, nor banish other flowers which may do homage to the beauty of a rose as courtiers to a queen. Let climbing roses drop in a veil from the terrace and smother with flower-spangled embroidery the garden walls, run riot over vaulted arcades, clamber up lofty obelisks . . . let there be a rose balloon weighed down by the struggling cupids, or the hollow ribs and bellying curves of an old-world ship . . . or one of those rose-castles which the French romance gave to the garden for a mimic siege in May . . . Such a Château d'Amour is represented on many a mediaeval casket and mirror-case. Ponderous mangonels are bombarding the fortress with monstrous blossoms, while from the battlements fair ladies hurl down roses still heavy with morning dew full in the faces of the attacking knights.

Clearly Sir George was not writing for the owners of suburban semis. However, for those of us who cannot stretch to rose-castles and ponderous mangonels there are still some lessons to be learned: roses can be used in a much freer way than was the norm in the early-twentieth-century rose garden. It was perhaps the lovers of old roses who most clearly demonstrated this: the exuberant growth and rich romance of the old varieties and their suitability for mixing with other plants have given rise to a style of rose garden that was not seen in the nineteenth century nor foreseen by the prophets Jekyll and Robinson, nor had it developed to the full until our most recent decades.

Sissinghurst represents the apogee of this style, though its development is not due to Victoria Sackville-West (1892–1962) alone. Vita was one of a coterie of aficionados of old roses of the early to mid-twentieth century which included Edward Ashdown Bunyard, the Hon. Robert James, Maud Messel, Arthur Tysilio Johnson, Sir Frederick Stern, Nancy Lindsay, Sir George Sitwell's son Sacheverell, Constance Spry, Hilda Murrell, James Mitchell and, still an important influence at the end of the century, Graham Thomas. Vita's importance in the history of rose gardens lies in her powerful advocacy of old roses through her weekly articles in *The Observer*, her books and her garden, which was and still is accessible to the public. Her exquisitely written portraits of the roses she loved captured the imagination of many gardeners and encouraged them to copy the example of Sissinghurst. However, the garden we see today is not as it was in Vita's time. Then the rose was still seen as being primarily an early summer flower. Vita herself considered that the display was "limited to one glorious month of midsummer." Since then, modern roses have extended it to last from spring to autumn; at Sissinghurst companion planting has become more varied, and culture, pruning and training have been optimized by three remarkable head gardeners.

The formal framework of the garden was laid out by Vita's husband Harold Nicolson (1886–1968) in 1932, though the roses were not planted until 1937. Vita's vision of her garden as "a tumble of roses and honeysuckle, figs and vines" has about it the naturalistic charm envisaged by Sir George Sitwell, and the roses she grew remain in the garden today, comprising the least changed element of Sissinghurst's planting. In its early days, the Rose Garden contained few companion plants other than irises (which were valued for their bold foliage contrast), lilies and, for later in the season, Japanese anemones.

The appointment of two energetic and visionary head gardeners, Pam Schwerdt and Sibylle Kreutzberger, in 1959 changed all that. They realized that the season could be extended without affecting the summer display of roses: for spring, tulips, wallflowers, primroses and polyanthus were added; onions such as *Allium hollandicum* and *A. cristophii* followed, coinciding with the early roses. For the peak of rose time, contrasts were provided by clouds of *Crambe cordifolia* and tall Spuria irises, breaking up the previously unrelieved rose foliage more effectively than the shorter Bearded varieties Harold and Vita had assembled. Cranesbills, catmints and campanulas also accompanied the roses, being followed by agapanthus, *Aster* × *frikartii* and annuals and tender perennials such as *Nicotiana* 'Lime Green', hybrid arctotis, argyranthemums and penstemons. Pam and Sibylle's constant striving for perfection, through improvements in planting, techniques and culture, continued uninterrupted after the garden's transfer to the National Trust in 1967 and is now carried on by Sarah Cook, head gardener since 1991.

At Sissinghurst the roses and the other planting may be seen as roughly equal partners in the design: neither one would work without the other. In other gardens in which old roses are planted informally within a formal structure and are complemented by generous quantities of companion plants, the roses predominate.

One of the best known of these is the National Trust's Mottisfont Abbey, where in 1972 the rose collection assembled by Graham Thomas was housed in the former kitchen garden. Down the center of the garden run imposing and generously scaled double borders planned to provide color from spring to summer, while all the surrounding rose beds and borders contain plants such as campanulas, columbines, pinks and white foxgloves chosen to flatter the roses.

Other impressive gardens of old roses, for example Helmingham Hall in Suffolk, contain similar companion planting. White foxgloves are also a feature here, valuable for the strong contrast of their spikes with the more amorphous roses. However, they do have a disadvantage: by the latter half of the rose season, the spikes may have just a small tuft of flower on top of an extremely lanky and often perversely wavy stem. Brave gardeners will cut these off as soon as the length of podded stem bare of flowers becomes excessive; however, an alternative approach, adopted at The Menagerie in Northamptonshire, is to use the shorter Foxy Group foxgloves, which are in any case much more in scale with bushes shorter than 5ft/1.5m. I normally despair of the seed houses' attempts to make graceful plants short and squat but such a modest reduction has its uses.

At Sudeley Castle in Gloucestershire, Jane Fearnley-Whittingstall, one of the most perceptive of recent authors on rose gardens, has designed a garden predominantly of old roses in formal box-edged beds in which companion plants need play only a minor role. The setting is stupendously romantic, with parkland to the south and east, a chapel to the north and the ruined castle to the west. The roses are pruned fairly hard, and though this does not allow them the free growth that some might consider a prerequisite of naturalism, it has other benefits: coupled with generous annual mulching, it encourages vigorous growth, relative freedom from disease and long flowering.

While informal rose planting largely using old roses was evolving throughout the twentieth century, roses for bedding were also undergoing a change: breeders transformed both the Floribunda rose and the Hybrid Tea in range and brilliance of color and in their ability to produce copious color from summer to fall. To the traditional rose colors were added strong yellows, oranges and bright vermilion scarlet; the comments of Foster-Melliar that the rose was unable to "keep up continual masses of color throughout the summer" and of Miss Jekyll ("the gorgeousness of brilliant bloom . . . is for other plants") simply no

A bed of roses at Helmingham Hall, Suffolk, edged with lavender and interplanted with white foxgloves. The bold spikes of the foxgloves provide an effective contrast of form with the roses.

longer applied. The rose had become a challenger to pelargoniums and petunias, offering competitive quantities of color with the bonus of superlative floral shape.

Not surprisingly, its perceived role in the garden changed from being principally a provider of quality blooms to being a source of color. By the 1920s, a bed of bush roses would display such strong color for so long that it became almost imperative to arrange the hues for optimum effect. Mrs Darlington discussed color in the rose garden in the *Rose Annual* of 1929 and 1930 and there was a further article by George Dillistone in 1934. Dillistone, best known today for his work at Castle Drogo, Devon, was the garden designer whose style most typified what was popular in early-twentieth-century Britain. His article in the 1928 annual shows a characteristic formal rose garden design of some 50 × 80yds/ 45 × 73m, typical in its elements and style of those found in almost every large garden of the time.

The popularity of public rose gardens in the mid-twentieth century was largely due to the transformation of the rose in the previous decades. Most extant rose gardens date from this period. After the very early International Rose Test Garden, Portland, Oregon (1917), there came Queen Mary's Rose Garden, Regent's Park (1931, replanted by Millar Gault, 1955-69); Hershey Rose Garden, Pennsylvania (1937); Parc de la Grange, Geneva (1941); Park of Roses, Columbus, Ohio (1952); Parque del Oeste, Madrid (1950s); Royal National Rose Society Gardens of the Rose, St Albans, Hertfordshire (1960); Westbroekpark, The Hague (1960); City of Belfast Rose Garden (1964); Parc de la Tête d'Or, Lyon (1964); Royal Botanical Gardens, Hamilton, Ontario (1967); Austrian Rosarium, Baden, Vienna (1967); the Rosarium of the German Rose Society, Westfalenpark, Dortmund (1969); St Anne's Park, Dublin (1970s) and the American Rose Center, Shreveport, Louisiana (1970s).

The partly ruined Sudeley Castle, set in the encircling Cotswold hills, makes a spectacularly romantic setting for this rose garden, late Victorian in design. Jane Fearnley-Whittingstall provided the present planting plans, punctuated by weeping standard roses such as 'New Dawn' here, in 1988. The roses beneath the standards are pruned fairly hard, which encourages rather late but long flowering, good health and even growth.

DAWN

These include some spectacular examples in which the color of roses combines with often superlative surrounding "borrowed landscape" and occasionally lakes and fountains to produce a memorable display. Most are formal; in those that are trial gardens, bed size and shape for each rose variety needs to be more or less identical and usually rectangular to provide a fair comparison, inevitably a limiting factor; however, some more recent gardens such as Westbroekpark and Parc de la Grange accommodate rectangular beds in a free-flowing informal design.

A particularly prodigious project in rose planting can be found in Aberdeen, Grampian, where some two million bushes have been used around the city, some in grand public gardens such as Duthie Park and Hazlehead Park but the vast majority of them to ornament almost every thoroughfare in the city. When I visited a year or so ago, I found Hazlehead to be most impressive, with two spacious and well-maintained square gardens filled with recent roses, many of them raised and selected locally by Cockers of Aberdeen. This is not a bad policy: it would clearly be unreasonable to expect a rose bred and selected in England to perform well in a Scottish climate (still less in North America or Australia) unless it had been shown to like the local conditions. The beds of Hybrid Teas and Floribundas are punctuated at intervals with standard roses – not I think, a success: the sameness of scale, foliage and flower does little to relieve the monotony, though the scale gives grandeur and the color provides impact.

The Queen Mother's Rose Garden at Hazlehead Park

Duthie Park is altogether different: perhaps less successful but far more interesting. Set in a glade among encircling trees is a substantial hill completely covered in roses. Sinuous interlocking blocks of Hybrid Teas and Floribundas wind their way on either side of a spiral path leading to the summit, where a viewing platform looks down the slopes through a gap in the trees to the park beyond. This is undoubtedly a spectacle and popular with visitors; but there is something unsubtle about the scheme that diminishes the viewer's pleasure. There are perhaps three reasons why I do not unreservedly enjoy this undoubted *tour de force*: first, the joy of coming across a rose mountain is offset by its failure to relate to the rest of the landscape; secondly, there is the monotony of rose foliage and flower used over a wide area, all of it in the same scale and with no relief of texture and structure that might be provided by some companion planting; thirdly (a problem affecting almost every United Kingdom local authority), standards of maintenance have clearly slipped below those originally specified and below the minimum required for the roses to survive in a state of tolerable health and attractiveness.

Here is not the place to bemoan the fact that local authorities, forced to cut expenditure and given a choice between reducing budgets on schools, hospitals or parks, have little option but to whittle away at parks first. They and their staff are doing their best in difficult circumstances, little helped by their public's failure to praise them when they do well or criticize, or even notice, when reduced standards are forced on them. But the lesson for all rose lovers is that roses need certain minimum standards: if these are no longer provided, they cease to be attractive and can even die. Sure, cutting out deadheading will only diminish their late display, not cause the roses to perish; but failure to spray, particularly in a large area of monoculture where disease problems are concentrated, will kill stone dead the most susceptible varieties and reduce others to a moribund, near leafless and ugly state; stopping the maintenance of humus content, and hence soil structure and fertility, by regular mulching will allow erosion and sometimes fatal loss of vigor.

At Duthie Park on my last visit, several rose groups were dead and others so reduced in health that they were inelegant when seen at close range from the encircling path; soil structure and humus content were visibly lacking; one wonders how much longer such planting can survive. It is perhaps unfair to single out one park to illustrate this point, particularly since it is run by the borough that has had the greatest commitment to the rose of any in Europe, and most other public parks suffer similar problems. But the lessons it shows affect all rose lovers: there is no point planting expanses of roses unless we are willing to give them the care they need; if we dislike spraying with synthetic pesticides and fungicides, or if we just do not get round to it at the crucial time, we should avoid all susceptible varieties; and we must always be prepared to keep the soil in good heart.

The most inspiring aspect of Duthie Park is that it points the way forward, showing that roses can be used in shapes other than rectangles to paint the landscape, to create the sort of spectacular gardens that became the hallmark of Roberto Burle Marx in Brazil. True, colors need to be judged with some subtlety: the Brazilian hues of many modern roses, as bright and brassy as any bromeliad, might look alien in the paler light of more temperate climates. There is no reason why other plants should not be combined with them to provide the variety of form and texture that the roses lack.

The hill of roses at Duthie Park in Aberdeen

Many informal rose gardens are unlike Duthie Park in that they are essentially wild, containing roses planted not in beds but randomly through grass or into shrubs and trees. This style of planting is the subject of a separate chapter (page 144). However, one interesting non-formal yet tamed rose garden was designed by Sir Geoffrey Jellicoe in 1959 for the 3rd Lord Astor at Cliveden, Buckinghamshire. Set in lawn in a glade among trees, this garden uses as its basis a painting by Paul Klee, *The Fruit* (1932), figuring a plum-shaped oval transected by a line which spirals within to make a series of overlapping shapes. A gravel path represents Klee's lines and the beds created by spaces between these are filled with shrub roses underplanted with ground cover.

Jellicoe considered that Klee was the most inspiring artist for landscapers because his paintings were so often based on biological forms. However, the vigorous shrub roses and the fairly sharp bends of the paths obscure the design so that it is sometimes almost impossible to discern the pleasing shapes of the beds. Like many of Jellicoe's designs, this is a scheme that can be appreciated to the full only if the viewer is provided with a plan and an explanation.

At Bagatelle in Paris, a relatively new and informal garden has been planted with Ground Cover and other roses on the fringes of woodland looking back across spacious lawns to the chateau. These are low-maintenance plantings with no edged beds and no fiddly pruning. This too points to a new era in the use of roses: they no longer need to be stiff and formal, and the work of growing them can be very substantially reduced from the traditional requirements of the Hybrid Tea. The development of the Patio rose has also offered new possibilities, both for brightly colored carpets and for front-of-the-border planting.

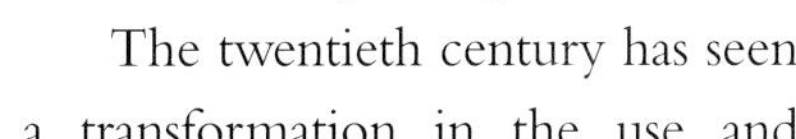

The twentieth century has seen a transformation in the use and character of roses. In 1890, roses old and new, shrub and bush, were valued for the beauty of their flowers but considered to be limited in their large-scale effect, difficult to associate with other plants, and incapable of gorgeousness. The skill and artistry of the gardeners of the last hundred years have shown how magnificence might be attained; breeders have produced roses of ever-more-powerful color and varied habit. Much has been accomplished, but the immense potential for the rose garden in the twenty-first century, exploiting the unique characteristics of more recent classes of rose, has yet to be fully realized.

Roses for Structure

Roses clothing the garden's essential designed elements – its structure – play a significant role in defining the walls of the garden room. Even the cleverest and most lavish built feature cannot supply the enjoyment of fitting design well furnished with beautiful plants.

Among garden structures intended to be clad with plants, pergolas are the most architectural and exert the strongest influence. Around the perimeter of the garden a pergola offers a viewing point, a green cloister, giving comfortable enclosure but presenting a series of framed views to the garden beyond. If the garden is large, a pergola placed across the center subdivides the available space, creating a more intimate and human scale. Pergolas have the added benefit of lending dappled shade. And they also present great scope for planting, provided they are not too heavily overcanopied by carpentry and foliage, when their interiors can be dank and dark, devoid of the flowers that should be their chiefest delight.

Though it is true that pergolas are often associated with the grandest gardens with more space and resources than most of us could muster, they can be adapted to smaller plots, including modest town or suburban gardens, and made from inexpensive and easily obtainable materials. Moreover, the problems and solutions of their planting apply largely to simpler arcades and catenaries and to the furnishing of fences and even of walls.

Pergolas of a simple kind were known in Italy in antiquity. These forward-projecting galleries of posts in front of houses were useful structures on which vines would be grown, and which also provided welcome shade. Later the word came to be used for covered walkways of masonry, brick or wood piers, topped with beams along and across the direction of the path beneath. To the purist, only structures that are square in section, with sturdy uprights and wooden cross-beams, are true pergolas, and it is in this sense that pergolas are discussed here. Walkways with round-topped roofs are more correctly arcades, while short, non-directional shelters covering a sitting area are loggias or arbors.

By the time the word "pergola" appeared in English in 1675 it was used for trellis- or carpentry-work structures that were much more elaborate than the Italian originals, often forming the *cabinets de verdure* that came to be such a feature of the gardens of William and Mary. An example can still be seen in their recently restored garden at Het Loo near Apeldoorn, where hornbeams are trained to the structure to produce a cool and shady green tunnel. It was not until the late nineteenth century that gardeners and architects – aided by the recently improved range of climbers, especially clematis and Rambler roses – realized that pergolas offered the opportunity for spectacularly profuse effects.

Edwin Lutyens, helped by planting plans from Gertrude Jekyll, was one of the first to capitalize on these opportunities, producing feats of architectonic legerdemain, some of them so astonishingly virtuosic that the architecture overwhelms even the most exuberant planting. Other architects such as Thomas Mawson and Harold Peto followed his example but in a rather lighter style, tending to use less megalithic supporting piers, including sometimes elegant and airy filigrees of treillage. When Miss Jekyll wrote her rose book (*Roses for English Gardens*, 1902), she commented that "every garden is now wanting a Pergola."

Perhaps more than any other garden writer before or since, Miss Jekyll provided some telling comments on the use, siting and planting of the rose-clad pergola. It "should be placed so that it is well seen from the sides . . . if they have not free air and space at the sides, the Roses will merely rush up and extend skyward where they will not be seen." "A pergola that crosses some open grassy space, such as might divide two portions of a garden, or that forms a middle line in the design of one complete garden scheme, is admirably suited for Roses, and a broad turf walk on each side will allow them to be seen to the best advantage." "A structure such as this . . . cannot just be dabbed down anywhere. It ought to lead distinctly from some clear beginning to some definite end."

Unless its architecture is unbearably bombastic, badly detailed or proportioned, or otherwise out of sympathy with the setting, a pergola should never be entirely obscured by its planting. The shape of the structure should always read clearly. In many cases, perhaps especially with treillage, it is the contrast of the structure with its furnishing plants that makes for exquisite effect.

A pergola with fairly stout and broad piers offers greater opportunities for displaying the roses, allowing the clothing of the verticals to provide as much show as the overcanopying roof. Miss Jekyll's observation that pergolas should be "well seen from the sides" is too often overlooked and worth remembering: though on the outside we do not have the benefit of dappled shade, or often the fragrance of the flowers, pergolas should also be beautiful from without.

A pergola at Polesden Lacey in Surrey

PAGES 56–57 *A Wichurana Rambler*

The classic pergola does require a good deal of space. Ideally, the piers of the pergola are spaced about 8–12ft/2.5–3.5m apart along the path. The beams joining the piers and forming the framework of the roof are generally stout and are furnished with further, slighter, laths or cross-members running either along the length of the path or from side to side. If laths are run lengthwise along the axis of path and pergola, the apparent length is exaggerated and viewers are encouraged to rush towards the end; if crosswise, the perceived width is increased and viewers are less strongly drawn towards the distant end; they tend to take their time and relax a little more. Thus optical trickery can be used apparently to lengthen a pergola that is too short or broaden one that is too narrow. Brick or stone paths can be laid with courses along or across the path to enhance the same effects.

Where there is room, the breadth of the pergola is usually determined by the width of path beneath needed for two people to walk comfortably side by side, that is about 6½ft/2m. Errant rose stems and a bed along the length of the pergola at the foot of the piers will require at least another 2ft/60cm of width. For smaller gardens, a narrower one-person pergola may be more appropriate, but it should still have an internal width of about 5ft/1.5m if it is not to feel uncomfortably constricted; the piers could be closer together, perhaps 6ft/1.8m, to maintain the proportions. All pergolas should be high enough for someone to walk comfortably upright inside without becoming entangled in roses; 7ft/2.2m clearance is perhaps the minimum.

If the pergola is sparingly clad with growth, there may be enough light beneath for a grass path, though brick or stone are more conventional. There is a tendency always to walk along the exact center of the pergola, causing a worn strip in grass unless the traffic is fairly light.

Pergolas running north–south will receive equal light on both sides and thus generally enough sun for any rose. However, if the orientation is east–west, one side will be sunny while the other is in the shadow of both pergola and planting. Especially if the planting is lush, some roses will grow and flower much less well on the shady side.

Rustic poles, usually of larch with the bark still attached, were immensely popular in the early twentieth century for making both pergolas and fences clad with Ramblers. Robinson was scathing: "Few things about country houses and gardens are worse in effect than the so-called 'rustic-work.' It is complex and ugly, its merit being that it rots away in a few years." Nevertheless, his *The English Flower Garden* showed several examples, one of them looking very like the surviving pergola at Polesden Lacey in Surrey. Rustic poles seem seldom to be used for pergolas today, perhaps because of their lack of durability (even with impeccable treatment such structures seldom last more than thirty years), or possibly because the slender poles usually offered make an unsatisfactorily flimsy-looking structure. Fatter poles (often sold as 10ft/3m lengths) should be selected for the uprights (to be set in the ground

ABOVE *Trained across arches, pergolas or catenaries, Rambler and Climbing roses will produce bloom from almost every node. However, varieties that have stiffly upright laterals will scarcely be seen from within the pergola. Those with pendulous side-shoots, such as Rambler 'Aglaia', shown here at Bagatelle in Paris, are more effective. 'Aglaia', introduced in 1896, was the first Rambler to have yellow flowers.*

RIGHT *The pergola at Bagatelle is grandly scaled, with ample headroom and arches spaced at an ideal distance to create a sense of enclosure. Box edging furnishes the sides of the path and masks the ankles of the roses, while a Lutyens bench provides both an effective focal point and a place to sit and enjoy the spectacle. The shadows of the cross-members on the path beneath break up what might otherwise be a dull expanse, and add a unifying element to the design.*

at 6–8ft/1.8–2.5m intervals) and for the top; thinner poles should be picked to create any lattice of subsidiary infill.

Henslow commented in 1922 on two sorts of pergola, squared timber versus rustic, and recommended purveyors of ready-made pergolas of each sort. For squared-timber pergolas of sawn teak, readers were advised to try Castle's Shipbreaking Co., whose advertisement shows at the top of the page a magnificent early-nineteenth-century man-o'war, transformed by the bottom of the page into a mediocre garden bench. It is interesting to speculate how many surviving pergolas of this period had colorful earlier lives on the high seas, perhaps even in Nelson's fleet. For rustic work, readers were referred to Mr E.J. Preece of Caerleon, whose advert shows a pretty but meanly proportioned section of fence with an archway only 30in/75cm wide and 5ft/1.5m high. Henslow makes the point that teak structures are usually more architectural and suited to positions nearer the house, whereas rustic work looks appropriate in the outer reaches of the garden; teak will last a lifetime but rustic work is for the short term. Some of the popularity of rustic work and its widespread adoption in suburban gardens may have been be linked to the new mobility of the middle classes, who no longer expected to stay in one house all their adult lives but planned to move before the larch rotted.

Wichurana Rambler 'Dorothy Perkins'

The feet of the posts were traditionally charred, producing tars to act as a preservative. Modern horticultural timber treatments offer much longer-lasting protection but are not absorbed if the wood is too green. Conversely, if the timber is well weathered, the bark tends to be loose; most gardeners prefer poles with the bark still attached rather than pale and shiny bare wood. If the bark is still clinging firmly, it too should be treated with horticultural preservative to make it last as long as possible. If not, the bark should be completely removed and the timber stained to render it a more acceptably muted color. The infill can be of horizontals and verticals alone or of diamond patterns, and the top of the poles may be fitted with simple finials or caps to prevent the entry of rot. The design of the infill must be pleasingly scaled and detailed and should remain discernible when clad with climbers.

For pergolas, Climbing roses can be ungainly, with few, thick stems only sporadically furnished with leaves; Ramblers are generally more accommodating and have more stems, better clad with foliage. Furthermore, the greater number of their shoots allows them to be trained out to cover more of the pergola. However, a Rambler that obligingly produces a dozen new shoots each year all of roughly equal length will require some of them to be substantially shortened to varying lengths if the piers of the pergola are to be attractively clad in blossom. The choice of variety depends on the size of the structure: ideally, the Rambler should be capable of reaching the top of the piers plus at least half of the distance across the "roof" of the pergola towards the adjacent piers, or typically about 13–16ft/4–5m. Thus Ramblers or other roses that only reach 7–10ft/2–3m, though suitable for pillars, will be rather too short for most pergolas. Conversely, the most vigorous Ramblers are rarely a good choice because they form a dense roof of foliage, confining the flowers to the top of the pergola where they cannot be seen from within. In 1917 Walter Easlea Jr criticized Miss Willmott's pergola for this reason: "I have seen the massive pergola at Warley Place and it is a fine structure, built to last for many years; but the majority of blossoms are out of view except from the windows of the mansion."

The heyday of the Wichurana Ramblers coincided with that of pergolas, arcades and other structures in the early twentieth century. The most famous of their ilk, 'Dorothy Perkins', became renowned even among non-gardeners. The English poet Alfred Noyes wrote: "The most prettily named English rose is the Dorothy Perkins; and Dorothy Perkins herself, one feels, must have been a very delightful person . . . she is one of the very few fairy godmothers of the garden who seem to convey their personal attraction through their names." Noyes' remarks notwithstanding, the rose was American, introduced by Jackson and Perkins in 1901.

Rosa wichurana had been adopted by rose breeders world-wide very soon after its introduction in 1891, and the first four Wichurana hybrids came from W.A. Manda's American nursery in 1897. Walter Easlea wrote in 1917 that " 'Dorothy Perkins' . . . is everywhere, and is something like a beautiful melody strummed constantly on a barrel organ, creating a distaste that is but natural." He found it fairly free of disease but by 1918 it was described as "ubiquitous, and . . . frequently blighted by mildew." In 1929 the eminent nurseryman Clarence Elliott wrote that "today there are gardeners who would gladly burn the last plant of Dorothy."

Rose cultivars tend to decline in vigor as they fall prey to fungal diseases that develop strains peculiar to a single cultivar and as they accumulate a scarcely less lethal collection of viruses. This is to some extent inevitable and almost impossible to reverse. Even if viruses can be removed by the wonders of modern science, few gardeners want to drench their roses in fungicide every fortnight throughout the growing and flowering season. In my days with the National Trust, replacements for Dorothy were a pressing requirement at a number of gardens, perhaps most notably at Polesden Lacey in Surrey, where it was used in large numbers but failed to get even to the top of the pillars of the garden's pergola, though it had once smothered the whole structure in bloom.

Wichurana Rambler 'Elisa Robichon'

Sometimes 'Debutante' could be a fairly successful substitute. On acid soils, 'Mrs F.W. Flight' would be a possibility, though she becomes chlorotic on lime, her yellow-green leaves clashing against rich pink flowers. It is perhaps the Super Series raised by Hetzel, including Super Dorothy® and Super Excelsa®, that today offers the best chance of vigor among all the Wichurana Ramblers, though with time we might also see the vigor and disease resistance of these decline. There can be little doubt that the poor health of some of the older Ramblers, coupled with the ramshackle state of most European pergolas after World War II, gave this style of gardening a reputation for moribund mediocrity; only in recent years has the nostalgic longing for the gardens of the past led to some conscientious efforts to recreate their glories.

Wichuranas may be classified as large- or small-flowered and as early or late flowering. Thus some such as 'François Juranville' and 'Fräulein Octavia Hesse' have relatively few large flowers in a cluster, while others like 'Dorothy Perkins' and 'Sander's White Rambler' have many small blooms. Early Wichuranas include 'Gerbe Rose', 'Aviateur Blériot' and 'Paul Noël'. For later in the season, the choice includes 'Crimson Shower' and 'Minnehaha'. Many Multiflora Ramblers date from the same period, though a few, such as 'Laure Davoust' (1843) and 'Polyantha Grandiflora' (1886), are earlier. Generally these have lighter, matt foliage, more flowers per stem and a stronger scent.

Some Wichuranas that are neither well known nor widely grown are astonishingly beautiful and should surely be taken up by enterprising nurseries. For example, I covet some of the Wichuranas with larger, more formal flowers grown at L'Haÿ-les-Roses; these include 'Edmond Proust', with nodding bunches of pale pink flowers rich rose at the heart, and 'Alexandre Tremouillet', delicate flesh pink, the outer petals fading to white. I am also particularly fond of 'Elisa Robichon', which I propagated from a sprig of flowers taken for identification from Gunby Hall in Lincolnshire in mid-summer. Perhaps the only other plant in the British Isles at the time was at Mottisfont Abbey, where it failed to meet with Graham Thomas's approval, having a poor-shaped flower. True, its flowers have few petals, informally arranged, but their profusion is remarkable and their delicate pink coloring, shaded with salmon and copper, charming. I think many gardeners today, no longer influenced by the strictures of the florists, would think its informality a positive virtue. With commendable vigor and resistance to mildew, it also has a generous scattering of blooms from the fading of its first flush until the onset of frost.

One of the morals of this story is that gardeners should never turn down the offer of a gift of propagating material, even if it is of quite the wrong sort and at the wrong time: Ramblers can often be easily propagated under the most unpromising circumstances. Another instance of this principle occurred when a *cri de cœur*

A broad arcade of elegant half-ellipse-topped arches at Stellenberg in South Africa. Climbing rose 'New Dawn', a repeat-flowering sport of 'Doctor W. Van Fleet', produces a profusion of nodding shell-pink blooms. Although the tiny beds at the foot of each rose and the surrounding expanse of gravel allow little opportunity for soil improvement, the rose seems vigorous enough to thrive. The box-edged parterre to the side of the arcade could easily be planted with bedding roses, though the small size of such beds and the impossibility of removing soil from the edging would make sterilization or resoiling difficult.

came from Sissinghurst: the 'Cooperi' in the White Garden had been killed by frost and none of the nurseries consulted could provide a replacement. Tiny, fleshy axillary shoots, taken (from the plant in my mother's garden) with a heel in mid-spring, produced well-rooted plantlets within a fortnight and the bare wall was quickly reclothed.

The shortcomings of some roses for general purposes can be seen as a benefit for pergolas. For example, though nodding blooms are often seen as a drawback and are seldom selected by rose breeders, they have distinct advantages for pergolas: here roses such as 'Climbing Ena Harkness' or, in favored climates, 'Climbing Devoniensis' and 'Maréchal Niel' display their blooms much better than their upward-facing kin. Ramblers with pendent bunches of bloom such as 'Adélaïde d'Orléans' and 'Edmond Proust' are supremely pretty.

Wichurana Rambler 'Edmond Proust'

On pergolas, as throughout the garden, roses combined with other plants can often be many times more beautiful than roses alone. Whatever climbers are planted with the roses, the success of the effect does not depend solely on color compatibility. The contrast of two or more sorts of flower, such as a fairly large clematis with small-flowered roses (or vice versa), a small rose with a large rose or the inclusion of a climber with an utterly different flower shape, such as a honeysuckle, can help. Another key to success is good timing: there is little point in deciding that two flowers would look beautiful together if they flower a month or more apart. Timing is a local matter. Combinations that might work with dazzling success in my home town in southern England will not necessarily flower at the same time in northern England or Scotland, and are even more unlikely to coincide further afield, in North America, South Africa or Australia. Observation of flowering times in your own area is essential. However, the following suggestions might provide some worthwhile starting points.

There are few Climbing or Rambler roses early enough to combine successfully with *Clematis montana* and other early clematis, wisterias or those popular subjects for tunnels and arcades, laburnums and the more flexible robinias (*Robinia hispida*, *R. boyntonii* and *R. kelseyi*). However, gardeners in favored areas (Z7 or warmer) could try Banksian roses in white or soft yellow or, in Z8, Cooper's Burma rose (*Rosa* 'Cooperi') or copper-flushed Fortune's double yellow rose (*R.* × *odorata* 'Pseudindica'). As usual, flowering seasons and thus the choice of varieties that will coincide with each other will vary from region to region but *Clematis montana* var. *wilsonii*, which usually blooms about a fortnight after the typical species, might prove useful. Later in the season, the flowering of late Wichuranas such as 'Crimson Shower' often coincides with that of Jackmanii and Viticella clematis.

Scent is an important asset for pergolas and all similar structures. Some of the Ramblers with the most pervasive scent, such as *Rosa mulliganii*, can be excessively vigorous and not all Ramblers and Climbing roses that are the right size have a scent that carries well. Combining with honeysuckles might be a solution. There are lots of excellent honeysuckles that will blend agreeably with roses: those with pale pink, peachy or cream tones are relatively easy to combine and are generally very fragrant. There are also several in hot colors that can be associated with red, orange, yellow or flame roses: these include *Lonicera* × *tellmanniana* (yellow), scarlet *L. sempervirens* (its narrow-leaved variant 'Cedar Lane' is especially good) and *L.* × *heckrotii* (flame red); however, the hot-colored sorts are generally less strongly scented. Most honeysuckles flower in

At West Dean in Sussex, the pergola designed by Harold Peto is spectacularly clad with the late-flowering Rambler 'Crimson Shower' and the Jackmanii clematis 'Victoria'. The effect depends on the rose being mixed well but not quite evenly with the clematis, achieved by spacing out the clematis stems as they grow back after pruning. The same rose could alternatively be used with a pink clematis such as 'Hagley Hybrid', while 'Victoria' would blend agreeably with a plum-purple or white Rambler.

early to mid-summer, though early Dutch honeysuckle (*L. periclymenum* 'Belgica') blooms rather earlier than most Climbing and Rambler roses.

Common jasmine (*Jasminum officinale*) is another excellent fragrant flower to mix with roses, though its first flush can come a little too soon to coincide with some. It continues to produce enough flower throughout the summer to generate a pleasing aroma, as does the more tender (Z9) and rather earlier *J. polyanthum*. *J.* × *stephanense* usually manages to bloom at exactly the right time to flower with roses, though (echoing the problem of *Rosa* 'Mrs F. W. Flight') the creamy yellow young shoots and often chlorotic-looking foliage can clash with its rich pink sweetly scented blooms.

Those blessed by Z9 or warmer climates can combine their roses with a much wider range of climbers, though there are few that can rival clematis or honeysuckle for sheer poise. Most maurandyas have flowers of blue, purple or crimson that are too dark to be telling from a distance, though they are charming at close range; they can be overwintered under glass or started early from seed in the hothouse and used as annuals. Their cousins the lophospermums include several with soft pink flowers (such as *Lophospermum erubescens*) that are rather more effective and have the same hardiness and cultural requirements, as does *Rhodochiton atrosanguineus*, a close relative whose purple-black hanging flowers are utterly charming though, again, almost invisible from afar.

Rambler 'Albertine' and Hybrid Perpetual 'Mrs John Laing' with honeysuckle and Vitis vinifera *in Helen Yemm's London garden*

Mutisias, though they have spectacular daisy flowers in pink or orange, are marred by untidy foliage but one daisy that I long to see back in our gardens (surely it should not be difficult to reintroduce) is the Mexican climbing dahlia, *Hidalgoa werckleі*. If tempted into early flower by starting under glass, its vermilion blooms could create stunning combinations with hot-colored late roses. There should be much potential for hybrids with dahlias, extending the color range and adding the fine and ferny dark foliage of, say, *Dahlia laciniata*, though one hopes the almost equal probability of introducing the worst stiff and lumpish vulgarity of some dahlias might be avoided.

Solanum crispum and its cultivar 'Glasnevin' are hardy enough for Z8 gardens, their purplish mauve flowers combining well with roses such as 'Climbing Iceberg'; however, the white potato vine, *S. jasminoides* 'Album', really needs a Z9 climate if it is to thrive out of doors and can be slow to reach flowering size (too late for most roses) if cut back by frosts. Cuttings overwintered under glass and grown to a substantial size before planting out should blend charmingly with Ramblers like 'Dorothy Perkins' or 'Debutante', though earlier roses like 'Paul Noël' would probably flower some weeks before the potato vine.

In climates with cool summers passion flowers are generally marred by an excess of dull foliage and too few flowers, but in warmer climates some of the choicer sorts such as *Passiflora* 'Amethyst', *P.* × *violacea*, *P.* × *belotii* and *P. caerulea* 'Constance Elliot' would be well worth trying. I would love to see *Tweedia caerulea* scrambling through a soft yellow or white rose, spangling it with its extraordinary kingfisher-blue flowers, though hot summers would be needed for long-enough shoots; gardeners from cooler climes could try the trick in a conservatory. Tecomarias in orange, yellow, crimson, scarlet or salmon could also be tried with those roses that provide a plentiful late flush of bloom.

Vines are often associated with roses on pergolas, partly because the pergola is historically their rightful and traditional home. However, most are rather too vigorous to share the same pier as a rose; generally each vine will need a pier to itself, intermingling only on the pergola's roof where it meets roses from adjoining piers. Some, including *Vitis vinifera* 'Incana' and *V.v.* 'Purpurea', have foliage that is attractive throughout the summer, though most vines, especially *V.v.* 'Purpurea', *V. belaii*, *V.* 'Brant' and *V. coignetiae*, are most spectacular in fall color. The dubiously named *V. belaii* (so called at Kew for many years but perhaps just a clone of *V. vinifera* that looks remarkably similar to *V.v.* 'Spetchley

Red') is perhaps the most dazzling scarlet of all true vines in autumn color; 'Purpurea' runs it close and has the additional advantages of attractively greyish shoots and leaves for most of the summer before flushing purple as its brief season of flaming red approaches. The Japanese glory vine, *V. coignetiae*, has perhaps the most handsome and most subtly shaded leaves of all vines, taking on tints of butter yellow, orange, russet, red and brown at its autumn apotheosis. Those wanting wispy vines sufficiently insubstantial to grow together with roses could try *Parthenocissus henryana*, whose dainty five-fingered leaves also turn scarlet in fall. It is true that it can be hard to find roses that will produce a significant quantity of bloom to harmonize with the vines at this season, though the hips of *Rosa helenae* or *R. multiflora* could create attractive combinations on more generously planted pergolas or in the wild garden.

Rosa *'Climbing Iceberg' with* Solanum crispum

One plant that requires little pampering is the common annual nasturtium. In its climbing forms this can be useful for furnishing the lower parts of the piers and blending with roses of warm colors. For nasturtiums, rich conditions, particularly in climates where summers are cool and moist, will encourage a mass of foliage with the only blooms hidden among the leaves; nitrogenous feed and water should therefore be sparingly given. In favored areas (Z9 or milder), evergreen *Berberidopsis corallina* could also be used to clothe the lower part of the piers on their shady side and would help conceal any ugly bases to the rose stems. *Sollya heterophylla*, as pure and remarkable a blue as the morning glory, could be used in similar climates in the same way.

Though there are few herbaceous perennial climbers to mix with roses on the pergola, perennial peas such as the various color forms of *Lathyrus latifolius* or *L. rotundifolius* would be admirable. It is possible that the climbing aconites from south-east Asia include odd individuals of a color pure enough and bright enough to be effective and whose flowering might just coincide with the roses. But of all the climbers that might be mixed with roses, the ones I would most like to see are some of the annuals. The genus *Ipomoea* (now containing plants that were once called *Pharbitis*, *Quamoclit*, *Mina* or *Convolvulus*) offers the most exciting opportunities of poise, clear color and contrasting flower shape. *Ipomoea lobata* (*Mina lobata*) has spikes of small flowers the shape of a chilli pepper, borne at exactly the same angle as each other in arithmetically decreasing size along the spike like a flight of porcelain ducks on a wall. Each floret shades from cream through yellow and coral to flame red and the flowers will blend happily with roses in scarlet, salmon, apricot, cream or white. All the other popular garden species have flowers that open into trumpets. *I. coccinea* (*Quamoclit coccinea*) has pure red flowers and, in its most attractive forms and also in its hybrid *I.* × *multifida*, finely divided leaves; it goes well with roses of similar color but even better with a noticeably lighter or deeper hue. *I. nil* (*Pharbitis nil*) is now available in several single colors and picotees. 'Chocolate' is the color of pale milk chocolate with a hint of salmon; I would like to see it scrambling through peachy salmon 'François Juranville' or 'Phyllis Bide', whose smaller flowers in tints of cream, soft yellow, peach and salmon might flatter it.

Ipomoea Early Call Mixed are hybrids of *I. nil* in colors including soft light vermilion, rich scarlet, maroon-crimson, salmon pink and that curious combination of pink overlying grey found also in some poppies. I think I would like to select individuals to blend with particular roses, a possibility if plants are started early in pots and planted out once they start to bloom. Most famous of all is the morning glory, *I. tricolor*, perhaps best in the azure 'Heavenly Blue', one of the rarest and most telling colors in all flowers and particularly effective with soft yellow or white. However, it is not a plant for those who venture into the garden only in the afternoon or early evening when it has faded. Those who, like Vita Sackville-West, want to enjoy a white garden at dusk might try *I. alba*, the

The central part of the Roseraie at L'Haÿ-les-Roses, called La Roseraie décorative, with its central pavilion and flanking arcades, was laid out in 1910. This coincided with the arrival of the term "decorative rose" for varieties showy enough to be used for their individual blooms. The spectacle would be difficult to achieve without the exceptionally vigorous Wichurana Rambler 'Alexandre Girault', one of the few roses capable of clothing such a large structure with sheets of bloom. A light covering of rose stems allows the treillage to remain visible and the blooms to be backlit by the sun. Neat box edgings and immaculate lawns contribute to the crisp formality of the design.

moonflower or *belle de nuit*, whose fragrant flowers would open then, to wither the following morning.

The difficulty with these annuals and with tender climbers overwintered under glass lies in getting them to bloom at the same time as the roses. They need to be started into vigorous growth early but not planted out until nights are warm. All such plants must have optimum cultivation while still in pots and when planted along the pergola. The snag is that pergolas usually have only a narrow and woefully inadequate bed for planting: it is hard to avoid the annuals being in direct competition with the roses; the roses usually win but even they are starved into achieving but a tiny fraction of their potential. This is unsatisfactory: pergolas justify the outlay in construction, planting and maintenance only if they froth, foam and tumble with cascades of the most beautiful flowers in a display of extravagant and luxurious opulence. The pergola design must allow adequate root run if the roses and their companion plants are to achieve their potential, or to attain anything more than a state of moribund twigginess. Any companion climbers must not compete for root run with the roses but must be planted at least 20in/50cm away, perhaps on the opposite side of the pier.

The beds along the foot of the pergola are often raised up, bounded by low retaining walls. Generally a width of at least 40in/1m (preferably rather more) is needed to allow optimum conditions for the roses and their companion climbers and to allow a carpet of plants to furnish the base. Generous shrub or herbaceous planting of any height – say 40in/1m or more high – would cause the inner sides of the beds to be rather shady; it would then be hard to ensure that these sides were well furnished and attractive. With lower planting (no more than about 20in/50cm), light penetration is not such a problem. Plants with a bold shape make a good choice; bergenias and hostas, for example, can cope with a little shade and would furnish and soften the hard edge of the pergola path. If the pergola's climbers do not cast too dense shade, a carpet of Ground Cover roses would also be a possibility here and would provide a unifying theme with the roses above. Other scrambling plants might be mixed unevenly with the Ground Cover roses, including annuals or tender perennials such as silver *Helichrysum petiolare* and *Senecio viravira* plus trailing petunias such as the Surfinia® Series, giving a tapestry of pleasing flower and foliage until the frosts.

The next chapter will discuss the advantages of spiralling the Ramblers around pillars, giving blossom from every node from top to toe. However, for pergolas this is rarely an option. There are several reasons: first, such spiral training only works well if the piers are broad and round in cross-section (they are usually square); secondly, to be spiralled round the full height of the pillars and yet still clothe the roof, the Rambler must produce substantially longer shoots that would be a nuisance along the pergola path unless frequently tied out of the way; thirdly, if roses are to be grown intimately mixed with clematis or other climbers spiral training becomes impossibly difficult.

If the pergola's piers are of stone, brick or rendered, it is necessary to devise some means of attaching the roses to them. If they are round, vertical galvanized or plastic-covered wires (black, brown or dull green, never viridian) held taut by vine eyes are the only option; loose and wavy wires look unbearably messy. The vine eyes should preferably be of brass or sherardized or galvanized steel and never of raw steel, which could rust and split the masonry. Sufficient numbers need to be used to prevent the climbers slumping down the wires. For square piers, horizontal wires are used, again held by vine eyes. These need to be spaced about 12–16in/30–40cm apart. If the piers are of brick, the wires should run along the mortar joints and the depths of the bricks will determine the spacing between successive wires (usually one wire to every three or four courses).

The problems of attachment do not occur with pergolas of trellis, where ties can easily be fixed around the laths. However, shoots passing through the mesh of the trellis can make pruning difficult and it is preferable to attach shoots always to the outside of the trellis and not to let them weave through the latticework. Such treillage gives a lighter effect than masonry, particularly if the wood is painted in a muted tone that harmonizes rather than contrasts with the accompanying foliage. The laths may be arranged as horizontals and verticals or in diamonds, usually evenly spaced.

One of the most splendid examples of the use of trelliswork was created by the 2nd Baron Aberconway in the early twentieth century at Bodnant in North Wales. A great semicircular bastion edged with a pergola gives splendid views to the valley beyond and below. Topped with urn finials pierced to match the trelliswork in lightness, the pergola is painted a blueish green *vert anglais*, a color sufficiently distinct from the foliage to allow the architecture to show but suitably muted and close enough to the leaf color to prevent the structure from dominating totally. A second curved pergola surrounds the base of the bastion on the Lower Rose Terrace below. As Graham Stuart Thomas observes, "At Bodnant . . . the climbers and ramblers are mixed with other things, which is how I prefer them." Bodnant's curved pergolas are directly contrary to Miss Jekyll's advice that they should run straight, but I feel they are a great success, holding the promise of hidden delights beyond. The stupendous curved treillage walk with central domed pavilion at L'Haÿ-les-Roses, perhaps strictly an arcade, also proves triumphantly that even Miss Jekyll could be wrong.

The pruning and training of the roses at Bodnant is exemplary, making the pattern of trained stems almost as remarkable and beautiful in winter bareness as in summer bloom. If built of masonry or brick, such a structure would have been impossibly oppressive and out of character with an area of garden some distance from the house where the countryside beyond is the only competing feature. That it has survived so long is a tribute to Lord Aberconway's foresight: he chose to have it constructed from hardwood teak rather than the more usual and much cheaper pine.

The traditional method of tying roses with willow withies is still used at L'Haÿ-les-Roses and Bagatelle.

The effect of arcades and catenaries is altogether lighter, more airy and less architectural than that of pergolas. This makes them less rigidly formal in feel and more suited to areas where architecture need not dominate as much as it does nearer the house.

Arcades, by definition a series of arches, may be made of lightweight wood – "rustic work," as recommended by William Paul in *The Rose Garden* (1848), anticipating the trend of fifty years later – or metal. It is possible to buy ready-made arches, often plastic-covered for durability, sometimes in segments that can be bolted together. These are often marred by ugly knuckles where uprights connect to the arched tops or to horizontals linking the arches, and the uprights are often too short to give comfortable clearance. I have never seen one I considered attractive, though I see no reason why these design faults should not easily be eliminated.

Mild steel arches are easily made by local blacksmiths or metal workshops and cost relatively little to produce, so that simple arcades are a cheaper option. Iron arches potentially have the disadvantage that they can become very hot in summer, scorching those parts of the rose stems that touch the hot metal, while in winter they may become so cold that they kill any touching stems, a particular problem in climates colder than Z7. In 1912 Walter Easlea wrote that he considered them essential but suggested interpolating black-painted bamboo canes between arch and stem to "prevent those frost bites and other injuries caused by contact with the iron in winter." Another problem of metal arches is that the maintenance of their surface can be difficult. Galvanizing them once they have been shaped is possible and they can then be primed and painted, using a light color if damage from chilling or scorching is to be minimized. Left unpainted, the garishly shiny galvanized surface will mellow to a dull battleship grey; however, such an area of unprotected zinc can prove toxic to some plants at the foot of each upright. If the simplest option of leaving the bare steel untreated to rust to a mellow brown-black is chosen, the problems of hot or cold bare metal should not prove lethal provided fairly vigorous Ramblers are used that will soon cast the metal into shade; wispy growers producing only one or two stems and little foliage cover are likely to be damaged. Unprotected mild steel will last several decades before it rusts away; my mother's garden

PAGES 74–75 *The gothic arches of this arcade in the garden of the Old Chapel, Chalford, Gloucestershire, are echoed in the white-painted seat set off-center in the bower beyond. Multiflora Rambler 'Veilchenblau' clothes the left-hand side of the arches and 'Six Hills Giant' catmint tumbles across the path.*

still has a couple of mild steel arches that are, I imagine, as old as the house (1908).

Such arcades could run parallel to paths or across and above them. Half-round-topped arches are perhaps the norm. An ogee top is also possible but I much prefer a half-ellipse shape, so popular in Regency architecture, perhaps particularly in Ireland. This seems to me to lend a much more spacious, gracious and comfortable feel to the arcade; furthermore, a path wide enough for two people to walk side by side would seem disproportionately high if over-topped by semicircular arches, and they would make pruning and training difficult. Of course, there will be some circumstances in which a sense of confinement is intended, perhaps as a deliberate contrast with airy openness beyond: in such cases, a path between catenaries or beneath an arcade wide enough for only a single pedestrian might be desirable.

Catenary chains swaddled with rope to protect plants from contact with the metal, at Bagatelle. The roughly finished poles will be hidden by roses at flowering time.

Gertrude Jekyll suggested that a short length of pergola (square in cross-section) could be placed at an important crossing in the garden and that rose arches of wood or iron could also be erected, for example at intervals of about 25ft/7.5m along the flower borders of the kitchen garden, thus similar in effect to the main axis of the garden at Giverny. She suggested setting the feet of the arches at the back of the borders. Enclosed arcades of closer arches, with their feet set in planting of larger herbaceous plants, shrubs or shrub roses 5ft/1.5m high or more, gain the benefit of comfortable enclosure but sacrifice their separateness from the surrounding planting and the opportunity for pleasing views out. As for pergolas, to retain distinctness and views, the planting to furnish the edge of the walk should be kept to a height of 40in/1m. Unlike pergolas, arcades usually admit plenty of light and so do not limit what might be grown beneath. This permits beds of small to middling-sized bush or Ground Cover roses, preferably with some companion planting, to form a more attractive furnishing to the edge.

Catenaries are by definition swags of chain suspended from posts. Though in gardens swags of rope are often used, chains have the advantage that their extra weight ensures that the swags follow a perfect parabola not deflected by any slight unevenness in the weight of rose stems that they carry. They have the same disadvantages as metal arches, namely the risks of overheating in sun and killing tender stems in cold climates. Gardeners have traditionally overcome this by swaddling the chains in thin rope so that the perfect parabolic shape is maintained but without any risk of damage to roses in extreme weather.

Like arcades, catenaries are most often placed along both sides of a main axis. For a more elaborate effect, it is perfectly possible to combine a catenary with an arcade, with swags alongside the path and arches over its top. Catenaries can also be used in a single row around the garden, often an effect found in smaller circular rosaries.

The depth of drop of the swags is determined by the way the garden is intended to be seen. Generally the swags will periodically interrupt the sightlines into the rest of the garden but allow a clear view from time to time. This is usually achieved by letting the swags drop to below the line of sight at their midpoint. However, grander catenaries in larger gardens can be taller, allowing a second lower swag but keeping the top swag above the sightlines. In such a scheme the top swag should curve more than the lower one, which should not be so low at its nadir that it interferes with any planting beneath (so the lower swag is unlikely to leave room for bush roses).

The fact that arcades and catenaries do not exclude light to the same extent as a pergola makes grass paths between paired catenaries or beneath arcades comparatively easy to achieve. However, such walks should not restrict pedestrians, through exuberant outgrowth from the sides or through excessively narrow arches, to the center of the grass path, causing an unsightly worn line down the middle.

The slender structure of arcades and catenaries makes it difficult to use more than one plant per pier, though some of the wispier climbers (*Maurandya*, *Rhodochiton*, *Lathyrus*, *Ipomoea* or

Solanum jasminoides 'Album') could easily be planted, not too close to the rose's roots, to twine through the rose. Other more vigorous climbers, for instance vines and most clematis, will need a pier to themselves, perhaps alternating along and across the rows with roses so that where climbers from adjacent piers meet there is an opportunity for roses and non-roses to mingle agreeably. The thinner supports can reveal all too clearly the boniness of some Climbing roses but there are many Ramblers that will produce just the right length of stems and enough of them to furnish well. Generally the slighter construction of arcades and catenaries will bear less overgrowth of climbers than is possible for pergolas, so the most vigorous roses and other climbers should be avoided.

Hedges are also part of the structure of the garden, walls built of shrubs and generally managed to maintain their shape and structure by pruning. They can vary from tidy edgings of dwarf roses only 6in /15cm high to screens of 7ft/2.2m or more, tall enough to contain the eye and provide complete enclosure. Though we occasionally see Rugosa roses or popular Floribundas such as Iceberg used as hedges, the potential for rose hedges has scarcely been tapped. The wilder-looking roses, including sweet-briar, 'Andersonii', 'Complicata', or *R.* × *hibernica* and some Ramblers, can be mixed with shrubs such as guelder rose, elder, lilac and philadelphus and woven through with honeysuckle to create a gloriously abundant and fragrant boundary. Exactly such hedges were found alongside the floral walk in almost every British landscape garden of the late eighteenth and early nineteenth centuries. It is astonishing that such effects have not been recreated and reworked, using also newer roses (though still of the same character) for more telling or longer-lasting effect. This sort of planting is similar to that discussed in the chapter on wild gardens (page 144) but the same principles may be applied to rather more sophisticated and highly bred roses used in hedges in the garden proper.

Solanum jasminoides *'Album'*

Where roses are the principal source of interest, mixtures of once- and perpetual-flowering varieties run the risk of abject failure: early summer sorts used alone are fine if we are content to enjoy the garden for the brief but glorious six weeks or so of their floraison; if we mix in 25 per cent (or even 50 per cent) of longer-flowering roses there are just not enough of these to carry the scheme on into late summer and autumn. With a half or more of the dominant plant out of flower, the scheme will sink under the weight of a hefty proportion of flowerless bushes with indifferent leaves. When it comes to mixed rose hedges there is a clear choice: either use early summer varieties alone, perhaps garlanded with clematis and honeysuckle, or plant longer-flowering roses, possibly intertwined with climbers that flower at the same time.

For early summer, many of the older sorts of rose, such as Gallicas, Albas, Summer Damasks, Mosses and Centifolias could be used. To last later into summer and autumn, Chinas, the larger Polyanthas, Hybrid Musks, Portland Damasks, Hybrid Perpetuals and David Austin's English roses would be ideal. Such hedges generally are only allotted a fairly narrow space and so the more spreading varieties are not suitable: for instance, a spreading Hybrid Musk such as 'Penelope' is often less fitting than an upright one such as 'Prosperity'. (David Austin's book *English Roses* gives helpful illustrations showing the habit of each variety, making selection simple.)

Though there is nothing wrong with a fairly low hedge of bush roses, hedges generally need to supply rather more division or enclosure and thus need to be a little taller. Several Polyanthas and

PAGES 78–79 *At Newby Hall in North Yorkshire, Multiflora Rambler 'Apple Blossom' (the only rose raised by the great American hybridist Luther Burbank that is still sold by nurseries) clothes rope swags held by brick piers. Purple smoke bush provides an effective foil for the roses and for lavender-blue* Campanula lactiflora.

Floribundas such as 'Mevrouw Nathalie Nypels' and Iceberg can be adapted to this need by pruning them less severely so that a hedge of up to 6ft/1.8m can be achieved. I would love to see a hedge of Iceberg woven through with morning glory or *Ipomoea lobata*. In a formal situation or where space is limited, pruning needs to be adapted to achieve an even hedge of the height and width required, rather than simply pruning to give maximum flower production. Henslow considered that annual shearing and removal of dead wood was perfectly adequate for rose hedges, a task made even easier today by electric clippers or even clearing saws. He also recommended planting a staggered row at 30in/75cm centers, a policy that ensures visual solidity. He recommended Sweet-briars (especially the Penzance Series), Rugosas, Chinas, Scotch Briars, Polyanthas and Hybrid Musks, though he considered it was best not to mix roses of different classes. Rugosas make superlative hedges for rougher sites and, if plants on their own roots are used, will sucker to become utterly impenetrable to most livestock; in such sites, mowing off excessively adventurous suckers is usually enough to contain the spread of the hedge.

The larger bush roses classed as Grandifloras in the United States, including such stalwarts as 'The Queen Elizabeth' and 'Fred Loads', are particularly suited to hedges of up to 6ft/1.8m. American gardeners have shown great skill in exploiting the many uses this extra height allows; if only British gardeners would be equally imaginative. Another way of using bush roses in hedges of this height is to alternate bushes with the same or a contrasting variety worked as half-standards. Bushes and half-standards can be alternated along a single line, though this runs a slight risk of the upper part of the standard's stem and its accompanying ties being too visible. Another method of using two heights but hiding the stems is to plant a double line of bushes set square with half-standards placed quincuncially in the interstices. A screen of this sort using Hybrid Tea 'Pink Suprême' can be seen in the Royal Horticultural Society's garden at Hyde Hall in Essex.

In this garden designed for the Chelsea Flower Show, the narrow arcade of timber, lightly clad with roses including 'Climbing Iceberg' and wisterias, is subtly painted blue-grey to harmonize with the restrained flower colors. Bush roses and perennials, among them alchemilla, Aquilegia vulgaris *'Nora Barlow' and* Viola *'Bowles' Black' help furnish the base. The urn, set against a plain background of dark foliage, transforms the quality of the ensemble; through its eighteenth-century association with the common inscription* "Et in Arcadia ego", *it makes a gentle pun.*

In many situations, roses used alone to create a hedge would not provide the necessary structure and formality. This can be overcome by adding structural elements such as a box edging and/or repeated architectural features such as topiary columns (square or round in cross-section), cones or pyramids; a round cross- section often works best where hedges follow a strong curve. Where structure and formality are not required, it will usually still be necessary to furnish the bases of the roses, using plants such as those suggested on pages 42–5. A different way to vary a rose hedge is to introduce another shrub, perhaps providing a contrast of leaf color or texture. Bronze-leaved plants such as *Berberis × ottawensis* 'Superba' or *Cotinus coggygria* 'Royal Purple' would be splendid with fiery red or orange roses and would also work with pale peach blends such as 'Perle d'Or'. Glaucous, silver- or gold-leaved shrubs could also be used, although strong variegation would run the risk of looking too frantic.

Where only a slight sense of containment is required, a hedge of bush roses can be used. There was a famous early example of this in Portland, Oregon, where more than three million bushes of 'Madame Caroline Testout' were planted along the walks of the city. A photograph in the 1916 *Rose Annual* shows one of the hedges in full bloom, though it would undoubtedly have looked even better with some other planting to furnish the base.

A hedge is usually substantial and three-dimensional, while a fence is effectively linear and offers a neat means of defining and containing an area if space is limited. The two different treatments may be highlighted by looking at alternative uses of sweet-briar, *Rosa rubiginosa*: at Hardwick Hall, in Derbyshire, it is used to create a large and billowing hedge, though still restricted from its potentially large size by fairly severe annual pruning; at Sissinghurst it is trained to the simplest of fences, a series of horizontal wires, in attractive and evenly spaced arcs, restricting its width and preventing it from encroaching on the adjacent path. The scent of its foliage is delicious, especially after a shower of rain.

Sweet-briar is a relatively stiff shrub to train against a fence, though similarly stiff Hybrid Musks were used in exactly this way until recently at Wisley; a Rambler or Climbing rose is a more usual choice, although any rose that is the right size to clothe the

*The neat and uniform growth of Rosa Mundi (*Rosa gallica *'Versicolor') makes it a popular subject for hedges, as here in a kitchen garden at Combe in Oxfordshire. Reversions to the unstriped* R. gallica *are common and part of its appeal.*

fence, and sufficiently pliant, could be used. Thus Hybrid Perpetuals and Bourbons are often ideal, their rather shorter stems making them perfectly suited to fences of 5ft/1.5m or a little less. Among the Hybrid Perpetuals, 'Reine des Violettes' is well adapted to fences, as are 'Souvenir du Docteur Jamain', 'Baron Girod de l'Ain', 'Roger Lambelin' and other prodigies that merit close inspection but would risk disease-ridden wretchedness against a wall. 'Reine des Violettes' is often seen as a grubby magenta sport, but it is well worth seeking out the slaty violet original; producing an abundance of new canes each year, it may be pruned like a Rambler, removing all but the new shoots. Also ideal for fences are exquisite Bourbons such as 'Reine Victoria', 'Madame Pierre Oger' and 'Souvenir de Madame Auguste Charles', martyrs all to mildew and blackspot in the dry warmth of a wall where lack of air circulation helps incubate fungal contagion.

Fences can be completely smothered in roses and other climbers so that any permanent structure disappears and the whole seems to be a hedge, a combination sometimes called a fedge. Miss Jekyll suggested similar screens using a framework of larch or oak poles fitted with coarse wire; the wire and whatever unsightliness lay beyond the screen were hidden by the roses. (However, some rosarians advise against the use of any sort of mesh because of the difficulty of disentangling shoots.) The fence can remain a feature and be only partly clad, its attractive design, color and surface qualities forming a part of the ensemble, as in trellis fences found at Bodnant. These are very like medieval examples such as that in a French translation of Boccaccio's *La Teseida* (1460), where a fence is shown interwoven with red and white roses.

Even such an airy structure as a fence or screen made of rustic poles offers substantial resistance against the wind and it is usually best not to make it higher than, say, 7ft/2.2m. Because it blocks little sunlight compared with a close-boarded fence, there is no risk of its roses suffering from lack of light.

Openwork fences may be used either around the boundary of the garden or as a screen to subdivide separate areas. However, such open fences cannot screen absolutely and should be used where a glimpse of what lies beyond is acceptable or desirable. The screen may contain an arch, also of rustic work, usually flat or of low pitch (about 30° to the horizontal); for a much more dramatic gothic effect, a steep pitch of about 60° could be used. Commentators on architectural taste, such as Sir John Betjeman, have pointed out that a pitch of about 45°, though common in recent buildings, rarely looks satisfactory. Rustic arches clad with roses may be used as a porch to a cottage or in isolation across a path, perhaps through a gap in a belt of shrubs, but look silly if standing forlorn in the open garden; they should be, in effect, a doorway through a wall, whether that be a hedge, a fence or an informal screen of generous planting.

Although, particularly in country gardens, I see nothing intrinsically wrong with it, rustic work has a reputation for suburban mediocrity, due to sometimes inappropriate siting or poor design. There is no reason why it should be limited to straight poles from garden centers or timber yards; I would love to see it used with all the wit and imagination shown by Thomas Wright (1711–86) in his designs for rustic grottoes, temples and tea houses, using far more interesting gnarled, forked and twisted timbers to create screens and structures of enchantment, enticement and even sometimes a hint of horror.

A charming and informal screen of grey-green-leaved Rosa soulieana *threaded through with perennial pea* Lathyrus latifolius *at Birlingham Manor in Worcestershire. Hiding a chain-link fence around a tennis court, this is a typical example of a fedge. While some fences have their climbers tightly trained to emphasize structure, looser training, as here, can help mask a less attractive feature.*

Close-boarded fences are usually intended to provide an impenetrable screen and, having little intrinsic beauty, to be well covered. Even when facing away from the sun (provided they are not beneath trees) such fences can be entirely clothed with roses and other climbers, trained to horizontal wires at roughly

18in/45cm intervals. The need to achieve complete cover requires a rather different sort of rose, one that produces enough shoots to train out across the entire area. The shoots should also be long enough to reach to the top of the fence. In these respects, roses for fences are similar to those for walls. However, fences do not generally cause the same acute disease and drought problems as walls, allowing use of varieties such as the Hybrid Perpetuals and Bourbons mentioned on page 82, which would need constant spraying if planted against a wall.

Rosarians have had differing views about the most suitable roses for walls. Henslow insisted that only large-flowered Climbing roses should be planted against the house and only Ramblers on garden walls. He gave no explanation, and there seems to be little difference in cultural suitability between garden and house walls; perhaps he felt that a greater degree of sophistication, complexity and gorgeousness was needed near the house. Henslow also advised using precious sunny walls for planting early and tender varieties like 'Climbing Devoniensis' and 'Maréchal Niel'. Robinson, on the other hand, heaped much scorn on those who tried (and failed) to grow these two varieties in anything less than ideal conditions. His alternative recommendations included the Noisettes 'William Allen Richardson', 'Céline Forestier' and 'Bouquet d'Or' and a host of Ramblers.

However, many Multiflora and Wichurana Ramblers do not thrive against a wall. In 1917 Herbert Oppenheimer advised readers to "plant none but the most disease-resisting roses against walls or in other confined positions; never use any Wichuraiana or multiflora scandens for a wall." H.H. Thomas concurred: "How difficult it is . . . to succeed with Crimson rambler and other similar roses on a hot wall. . . . How fascinating on a warm wall are the climbing Teas . . . yet how difficult anywhere else . . . hardy ramblers . . . languish on precious walls for the lack of fresh, sweet air about their shoots, while other far lovelier roses, that would be supremely happy there are neglected and forgotten."

Whatever their differences, all are agreed that health is a key factor. Walls encourage not only blackspot and mildew but also rust and spider mite, and all but the most resistant strains are vulnerable to disease in such a confined position. Gardeners – particularly those who want to avoid using synthetic pesticides – will be well advised to avoid planting susceptible varieties. However, despite Oppenheimer's and Henslow's comments, there are some Ramblers, notably those with a high proportion of China blood (such as the Noisettes) or of Hybrid Tea blood (such as 'Albertine and 'New Dawn'), that will thrive on a sunny wall.

House walls may be generously clad with roses up to two storeys or even higher; the height chosen will often depend on how high the gardener is prepared to climb, not only for annual pruning but for tying in and any spraying. (Powered sprayers can be used to drive sprays from ground level up to the top of most domestic buildings but tend to cause more spray drift, wastage and thus environmental damage, nor are any resident nesting birds likely to welcome them.) The part of the wall to be covered with roses should be wired with horizontal plastic-covered or galvanized wires held with vine eyes, as for masonry pergolas, set about 18in/45cm apart and running along the courses if the building is of masonry, brick or clapboard. If the wall is rendered, a spirit level should be used to ensure that the wires are absolutely horizontal.

A traditional alternative to fixing the plants directly to the wall, sometimes still seen on old French or Regency English buildings, is the use of panels of treillage. These can be very pretty if the building is regular and formal in design but can be difficult to accommodate if it is of more random shape. The panels should be held about 1in/25mm clear of the wall to allow ties to be worked through the laths, always attaching the rose stems to the

RIGHT *Ramblers 'Veilchenblau' and 'Félicité Perpétue' mingle with self-clinging, fragrant, filigree* Trachelospermum asiaticum *above Foxy Group foxgloves at Stellenberg. Though hardy to Z7, the trachelospermum needs fairly hot summers if it is to flower well; if the wall has to be painted, it will need to be detached and given support thereafter.*

PAGES 86–87 *Wichurana Rambler 'Crimson Shower', trained along a wall at Heale House in Wiltshire. Galvanized wires are held by vine eyes, both on the side and along the top of the wall. These help horizontal training of the rose stems so that every node can produce a lateral shoot and a spray of flowers, particularly effective when the blooms break the hard line of the top of the wall and are lit from behind by the sun. Though their color is muted and unobtrusive against the stonework, the wires would look better if properly tensioned and straight. Tar twine is used to secure the shoots, ideally tied in a figure-of-eight loop around stem and wire and doubled around the stems to reduce pressure and chafing.*

front of the laths and never allowing stems to make their way behind where they can cause difficulties at pruning time. Even this little gap allows the circulation of fresh air and makes all the difference between success and failure. The panels can be made more decorative by adding borders, cut-out corners and other details, using a change from square-mounted to diamond trellis to pick out the design. Such a treatment will require a less solid covering of plants so that the grace of the design is not obscured.

A long and high expanse of wall can accommodate the most rampant roses and also the more vigorous non-rose climbers, which can be used both to complement the roses and to hide the bare stems at the base of Climbing varieties. With such large areas, intimate combinations of plants too big for pergolas are possible, such as roses with vines or *Actinidia kolomikta*. In the garden of friends in Yorkshire this latter is woven through with 'Madame Grégoire Staechelin', the pink-tipped leaves of the actinidia exactly matching the petals of the rose. In a kitchen garden, roses and companion climbers can fill the gaps between and above trained wall fruit, providing interest from the time the fruit blossom fades all through the summer until the crop assumes the ripe and decorative tints of autumn.

Climbing rose 'Madame Grégoire Staechelin' with Actinidia kolomikta

The opportunity of using a large area for bold and spectacular effect should not be missed: the sight of an entire wall of the South Cottage at Sissinghurst covered with 'Madame Alfred Carrière' is astonishing. Climbers that are too large for pergolas can be used with roses in such positions to make refreshingly different and striking combinations.

Walls are not just sustaining props for the more vigorous plants. If they are sunny, they will permit the use of roses and wall plants suited to climates with winters one zone or so more favored than is the prevailing local norm. This makes it possible to grow in Z7 many roses that are not quite hardy enough for the open garden or need a bit more warmth for adequate flower production, such as 'Cooperi', and the more tender Noisettes, Teas and Climbing Chinas. Thus for Z7 climates (typical of much of the southern United States) a Z8 combination of, for example, a Banksian rose weaving through golden fremontodendron could create a pleasing harmony (but beware of the fremontodendron's irritant hairs when pruning or training). On the West Coast, *Rosa banksiae* 'Lutea' with a ceanothus such as *Ceanothus impressus*, *C. dentatus*, *C. arboreus* or any of their hybrids will make a classic combination and contrast.

Shrubs such as ceanothus and fremontodendron are usually a bit too stiff to train to pergolas but with a little persuasion may be spread out to cover a substantial area of wall.

Even if we agree with Henslow in preferring larger and more complex blooms on the house walls than on the walls of the garden, flower qualities alone cannot be the primary consideration in choosing a rose variety to fill a particular area of wall. The choice of variety must depend largely on the site to be filled and how the growth characteristics of the various candidates are fitted to it. Generally Climbing roses need considerable horizontal spread if their stems are to be trained lower and lower in successive years, to encourage flowering shoots from every node, a good covering of foliage and as few ugly bare stems as possible. This means they are not best suited to, for instance, the narrow spaces between windows. On the other hand, such spaces are often ideal places to accommodate a Rambler or even a pillar rose, with the proviso already discussed that it should be disease-resistant. The size and vigor of the rose should always be matched to the area it has to fill. This is perfectly judged at Haddon Hall in Derbyshire where 'Albertine' exactly fits the panels of wall beneath and above the ancient bay window.

Another important consideration is how the color of the rose will suit its background. Brick, particularly shiny-surfaced and fiercely red engineering brick that scarcely mellows in a hundred years, can clash horribly with some colors. Even red roses of similar tone might not benefit from such a backdrop, the blooms being substantially camouflaged by their surroundings; similarly a white-painted wall can dominate the palest roses. Some strongly colored local stones or stridently painted wood or aluminium siding will also fail to flatter some rose colors.

For trellis that is meant to be seen, color is important too. Old examples have usually been regularly painted, most frequently in a dark green or blue-green *vert anglais*. It should be possible, perhaps by making the panels detachable, to paint the trellis without painting the wall. A preservative horticultural wood stain in dark green or brown would be an easy alternative to painting. However, trellis can be purely functional rather than decorative: in the Jardin des Présentateurs at Bagatelle, the entire surface of a long wall is covered with plain treillage used just for support and completely hidden by a mass of roses mixed with clematis.

Noisette 'Madame Alfred Carrière', covering the South Cottage at Sissinghurst

It is occasionally suggested that roses should be planted about 16in/40cm away from the wall so that they are not in the rain shadow of the house. This is particularly useful for sunny aspects, though there is usually less of a problem against shady walls or those facing the prevailing wind and rain. Roses suffering from drought at the foot of a wall can and should of course be helped by regular watering.

Roses may also be used to clothe the interior walls and, perhaps even more successfully, the roofs of conservatories. In temperate climates this presents the opportunity to use varieties that thrive in warmer, drier conditions, such as Climbing Teas, Climbing Chinas and Noisettes. Chief among these has been 'Maréchal Niel', whose soft yellow blooms of perfect form can make a spectacular sight. I once worked in a greenhouse devoted to this variety, though peach trees were allowed the secondary role of covering the back wall. It was more usual for roses to be planted to cover the back wall and thence the roof; however, trained like a grape vine, the main stems of these roses were spread out horizontally along the front of the greenhouse, with cordons of younger stems running to the apex. If the rootstocks of roses are planted outside and led in through holes in the front wall, as is often the case with vines, it is easier to keep up the good practices of plenty of watering and the occasional application of liquid feed. The rose culture at my holiday job was exemplary, and the entire roof was covered with healthy green foliage and massed in late spring with the nodding yellow blooms.

Though 'Maréchal Niel' seems long to have been the most popular glasshouse climbing rose, others such as 'Climbing Niphetos' and 'Climbing Devoniensis' were frequently grown, though these are often too vigorous; the bush forms of the latter two can cover an area of wall 10ft/3m or more square and are often a better choice. Other roses said to be particularly good under glass include 'Climbing Ophelia', 'Climbing Madame Abel Chatenay' and, though it flowers for only a few weeks in spring, Fortune's double yellow rose, *Rosa* × *odorata* 'Pseudindica'.

As authors such as Walter Easlea have noted, the trick in growing roses under glass lies not so much in heating, for in a Z7 or warmer climate it is not essential (though a little can boost growth and flowering during cold dull spells). Everything depends upon adequate ventilation: if the air is too damp, mildew will proliferate; if it is too dry, spider mite will suck the sap from every leaf, leaving it crisp and brown, sinisterly cocooned in a fine web like an unfortunate victim from a horror movie. With plenty of air in moist conditions, and damping down when the atmosphere is too dry, these pitfalls can be avoided. However, almost all conservatories sold commercially are not provided with sufficient ventilation. Those who want to grow plants in their conservatory, not just roses but almost all other genera, must either get their conservatories custom-built or at the very least be prepared to add more vents.

Other features in the structure of the garden include temples, bowers, arbors, loggias, summerhouses and covered seats.

Rose temples were recommended by Paul and Hibberd as viewing points from which the whole garden could be surveyed.

Usually square or circular in ground plan and surrounded by a colonnade or arcade with or without a roof, they also acted as focal points for the entire design.

Wire rose temples were very popular in the late nineteenth and early twentieth centuries. A few survive, for example at Waddesdon Manor in Buckinghamshire and, now in the kitchen garden, at Arley Hall in Cheshire. Immensely pretty if well designed and proportioned, these look best if only lightly clad with the most dainty of Ramblers. Such frail structures must be galvanized and painted if they are to survive. Their delicacy lends itself to a fairly light paint color such as pale *vert anglais* or broken white.

William Paul shows a simple ironwork example in the garden of John Warner at Hoddesdon; it is based on eight ogee arches encircling and overcanopying a mound at the center of the garden. About 20ft/6m across, the central pole of the temple seems to have supported a circular seat. The scheme is superficially like the arbor in the White Garden at Sissinghurst designed by Nigel Nicolson. However, I imagine I would feel somewhat exposed sitting here and would prefer an arbor or gazebo, a place to sit and survey the garden, to one side of the garden, as we find today at Bagatelle and the main pavilion of the Roseraie at L'Haÿ-les-Roses.

Hips on Rosa multiflora *in autumn*

Though not on high ground, the bower in the extension rose garden at Mottisfont Abbey perhaps has its origins in Paul's designs: substantial octagonal wooden posts with iron arches springing some 16in/40cm below their tops support alternately 'Debutante' and 'Bleu Magenta' Ramblers. Provided that these have a good growing season with ample rain, even a couple of stems over the top of each arch is enough to yield generous sprays of blossom covering the arches the following year. However, a dry summer on Mottisfont's hungry chalk can sometimes mean that the bower is not covered and looks a little bare. This is not helped by the narrowness of the bed around its base, allowing little opportunity for soil amelioration.

The terms arbor and bower are interchangeable, both meaning a shady retreat, usually of latticework and covered with climbing plants. Arbors and covered seats are incidental features, occasionally used as a focal point for the end of a vista or path, though they are rarely the linch-pin of the design. Miss Jekyll reserved a special recommendation for "the simple old Rose arbour, by no means so often seen as it might well be, [which] should be in every modest garden. A Dundee Rambler on one side to cover the top, and an Aimée Vibert, or an alba kept to pillar height, to clothe the other side, will be an ample furnishing." She adds that the backing of a wall or hedge of box or yew will help and that even for "a more important structure . . . some free roses at its opening offer a charming invitation to enter and rest in grateful shade." Arbors, loggias and summer-houses are thus usually places for repose rather than the contemplation of spectacle. A charming example at Villandry where four circular arbors surround the main crossing of the garden has its roots in medieval design. Exactly the same design can be seen in a plate by Kip and Knyff for Tortworth from Sir Robert Atkyns' *The Ancient and Present State of Glocestershire* (1712) in which fifty-eight houses and their surrounding formal gardens can be seen.

In the clothing of the garden's structure, the Ramblers have proved more useful than any other class of rose. It is a matter both of regret and of hope and excitement for the future that so few rambling species have been used as the parents of new roses. Even the likes of *Rosa wichurana*, *R. multiflora* and *R. sempervirens* have

Rambler 'Polyantha Grandiflora' on a close-boarded house at Motveka in New Zealand, with peonies, delphiniums and lemon verbena. The Rambler, introduced by French rose breeder Bernaix in 1886, is one of several known under the confused name of Rosa gentiliana. *Commonly misidentified as 'Wedding Day', it differs in its drawn-out leaflet tips, slightly overlapping petals and fragrance of oranges; it does not develop the unsightly blotches after rain that mar 'Wedding Day'.*

seldom been crossed with Hybrid Teas or Floribundas in bright modern colors. True, we would not all want Ramblers in these hues and they would not blend happily with old-fashioned varieties in gentler tones, but they would surely find some striking new uses that would extend the versatility of roses in our gardens. And we still lack Ramblers that are truly perpetual-flowering.

Moreover, the three rambling species named above surely do not have a monopoly of desirable characteristics to combine with bush roses to make first-rate new Ramblers. What of the blue-grey foliage of *Rosa brunonii* 'La Mortola' or *R. soulieana*, the feathery leaves of *R. multiflora* 'Watsoniana', or the abundant flowers and fragrance of *R. mulliganii*? The rose is already the most useful genus for furnishing the structure of our gardens. In ten or twenty years nurseries, and even amateurs, could extend this versatility dramatically. The coming decades could be the most exciting for rose lovers since the time of Josephine and Malmaison, the garden that first demonstrated the full potential of the rose.

LEFT *An elegant summerhouse at Hailsham Grange, East Sussex, generously clad with Rambler 'Goldfinch'. Though the effect of tumbling swags of bloom is gloriously romantic, the Rambler has reached a size at which it threatens to mask the architecture of the building and block the views from inside to the garden beyond. The greens and yellows of the companion planting of euphorbias, anthemis and alchemillas provide a muted background that avoids upstaging the rose and its support.*

PAGES 94–95 *Rambler 'Adélaïde d'Orléans' and clematis 'Perle d'Azur' and 'Beauty of Worcester' clothe the central arbor in a Monmouthshire garden. Giant oat grass* Stipa gigantea *and rose 'Fantin-Latour' frame the view. In the distance beyond are trained pillars of Rambler 'Goldfinch'.*

Roses as Punctuation

In the garden as in writing, punctuation is needed to clarify structure and meanings. A garden without punctuation is like prose without full stops or music without a beat.

If you compare a garden with a book and each separate area in it with a chapter of the book, within each chapter are paragraphs, elements of the design that have some separate coherence, such as a vista, a border or a bed. Through each of these we can perceive beginnings and ends of planting themes that might be thought to represent sentences within the paragraph, that can be shown to be separate by the design equivalent of a full stop. Where garden sentences are extensive, they can be separated into phrases by less marked accents equivalent to semicolons or commas.

We all recognize the horticultural exclamation mark, the termination of a bold design statement in the garden that deliberately draws attention to itself as a focal point. This is a useful device but, as in prose, it can be tedious in its peremptory demands for attention if overused, and it does not lead to tranquillity. However, more liberal use is permissible in gardens seen infrequently and meant to excite, such as public parks or gardens. Where the termination of an element of design does not need such pointed attention, a less strident feature can be used to close it, a full stop rather than an exclamation mark.

The elements of garden punctuation covered below start with the most emphatic, the exclamation marks of cones, columns and pyramids, and progress to marks of less structural significance such as standards or roses in pots, whose function can be equivalent to a full stop, a semicolon or a comma, depending on the situation. These can be used repeatedly within a design element, for instance along a border or terrace, and can give coherence without unduly interrupting the flow. Even less obtrusive elements such as repeated rose balloons or domes can punctuate in a similar way provided they can be seen as distinct from the surrounding planting.

The earliest rosaries contained elements that could be adapted to ornament gardens of today, providing punctuation and focal points: in the nineteenth century for example there were the basket beds of Humphry Repton, Loudon's cones of Ramblers capable of 40ft/12m shoots, the 18ft/5.5m standards at Versailles worked with twenty different varieties, William Prince's rose-trained wire pyramids, and his friend's 30ft/9m pillars of 'Laure Davoust' in Geneva. Even within living memory, the *Rose Annual* showed a remarkable column of 'Seagull' 22ft/6.8m high covered in bloom from top to toe. Compared with such virtuoso performances, the modern use of roses for punctuation is tame and unimaginative, using scarcely a fraction of the rose's immense potential.

True, trellis obelisks and willow wigwams are common enough but they are too often used in an apologetic way, with only a spindly top emerging from the surrounding planting. What was twenty or more feet high in Josephine's or Loudon's day has shrunk to little more than three feet today. I find this disappointing, an opportunity wasted, most of the effort of planting and training squandered to produce less than eighteen inches of apex a few inches wide peeping timidly above the encircling plants. It seems as though gardeners become more and more fainthearted as time goes by, scared of any daring elements in their gardens lest they breach some cardinal rule of good taste.

To be effective as a focus, to provide the required frisson, such vegetable exclamation marks need to be related to the height of the viewer and almost always taller. For instance, a garden for 6ft/1.8m people needs such accents to be at least 7ft/2.2m high; at least half of this height should stand above its surroundings.

At Bagatelle we see a much bolder approach, with columns of

about 10ft/3m immaculately swathed throughout their height and smothered in bloom. Perhaps the most effective variety is Climbing Gold Bunny (syns. Climbing Gold Badge, Climbing Rimosa) with large, bright yellow flowers. 10ft/3m is perhaps an optimum height for bold effect in a garden of reasonable size: tall enough to be impressive but not too tall for training to be tackled from step ladders. Those who want to be more daring (and have the space) could create even taller structures, planted with several roses, and deal with training from scaffolding towers or maybe a platform hoist, hired by the day when needed.

It takes time for gardeners to realize the potential modern mechanical marvels offer for spectacular new styles of gardening. Almost certainly the most effective example of the exploitation of this potential is the superb Scottish garden made during the 1990s by Charles Jencks, using earth-moving machinery to create lakes and earthworks of exquisite form, all with a tiny fraction of the effort that would have been needed in the days of Capability Brown. We have become used to seeing platform hoists in gardens, brought in to deal with problems such as monstrously overgrown topiary. But why have we not used such machines to make dramatic new topiary, trained or clipped, formal or informal? The interplay of shapes, geometrical or irregular, arranged in a balanced and attractive way, could be much more cheaply and easily achieved through topiary or climbers trained to supports than by stonework or brick structures. Modern techniques make spectacular features comparable to the immense standard roses of Versailles or the towering rose cones of Loudon relatively easy to achieve; no longer would they be astonishing feats of perseverance in the face of perverse difficulty. Victorians with the imagination of Joseph Paxton would have relished the opportunity such machines offer to make prodigious, dazzling and beautiful set pieces.

Rosa *Climbing Gold Badge at Bagatelle*

PAGES 96–97 *Multiflora Rambler 'Laure Davoust'*

The setting of cones, columns or pyramids needs careful consideration. Are repeated accents required, to provide a unifying theme, or simply a single focal point? Should they be set among planting or stand in splendid isolation on a lawn? If the latter, they will probably need some furnishing at the base. A plinth of box is possible, square, round or any other shape desired, leaving the center sufficiently open to allow the roses to grow without undue competition and giving access to the ground for mulching, while avoiding a large and visually disturbing gap. Such shapes can also be used formally, perhaps with heights diminishing along an axis to exaggerate perspective.

There are several possible materials from which a frame may be constructed. A simple structure of poles is often perfectly acceptable, for the roses will hide the poles throughout most of the year. I am not a fan of single poles: even if they have truncated side branches still attached, they provide a narrow, rather spindly and weak accent. A single plant of most Ramblers or Climbing roses is capable of furnishing a broader structure based on three or more uprights to provide something more definite and architectural. A metal framework is also possible, though the caveats discussed in relation to arcades (see page 73) should be borne in mind, especially if the frame is to have a dark surface and be only lightly clad with roses. The wire pyramids recommended by Prince sound attractive, though good-quality wire structures of reasonable size are likely to be costly. Wooden trellis is a popular alternative that could be more imaginatively shaped than is usual, perhaps even based on centuries-old plans, such as one of the simple designs shown in Jan van der Groen's *Den Nederlandtsen Hovenier* (1669). If the frame is pleasingly architectural in its own right, it is probably preferable not to smother it beneath roses but to leave the structure partly visible.

The roses need to be selected with care. Unless only a light covering of foliage and a scattering of blossom are needed, they should be trained spirally round the support to produce flowering shoots from most nodes; the variety chosen should therefore be capable of producing stems roughly two or three times the height of the support. One of the recently introduced Climbing Miniature roses might well provide the right scale for the small garden, though some of these are a little short for full-scale pillars, cones, or pyramids. Spiral training makes mixing with clematis difficult to achieve and the clematis would have to be tied in at fortnightly intervals throughout the growing season. However, alternate uprights of clematis and rose could be very effective, particularly if roses and clematis that flower simultaneously are chosen. Annual climbers, perhaps especially *Ipomoea* species such as *I. lobata*, could be woven through the rose, though the annuals should not be planted where their roots are in competition with those of the rose. Perennial peas such as *Lathyrus grandiflorus* and *L. latifolius* could be used in the same way.

It will be easier to take down, prune and retrain the roses if they are fixed only to the outside of the support; if trellis is used, stems weaving between the laths can make retraining very tiresome. Large blooms look out of proportion on small structures: for all but the biggest structures in the grandest gardens Ramblers with their smaller flowers are more likely to be in scale than Climbing roses. When clothing taller structures, it is worth remembering that dark-colored roses will not show well against a background of light sky (crimson and purple both look black against a white sky) or of somber yew. Yellow roses can look stunning against blue sky, though this combination might be too strident for some settings. Conversely, pale colors can look washed out and ineffective against white cloud, though they can work well against a dark background.

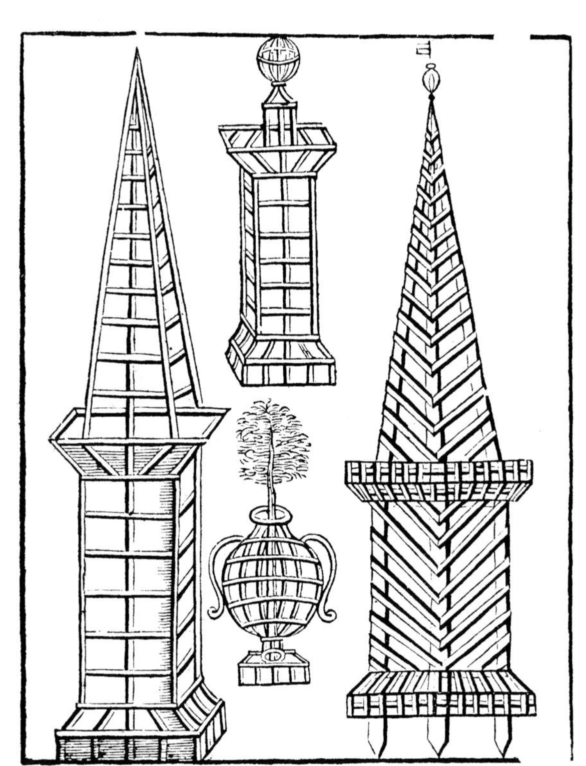

Treillage obelisk designs taken from Den Nederlandtsen Hovenier *by Jan van der Groen*

Such upright punctuation may be too stark for some schemes and an altogether flatter or rounder shape may suffice – perhaps a full stop rather than an exclamation mark. At Castle Howard in Yorkshire, the rose garden contains low trellis pyramids broader than they are high, an idea that could be effective in some circumstances, though here they scarcely show among the exuberant shrub roses. The balloons of roses mentioned by Mrs Gore in her *Book of Roses* (1838) were formed simply by tying together the stems of Boursault or Multiflora Ramblers. They could equally be achieved by training roses to supports like the iron-framed balloons at Powis Castle in North Wales, and in either case would provide an altogether softer and less insistent accent than a column or obelisk. However, such balloons still need to be higher than the surrounding planting if they are to make an effective impression. Lower still, domes, formed either by training the stems of the rose, as for 'Madame Lauriol de Barny' at Sissinghurst, or by providing a metal framework, could also be used, although they would likewise need to be taller than the encircling plants if they were to read as punctuation marks.

Balloons or domes would work equally well as incidents on a lawn, though they would probably need planting around the base to hide bare stems. Basket beds, planted with roses alone or a mixture of roses and other plants, could also subdivide and articulate areas of lawn, if positioned tellingly, as are those in the garden designed by Sir Geoffrey Jellicoe at Horstead Place in Sussex. This scheme is reminiscent of Repton's lawn scattered with basket beds at the Royal Pavilion in Brighton.

Standards are perhaps the simplest of all accents, although they still have something of the stigma of their unsympathetic over-use, so vehemently criticized by William Robinson in the nineteenth century. Their advantages were encapsulated by the Essex rose

ABOVE *The Rose Garden at Bagatelle, with a view towards the Orangery. The simple plan of box-edged beds separated by gravel paths is made more elaborate, even slightly frantic, but undoubtedly spectacular, by the numerous standard roses, pillars and topiary cones that punctuate the design.*

PAGES 102–103 *The Queen's Garden at Sudeley Castle consists essentially of four quarters, each containing a circular bed surrounded by four others. Each of the outer beds has a standard rose at the corner to punctuate an otherwise flat parterre. This view across the corners of three beds shows from left to right standards of 'Laure Davoust', 'François Juranville' and 'Albéric Barbier' contrasted against the encircling yew hedge. The exquisite Multiflora Rambler 'Laure Davoust' opens rose pink and ages to palest blush. It is sometimes known as 'Abbandonata', a curious name for a rose that is widely known and grown in Italy as well as in its native France, though scarcer elsewhere than it should be.*

Standards of Wichurana Ramblers 'Albéric Barbier' (on the left) and 'Léontine Gervais' add emphasis to the placing of a wrought-iron bench in a Staffordshire garden designed by Jane Fearnley-Whittingstall. Alchemilla mollis *furnishes the front of the bed, while the spiky leaves of* Sisyrinchium striatum *provide a contrast of texture. The pale yellow flowers of the sisyrinchium are gentle enough not to clash with pink roses.*

grower C.E. Cant in 1919: it "brings the head free of other growths, and into a brighter atmosphere" and can "break the dead level of the Rose garden, where beds of dwarfs are arranged." He went on to warn that "Only those varieties which make good heads, are free-flowering, and carry healthy foliage, are worth growing."

With standard Hybrid Teas and most Floribundas, raising the bush aloft draws attention to the coarseness of the foliage, the ugly jumble of branches at the base and the paraphernalia of stakes and ties needed to support them. But with weeping standards, any ugly infrastructure is hidden by a cascade of blossom.

As with columns and obelisks, the twentieth century has seen a downward trend in the height of weeping standards. Whereas Dean Hole in the late nineteenth century recommended 6–8ft/1.8–2.5m briar rootstocks, H.R. Darlington in 1941 considered that 5ft/1.5m was the optimum height. Today 50in/1.25m is the norm. In this case, a fear of apparent extravagance and ostentation is not solely to blame. As Darlington explained, echoing the comments of B.W. Price some years earlier, the taller the rootstock, the less vigorous the scions; even roses on a 6ft/1.8m stem would not maintain adequate vigor over a reasonable number of years; the head of the rose would become too scantily furnished with stems. Furthermore, Darlington warned that taller standards were more susceptible to wind damage. Nevertheless, Bertram Park in 1956 thought that a 6ft/1.8m stem produced the most attractive effect, the height also chosen as the optimum by George M. Taylor in 1939. I am inclined to agree with them that standards of Ramblers should ideally have 5–6ft/1.5–1.8m stems. This extra height allows the Ramblers their full potential for producing elegantly hanging stems visible from top to bottom without their becoming entangled with the underplanting; and in most cases a good support and strong ties will provide sufficient safeguard against wind damage. For some virtuosic effects, and in larger gardens, we might want standards that are even taller.

As Price's experiments proved, the choice of rootstock limits the possible height of a standard; if we want to create taller standards, different rootstocks must be used. It is interesting to note that although Miss Jekyll considered in 1902 that only *Rosa canina* was suitable for standard stocks, earlier authors recommended a range of species and the Noisette 'Manettii'. Since World War II, Rugosa stocks such as 'Hollandica' have become more common. Clearly the 18ft/5.5m standards at Malmaison were too tall to have been grafted on to briar or Rugosa stocks but were probably budded on to a vigorous Rambler. Some enterprising rosarian might try experimenting with Rambler species as rootstocks to see if such virtuosity is achievable. In any event, discerning gardeners will not necessarily want their stocks to be a standard 50in/1.25m unless it is the perfect height for their own requirements; they will be prepared to find a nursery willing to produce plants to their precise needs and to wait an extra couple of years until their roses are ready. For informal schemes, standards of even height could introduce an altogether unwelcome element of uniformity.

The *Rose Annual* abounded in discussions about standard roses over the years, some of them contradictory. However, there was total agreement that weeping standards must have space to be seen to full advantage and to achieve even growth around their circumference; a number of rosarians suggested growing them in isolation on lawns or at intervals along a drive, treatments that might seem a little unsubtle today. But what is wrong with unsubtlety? In some situations, such as public parks, seen occasionally and perhaps fleetingly, features that delight by making an immediate impact are preferable to those that reveal subtleties of color, proportion and architecture only over long inspection. It has to be admitted that in private gardens, subjected daily to the critical eyes of their creators, the unsubtle is only tolerable if it is allied to perfectly judged characteristics such as scale, shape and color that make for more lasting enjoyment.

Rosarians of the last century have shown less consensus over training: some insist that weeping standards need an "umbrella" trainer; others, such as Walter Easlea and George Taylor, consider this sort of frame an eyesore, a disfigurement and "an abomination to the lover of natural beauty." A simple hoop tied within the canopy of rose stems is all that is needed to ensure the shoots are evenly spaced around the perimeter of the head without destroying the natural grace of the cascading stems. Easlea and Taylor's judgment tallies with Miss Jekyll's teachings that formal gardens need exuberantly informal planting. Thus, the placing of standards and their uniform height can give formality, but allowing their shape to be as loosely natural and graceful as possible produces a more beautiful effect. This is still a useful precept: if we must use umbrella trainers, it is perhaps best to avoid the temptation to tie every stem rigidly to the frame to produce a perfectly uniform

mushroom; only occasional ties should be needed, to distribute stems evenly throughout the head of the plant and to avoid chafing against the frame or between adjacent shoots.

Much of the *Rose Annual*'s discussion centered on Wichurana Ramblers. Smaller-flowered sorts such as 'Dorothy Perkins', 'Excelsa' and 'Sander's White Rambler' were universally praised as being ideally suited for use as weeping standards; as indeed they are. Those with fewer shoots and/or larger flowers received slightly qualified commendation, partly because they tend to need more training and thus look less graceful. Walter Easlea liked to supplement Wichuranas with weeping standards of some of the older Ramblers such as 'Félicité Perpétue', 'Dundee Rambler' and 'Flora', not just for variety but for their delicious fragrance. He also suggested several rose species, shrubs as well as Ramblers, for tall standards. These included *Rosa mulliganii*, *R. glauca*, *R. hugonis*, *R. pimpinellifolia* 'Grandiflora' and *R. willmottiae*; I am not convinced that the more upright of them can have been a success. Easlea advised that some Ramblers did not need such rigorous pruning if grown as standards: most, and especially larger-flowered sorts such as 'Albéric Barbier', would still throw out productive flowering laterals from two- or three-year-old main shoots. He dismissed varieties such as 'Albertine', 'Paul's Scarlet Climber' and 'Blush Rambler' because they were too wayward; a tolerable result could be achieved through training with guy strings but this needed skill.

George Taylor expressed qualified agreement with his friend Easlea but considered his strings ugly and laborious, though he would tolerate trainers for 'François Juranville', 'Hiawatha', 'Léontine Gervais' and 'Albéric Barbier'. However, he added to Easlea's list of unsuitable varieties a few more he thought "really hopeless," because too stiff and coarse in growth. These included 'Chaplin's Pink Climber', 'Gloire de Dijon' and 'American Pillar'.

In 1941, in a blockaded Britain with paper desperately scarce, it was bold of the *Rose Annual*'s editor to run a 32-page survey of roses for weeping standards, probably the most extensive account of the subject ever published. It is touching that amateur gardening should continue in such times of turmoil, though many of the grandest gardens lost their staff to the armed forces and went into

Multiflora Rambler 'Neige d'Avril', grown as a weeping standard at L'Haÿ-les-Roses; this is a useful early-flowering creamy white variety that should be more widely grown.

rapid and irreversible decline. H.R. Darlington collated the comments and opinions of the most eminent rosarians about training, culture and appropriate varieties. He included some helpful advice, such as the warning that standards in front of a shrubbery are apt to become one-sided and the tip that training is often unnecessary, though a hoop of wood or wire can help the spacing of the stems. The views on varieties confirmed those of earlier authors, 'Dorothy Perkins', 'Excelsa' and 'Sander's White Rambler' still being held to be the best. An amateur rose grower, Mrs Corbett, interestingly recommended 'Elisa Robichon', not only for its abundant production of lax and graceful shoots but also for its generous autumn flowering.

Weeping standard roses are so much less common in Britain today than they were in 1941 that British gardeners associate them more with the gardens of France, where superlative examples are still quite common. Of all French gardens where they are used to spectacularly breathtaking effect, Monet's Giverny is perhaps the most famous. Not all the standard roses here weep, the Hybrid Musk 'Robin Hood' and Floribunda 'The Queen Elizabeth' among them, but the weeping standards are much the most effective. Some are grafted to relatively short stocks and made to weep by training to an umbrella frame, to produce a *cloche* (bell) or *champignon* (mushroom) shape, as for the Floribunda Centenaire de Lourdes®. The modern Ground Cover rose Palissade Rose (syn. Heidekönigin®) weeps naturally without so much forceful persuasion. But perhaps most effective of all are the Wichurana Ramblers such as 'François Juranville', grafted to a relatively tall 6ft/1.8m stem and tumbling down to almost meet the carpet of poppies, irises, peonies and sweet rocket beneath.

Wichuranas are not the only group capable of forming excellent weeping standards. At L'Haÿ-les-Roses, 'Neige d'Avril' is a first-rate Multiflora; its name is a little optimistic, though it does flower there in late spring ahead of most other Ramblers. Perhaps my favorite Multiflora for this use is 'Laure Davoust', seen to stunning effect at Sudeley Castle, where 'May Queen' and 'Félicité Perpétue' are also admirable. 'Raubritter' is sometimes seen trained as a standard, though rarely offered by nurseries, and many Ground

Wichurana Rambler 'Paul Noël', grown as a weeping standard at Bagatelle. Another Wichurana Rambler, 'Paul Transon', looks almost identical and flowers about a fortnight later.

Cover roses, particularly those with abundant lax stems and good foliage, should prove excellent. Pink Flower Carpet™ is a common and good example. Climbing Miniatures can sometimes be bought as weeping standards, usually on 18–24in/45–60cm stems, and would be pretty where a much smaller scale is appropriate, though as with all Miniatures there is a risk of their looking too precious.

However, I would not mind them used singly or perhaps even better as a group in order to raise the height of other planting (provided the jumble of stems is hidden), nor would I object to standards of variable and graded heights being used to create a bank of roses (cheaper and easier than importing vast quantities of soil). Most of the same problems apply to Floribundas, though foliage and flowers are often less coarse. Polyanthas and their allies are rather better, their flower size usually just about perfect for a head of this size. 'The Fairy' and 'Ballerina' can be persuaded to weep just enough to cover the base of the head; the latter is sometimes classed as a Hybrid Musk, a class with a very similar parentage. 'White Pet' is one of the most popular, a great feature in the potager at Barnsley House and blessed with neat growth and good foliage.

Rosa *'Ballerina'*

Full standards of bush roses are budded at a height of 40in/1m (until the 1940s 4ft/1.2m was more usual), and half-standards at 30in/75cm. Roses of smaller habit and flower tend to be budded on a shorter stock, usually 30in/75cm for Patio varieties and 18in/45cm for Miniatures. Smaller-growing Ground Cover roses are usually worked on a 40in/1m stock. If these heights do not fit your exact requirements, you will have to get plants budded to order and be prepared to pay extra and wait longer, though such a sacrifice is worth while to get scale and proportions precisely right, so important if the garden's punctuation is to harmonize with the rest of the design.

The growing of roses in pots is a useful technique that allows another sort of punctuation, whether the pots are to be placed formally – perhaps along a terrace or a broad walk – or informally. It is true that many uses of pots, for instance in a conservatory, cannot strictly be considered as punctuation. However, they need to be given light and air on all sides to develop evenly and thus prefer to be stood apart from other planting. This means that in the open garden they must usually work as punctuation if they are to flourish and be relevant to the design, rather than appearing as superfluous frippery.

Though the techniques of pot culture were developed as a means of growing early exhibition roses, most are relevant to growing roses in pots for outdoor punctuations. As it is too small a subject for a separate chapter, pot culture of roses for the conservatory will also be briefly discussed here.

Most rosarians grew their roses thus to force them for spring flower shows and produced innumerable stalky bushes in 6-8in/15-20cm pots. These had to be pruned to an upright stem and encouraged to grow up without spreading sideways so that the maximum number of pots could be accommodated. It did not worry these eminent growers that the result was hideous: the quality of individual blooms was all that mattered. However, there are a couple of descriptions of approaches that are of relevance for those who want to use roses in pots to enhance the beauty of the garden.

There was an extraordinary culture of roses for cut flowers by George Beckwith of Hoddesdon (*c.*1821–98), a pioneer of market gardening under glass, who supplied not only the British markets but those in Paris too, growing as many as three thousand potted

Standards of 'White Pet' grow among lavenders around the center of the potager in Rosemary Verey's garden at Barnsley House, Gloucestershire. The bush form of the deliciously scented Rambler 'Félicité Perpétue', this is classed as a Polyantha, although unlike others of this class it does not include Rosa multiflora *in its parentage. The weight of blooms is usually enough to pull down the stems to hide the ugly base of the head.*

roses each of numerous varieties. The salient points for today's rose grower are first that, with careful timing and accurate heating, it is possible to persuade roses to flower under glass from autumn until spring; secondly, those who want to grow roses with good individual blooms in a conservatory could do worse than picking commercial cut-flower varieties (such as today's Garnettes) which are selected for exactly this sort of culture.

The 1925 *Rose Annual* contains the most useful collection of accounts by several leading rosarians on different techniques of pot culture. Here Walter Easlea recalled the glorious achievements of the 1870s, when potted roses with two hundred blooms were not uncommon. Three of the cultivars he recommended are still offered by nurseries, 'Her Majesty' (Hybrid Perpetual), 'Coupe d' Hébé' (Bourbon) and 'Juno' (Centifolia). He also mentioned pot roses for decorating the house, recommending placing canes round the outside of the pot to train the stems. This kept the bush open, encouraged better growth and ripening of the shoots and minimized disease. This remains good advice for potted roses wherever they are to be used.

Easlea gives no explanation of how the largest and most prodigious potted roses were achieved, though there is some discussion in the Revd Foster-Melliar's *The Book of the Rose*. Here we are told that it is all very simple and that:

> patience and care for several years in disbudding and tying out the required shoots at the proper distances from each other are all that is required. I have been told it would often take a man three days to tie out and wire one of these big plants. The lower shoots were given sufficient lateral direction by long ties fastened to wire surrounding the pot; and these were pruned first to give them a start over the central upright shoots, which would otherwise get more than their share of the sap. A pyramid or cone was the usual shape aimed at, but sorts of short stiff growth were sometimes trained in globular form.

Foster-Melliar recalls a potted plant of 'Charles Lawson' 8ft/ 2.5m high and 7ft/2.2m through, with three to four hundred blooms on it at the same time, as 'a grand sight'.

Easlea considered that very double varieties did not perform well under glass but recommended 'Betty Uprichard', 'Melanie Soupert' and 'Madame Butterfly'; a later recommendation was 'Crimson Glory'. He also mentioned well-flowered Ramblers in 10–12in/25–30cm pots. It would be perverse to go to the trouble of growing Ramblers to be used outside in pots but they could be grown this way for the conservatory. In the same issue, George Burch, a rose nurseryman, recommended Hybrid Teas (for example, 'Madame Caroline Testout' for her remarkably large blooms) and Teas for pot culture but also said that Hybrid Perpetuals such as 'Frau Karl Druschki', 'Mrs John Laing' and 'Hugh Dickson' were good where space allowed. The 1931 annual contained a discussion of Polyanthas in strangely small 6in/15cm pots by Sir Edward Holland, a past President of the National Rose Society; among those he recommended, 'Coral Cluster' and 'Cécile Brünner' are still widely grown. The landscape architect Richard Sudell was more interested in garden effect and wrote in 1933 of growing roses in tubs: oak half-barrels with iron hoops were good for outdoor use and allowed bushes to become large and well furnished. For the conservatory teak tubs with brass hoops were recommended; however, these are rare today.

Some of the cultural recommendations remain relevant: roses to be potted will flourish only if already growing vigorously; weakly growing plants should be avoided. Roots on bought-in roses or those lifted from the open garden should be shortened to about 6in/15cm and the tops pruned to about 12in/30cm. Good compost is essential, preferably based on the finest loam with well-rotted manure, hoof and horn and a source of potash (bonfire ash) added; grit or sharp sand may be needed to improve drainage, for which the pot should also be well crocked. For mid-spring bloom, roses should be brought into a glasshouse with a temperature of about 7C/45°F at night and 10C/50°F by day and started gently into growth in midwinter. Good ventilation is essential to minimize damage by mildew and spider mite. If the roses are pruned after their first flush, a second flush will follow, after which the roses can be rested out of doors. Potted roses do not need annual repotting but it is good practice to resoil the top of the pot each spring to maintain fertility. Nowadays, composts often contain water-retentive polymer to reduce the risk of drying out, and also possibly a slow-release fertilizer. However, in hot climates and under glass there is a risk that the fertilizer can break down all too rapidly, causing a sudden concentration strong enough to kill the roses' roots.

Today the popularity of growing plants in containers is linked to the recognition of their usefulness for punctuation and for furnishing areas such as patios and terraces. It is also due to the current availability of many attractive containers, especially those made in terracotta. It is doubtful whether Hybrid Teas and Floribundas would be our first choice: grown singly, their habit and foliage is generally much too coarse. However, many of the newer sorts of rose are ideally suited to this sort of culture, perhaps especially Ground Cover roses: those with small and neat foliage and a fairly lax habit can furnish a container of moderate size and drape themselves gracefully over its edge. 'The Fairy', classed as a Polyantha but with the lax and spreading habit of a Ground Cover rose, is a well-known and old variety that is perfectly adapted to this sort of use. Many Patio roses would also work well, generally having a neater habit and less coarse foliage than Hybrid Teas and Floribundas. Where a smaller scale is needed, perhaps on the patio of a small garden or especially in conservatories, Miniature roses could be used and are extremely easily and quickly raised from cuttings. At such close range, their small leaves would appear less offensively coarse than the usual run of bush roses. The Climbing Miniatures seem very promising, being able to clothe the edge of containers gracefully but also having the potential and ideal scale for hanging baskets, both out of doors and under glass. I would also like to see them trained as cones in large containers, the potted equivalent of the exclamation mark.

Ground Cover rose Pink Flower Carpet™, *with (on the left) Polyantha rose 'The Fairy'.*

In the open garden, roses in pots can be used to subdivide a long terrace into manageable 'sentences', either placed at intervals along a path or along a terrace's retaining wall or balustrade. I think my favorite combination for such treatment would be a terracotta pot in imitation basket weave planted with a Ground Cover rose, though its color must be chosen not to clash with the pot. On a patio, containers can subdivide and articulate spaces or frame a view to the garden. They may also be used at the crossing of paths, either in the interstices or to mark the center of the crossing.

Pots or containers can be removed to a nursery area once their contents have passed out of flower, to be replaced with other plants for winter or spring. If liners are fitted, this need not necessitate having two expensive sets of containers. Galvanized metal liners used to be traditional, even though they were toxic to some plants, but glass-reinforced polymer liners are more usual today. Thus while one season's plants are enjoying their moment of glory in the garden, those for the next season will already be growing in liners behind the scenes. Larger containers need not be restricted to roses alone: though the floral complexity of most roses is not flattered by other fussy small-scale planting, a couple of additional plants might create a pleasing effect. Some summer bedding plants, perhaps the silver foliage of *Senecio viravira* or *Helichrysum petiolare* with a trailing petunia, can work effectively with roses, though their propagation needs to be timed so that they are at their best when the roses flower.

In the two centuries since Josephine made her Malmaison garden various styles of using roses for punctuation have come and gone. Many were remarkable for their panache and would still ornament our gardens effectively today. Others, such as Foster-Melliar's potted monsters, each requiring weeks of work for a few days' dazzling display, were extravagantly wasteful of time and skill and are justly unlikely to regain their popularity. Today's roses can be used for all the punctuation purposes of the past, plus many more we are only beginning to appreciate. They have greater variety of form, flowering period and color and should be much more imaginatively used, whether to provide focal points of bright bloom or to establish rhythms of repeated accents. Recent decades have seen important advances in rose breeding to supply new classes of rose that have yet to be widely and effectively used for punctuation in the garden. The potential for even more sorts of hybrid is immense. Provided we remain aware of this potential and exploit it to the full, the future will be rosy.

Roses in
Mixed
Borders

In the modern mixed border there is usually an interplay between herbaceous perennials and shrubs, perhaps with the addition of annuals and bulbs. Roses are often an essential part of the cast.

When the term "mixed border" was first used in the early nineteenth century, it was applied to quite a different style of planting. The mixed border as we understand it today evolved principally in the years between the two world wars, though it is only in the last few decades that gardeners generally have become aware of its beauty and usefulness and have come to understand how to combine plants to make one. Even in 1948, Arthur Hellyer wrote in *The Amateur Gardener* about the alternative to herbaceous borders which "for want of a better name I call . . . the 'mixed border'," the quotation marks implying that his readers were not expected to be familiar with the term.

While in rose gardens, by definition, the roses always predominate, in a mixed border roses will usually account for no more than a third of the planting. The rose groups in mixed borders tend to be isolated from each other by other plants. In a rose garden, other plants are the seasoning, the salt and pepper needed to bring out the flavour of the roses by flattering them with contrasting form or hiding their worst defects; in a mixed border, the other plants are just as important ingredients of the recipe as the roses themselves.

In the early nineteenth century, the term mixed or mingled border described a style of planting in which herbaceous plants of different sorts and colors were repeated at regular intervals so that they were thoroughly intermingled; their colors were alternated to make them show up as distinctly as possible. Early advocates of the style such as Loudon did not suggest mixing shrubs and herbaceous plants intimately together in the one border. Admittedly, some early border plans show a shrubbery with herbaceous plants fringing the front, but there is none of the thorough mingling of the two sorts of plant that is usual today. There is perhaps more discussion of herbaceous planting in front of shrub borders in German literature, with designers such as Hermann Jaeger (1815–?91) and Theodor Ruempler (1817–91) illustrating the use of bold perennials to furnish the transition from large, tall shrubs to lawn. The rose garden set in glades, as described by William Paul and Joshua Major some fifty years after Loudon, encircled by large shrubs and fronted by roses, had some elements of the modern style but still the planting was not thoroughly mixed and the rosarians' stubborn belief that roses should not be mixed with other plants remained the norm.

The change from the historic to the modern definition of the mixed border occurred in the lifetime of William Robinson. His *Hardy Flowers* (1871) mentioned mixed borders of several sorts, still related to the historic use of the term, though by then he advocated a less rigid and dogmatic approach: there could be mixed borders of hardy perennials, of bedding plants or of shrubs, though each sort remained essentially unmixed; the repetition of each variety on a regular grid was a recipe for tedious ugliness that should no longer be followed. However, he did suggest including bold bedding plants such as cannas with perennials and incorporating some perennials and lilies between shrubs.

The combination of herbaceous plants with shrubs figured more prominently in his *The English Flower Garden* (1883). Robinson wrote: "A frequent way in which people attempt to cultivate flowers is in what is called the 'mixed border,' often made on the edge of a shrubbery the roots of which leave little food or even light for the flowers." Such attempts were, he felt, usually unsuccessful. There should be no straight line dividing shrubs and herbaceous plants; generous gaps furnished with herbaceous flowers should be left between the shrubs, with some shrubs coming right to the front of the border. There was no suggestion of using roses in such schemes.

Miss Jekyll discussed mixed borders in *Wood and Garden* (1899), mentioning dozens of hardy herbaceous plants plus cannas, dahlias, yuccas and hydrangeas, a scheme no more mixed than the borders described by Robinson in *Hardy Flowers* almost thirty years earlier, and not comparable with the mixed borders of today. In over a hundred plates in Penelope Hobhouse and Christopher Woods' book on *Painted Gardens: English Watercolours 1850–1914*, not one shows a mixed border in the modern sense. So by 1914 not even the great prophets of gardening Jekyll and Robinson had recognized and exploited fully the advantages of the mixed border, nor had they shown the valuable role roses could play in them.

The reduced availability of gardeners during and after World War I focused gardeners' attention on garden features that were less labor-intensive than the traditional herbaceous border. In many gardens they were swept away and replaced by what Graham Stuart Thomas calls "an unfortunate development," the shrub border. The most skilled of designers have difficulty in creating a thoroughly pleasing border of shrubs alone, even if they include roses. The scale of a group of large shrubs is disproportionately big in all but the grandest gardens; if their flowers are attractive, their foliage texture and structure are usually tediously amorphous; most are dull after early summer. While there are many herbaceous and mixed borders that might be called excellent, even rarely great, I have not seen one shrub border that is thoroughly satisfactory. But although aberrant shrub borders predominated, a few mixed borders were created in the years between the wars. The development of the modern mixed border owes much to four pioneers. The first of these, Lawrence Johnston (1871–1948), created the garden at Hidcote Manor in Gloucestershire from 1908 onwards, incorporating within the structure of a grand garden elements of cottage gardening. These included repetition of key plants and scattering of odd plants away from the main group. Photographs of Hidcote taken in the 1930s, particularly of the Old Garden, show larger roses and some shrubs mixed with predominantly herbaceous planting.

'Thisbe', one of the Hybrid Musks, a versatile group for using in mixed borders

PAGES 112–113 Rosa *'Bonica' with* Diascia vigilis

Johnston's friend the Hon. Robert (Bobbie) James (*c.*1873–1960) was a leading influence in rekindling the popularity of old roses. His garden, St Nicholas, near Richmond, Yorkshire, survives under the stewardship of his widow, Lady Serena James. In an article in the 1953 *Journal of the Royal Horticultural Society*, James, claiming to be describing the borders in an imaginary garden, wrote about a typical mixed border of the kind that we would recognize today. Though most of the herbaceous planting at St Nicholas has disappeared since James's death, the borders he made there in the years from about 1908 onwards must have been much like the one he discussed, which contained roughly equal quantities of roses, other shrubs and herbaceous plants.

His article describes a backbone of shrubs including a few evergreens, with rhododendrons at the far end of the border to give solidity. Generous quantities of herbaceous plants, bulbs and some annuals were worked between and in front of the shrubs. Colors were chosen to flatter whatever James considered to be the typical hue of the season. Thus yellow was favored in spring, blue in summer, and brown, with red and orange flowers, in autumn, while white "attracts the eye and should be used with great discretion."

In spring the display started with bulbs, wallflowers, primroses, forget-me-nots and peonies, along with berberis, broom, daphne

The garden at Broughton Castle in Oxfordshire contains some excellent mixed borders designed by Lanning Roper. Here roses such as 'Fantin-Latour', with other shrubs, including philadelphus, and clouds of Crambe cordifolia *provide bulk at the back of the border, with Rambler rose 'Albertine' on the wall behind to carry the border's display upwards. The color scheme of pinks with blue delphiniums and white campanulas plus dusky purple* Allium cernuum *is saved from blandness by piquant* Alchemilla mollis *and golden feverfew. The front of the border has a York stone edging over which lavenders, cranesbills, pinks and lamb's ears can flop to soften the hard line.*

and lilies. Summer flowers included violas, campanulas and lilies, plus annual white tobacco and mignonette. After a spell with relatively few flowers, autumn brought "a new lease of life" with salvias, sternbergias, crocus, Michaelmas daisies and chrysanthemums. He considered the two greatest advantages of the mixed over the herbaceous border to be the reduction in labor (less splitting, digging and staking) and its colorful twigs and rose hips, which meant the border was never naked even in winter. Altogether he seems to have been the most advanced early theorist of the mixed border; however, his significance to our story is that he was probably the first to consider that the rose was its most important plant:

> There is one order of bushes . . . which for borders of this kind must, I think, take first place and that is the Rose, and I refer particularly to the so-called old Rose or bush Rose. Here we have something to which I would give full marks. The flowers are incontestably lovely – they have scent, they have profusion, they have charm, and are semi-evergreen. True most of them only flower once in the season but they do it so wonderfully and would impart to the border that something personal which to my way of thinking is the first essential of a good flower garden.

However, James had reservations about Hybrid Teas and Floribundas: "few of them are pleasing plants and should certainly be underplanted with such things as *Viola cornuta* and pansies."

Another early pioneer of the mixed border was plantsman Arthur Tysilio Johnson (1873–1956). In his *The Garden Today* (1938), reprinted from weekly articles in *The Sunday Times,* he devoted a chapter to the subject of mixed versus herbaceous borders. Writing that "summer's crowning triumph, 'the herbaceous,' has held a place of eminence above the common round," he held that "there came a time when it seemed that this old retainer – always costly in maintenance – would have to be modified or done away with. Its toll on our time and money was heavier than changed conditions would allow. So the mixed border came into being."

Johnson wrote as someone who loved individual plants: his motives in championing the mixed border seem to have been primarily to reduce labor and secondly to provide a setting where each of the plants he loved could be seen to best advantage, rather than trying to create a symphonic and color co-ordinated whole. He advised including mostly evergreen shrubs (especially spring-flowering genera like camellias and rhododendrons), "a few non-evergreens, such as the single roses (*Moyesii* and *Hugonis*)" plus herbaceous plants. He felt that the old roses were best used in the formal "period" garden and should not be mixed with the new Floribunda and Polyantha varieties of the day, which he used for bedding only; roses can have played no more than a minor role in his mixed borders.

In contrast, the numerous color-schemed mixed borders planted by Phyllis Reiss (d.1961) in her garden at Tintinhull, in Somerset, included roses of every sort, among them Floribundas, modern Shrubs, old and species roses. A significant feature of Mrs Reiss's planting was the incorporation of bush roses into the mixed border, a practice not sanctioned by A.T. Johnson and one which Bobbie James allowed only with strict provisos.

Though these few pioneers showed the way in developing mixed borders, some of the most eminent names in planting design seem to have had little involvement. The archetypal mixed border does not appear in the designs of Beatrix Farrand or Percy Cane, nor in the Sissinghurst of Vita Sackville-West's day. But after World War II mixed borders rapidly became more popular and began to incorporate more roses.

The first major work on the subject, Christopher Lloyd's *The Mixed Border* (1957), championed the use of roses but showed that the rosarians' dogma of separation had not entirely disappeared: "Far greater use should be made of roses in mixed borders. There still lurks in most of us a deep-seated prejudice against associating roses with other plants . . . it must surely be admitted, in appraising a rose bush at any time in the year when its shape is not actually obliterated with blossom, that it is either exceedingly ungainly or merely a shapeless mess."

By this time a new generation of gardeners had taken over from the four pioneers and were successfully using roses in mixed borders. Perhaps the most prolific and influential of these were Lanning Roper (1912–83) and Graham Stuart Thomas, both of whose schemes prominently feature roses. Roper admired Mrs Reiss's Tintinhull planting and had visited frequently. His most productive period, in the 1960s and 1970s, coincided with the rise of the art of garden photography in color. Many of his best schemes appeared in popular magazines and encouraged numerous imitations, perhaps most noticeably in the gardens created for successive Chelsea Flower Shows. His borders were usually mixed, with a third or more of the shrubs being roses. Repeat-flowering varieties were favored, especially Rugosas and Hybrid Musks, with the addition of some bush roses and a few once-flowering varieties such as 'Raubritter'.

Graham Thomas has perhaps been the most insidiously influential of late-twentieth-century designers of planting, through his work as Gardens Adviser to the National Trust from 1956 to 1973 and subsequently as their Gardens Consultant. When he joined the Trust, his knowledge of roses old and new was already legendary, acquired and augmented through his work at Sunningdale Nursery where he gathered a remarkable collection of old roses, the basis of the National Collection at Mottisfont Abbey in Hampshire. Since then he has enriched and enhanced borders in all the Trust properties where he has advised, almost all of them open to the public, and has thus influenced planting in most British gardens. He has used not only the old shrub roses in borders for early summer but modern repeat-flowering shrub roses and bush roses too. A disliker of herbaceous borders, Graham Thomas thinks that mixed borders are essential in every garden and that it is only the mixture of herbaceous plants with bulbs, shrubs and the occasional small tree that can supply the necessary richness of planting.

So omnipresent did the style of mixed planting with roses become in the 1960s and 1970s that a rebellion against it was inevitable, especially as it had generally been made more "tasteful" by the use of Jekyllian combinations in a restricted and muted color range. The 1980s saw a rehabilitation of hot colors such as scarlet, orange and red. There was also the return of the dahlia to favor, after decades of being considered too coarse to be allowed out of the cutting border or kitchen garden.

The dahlia has similar design uses to the rose: both have large round flowers, generally indifferent foliage and a wide color range. Certainly, their differences make them not entirely interchangeable: the rose can have blooms of more informal shape and often exquisite fragrance, with bushes possessing bulk early in the season; the dahlia has more formal, geometric blooms, is slow to fill the middle and back ranks of the border but often has fewer disease problems. The rose is more romantic, the dahlia sometimes more dramatic, particularly for late bright color. When large round flowers are needed, however, gardeners should forget prejudices about either genus and just think which would supply the required effect at the right time.

The voice of Christopher Lloyd has been particularly influential in the continuing rebellion against a suffocating softness and timidity in the use of color. His predilection for bright contrasts and bold foliage effects, known to gardeners as early as the 1950s, has at last in the 1990s received such widespread acceptance that it looks set to become the norm: the danger is that for those who forget that he also values harmonies, excitement will replace the tranquil gardens of thirty years ago and the garden will become as endlessly thrilling as a rollercoaster ride, and about as restful.

Christopher Lloyd has replanted the Old Rose Garden at Great Dixter using mainly tender foliage plants and flowers to create a dazzling Rousseauesque effect reminiscent of Victorian tropical bedding. The principal plants include cannas, pelargoniums, begonias (both foliage and flowering sorts), spiky Cactus dahlias, fiery coleus, palms, phormiums, colocasias and bananas. A few roses such as Floribunda 'Chanelle' and the Hybrid Musk 'Madge' are retained in a large block of planting that still has many of the characteristics of the mixed border, though it is not linear. Delightful as these roses are, they are the least extrovert of all the plants in this part of the garden. And otherwise the role of plants with large round flowers has been surrendered almost entirely to the dahlia. I feel that modern roses, especially the more flamboyant varieties, some perhaps with dark foliage, could play a greater part in this style. Such a scheme could be repeated in many gardens, perhaps with the addition of other showy bedding and foliage plants such as tall African marigolds, the larger New Guinea impatiens, rampaging Surfinia® petunias and wigandias. Only the most extravagant modern roses in the hottest colors can hold their own in such company. More modest and subtle varieties would be lost in the mêlée.

Another modern approach to planting that has recently achieved popularity in both the British Isles and North America originated in German gardens where plants are chosen to be ecologically suited to their site and stay in equilibrium with their neighbors over many years. This style lends itself to informal planting for which some species roses and more natural-looking hybrids are suited and is more akin to the planting discussed in the next chapter, on wild gardens.

Over their first century, mixed borders with roses have risen in popularity primarily because of three factors. First, garden design ceased to be dominated by great estates, where a separate area could be devoted to each favored genus; instead the same space had to accommodate all the plants gardeners wanted to grow, including roses. Secondly, a growing awareness of the importance of the architecture, structure and texture of planting, inspired largely by the writings of Miss Jekyll, made gardeners realize that rose foliage alone could be extremely dull, though its faults could be mitigated by companion plants. Thirdly, gardeners were no longer willing to tolerate planting that had a short season of one or two months but wanted a longer-lasting display. This became a requirement also in gardens of stately homes open to the public, where single-season borders were a recipe for disappointment and ensured that garden lovers would visit only during the borders' peak period and not at other times of year.

The more reliably recurrent-flowering nature of modern bush and shrub roses has helped the trend towards continual display that has made the mixed border a popular feature. The appearance of classes such as Rugosas and Hybrid Musks in the years around 1900 made it possible to create a much longer-lasting show. The taller Hybrid Teas and Floribundas, including those roses intermediate between the two which are classed as Grandifloras in the United States, should also prove excellent for mixed borders. The bold and sculptural shape of many roses, their relatively large flower size, long season and wide range of colors give them a vital role in the mixed border.

It is true that, used as single plants, some Floribundas and most Hybrid Teas have blooms that are disproportionately large to the size of plant. This is particularly relevant in the small garden where the largest rose blooms can look out of scale. It may be that in truly tiny gardens Hybrid Teas should be avoided altogether, and Floribundas, Patio and Miniature roses of more fitting flower size favored instead. Bush roses are a little small for grand borders unless several are grouped together to match the scale of other plant groups. This is exactly the way we automatically use most herbaceous plants, not singly but arranged in groups according to the scale of the border. The same treatment is necessary for roses.

The value of the mixed border, and the reason why it is held in such high esteem by the likes of Graham Thomas, lies in the bulk that shrubs, and even small trees, can add to herbaceous planting, plus the extra benefits of their winter structure. The greater height and substance of mixed borders allows them to be used as boundaries between adjacent gardens or garden rooms and can make the grandest borders even more imposing.

Although lots of modern roses can flower all summer long and into the autumn, many of those we might like to grow have a relatively short season, usually in early summer. Those fortunate enough to have space for single-season borders can avoid the late summer and autumn dullness of these roses by segregating them into an early summer mixed border and reserve the perpetual-flowering varieties for use in borders designed to perform non-stop from spring to fall. If we have room for only one border, the occasional much-loved once-flowering rose can be accommodated, though if there are too many, the interplay of colors and textures will be disastrously interrupted by non-functional and amorphous green for too much of the year.

As a rough rule of thumb, a border needs at least one-third, and preferably half, of its plants performing at any one time if the relationships between its colors and textures are to continue to work. Too many non-performers can kill a planned effect stone dead. The converse of this rule is that for a plant to be successful in a border, it must perform for at least one-third and preferably half of the border's season. A border that ceases to dazzle only in winter usually has a seven or eight months' season; a rose that flowers for less than two months cannot pull its weight in such a setting.

There are some roses that have more than one trick, for example attractive hips (though these are rarely showy enough to make an impact, unless they have the profusion and bold shape of *Rosa moyesii*); good autumn color is another bonus. Either of these assets can increase the rose's performance time so that it fully justifies inclusion. Such strict criteria applied to shrubs show just how few perform as well as roses: though fine for the early summer border, the likes of philadelphus, deutzia and weigela are simply not good enough if longer display is required.

Rosa *'Geranium' in the Purple Border at Sissinghurst. In a color scheme that, ranging from magenta to lavender blue, runs the risk of being leaden, this* R. moyesii *hybrid, with its cherry-red summer flowers and bold-shaped orange-red hips in autumn and winter, provides a lively contrast.*

The major criticism of this approach is that only shrubs with freakish foliage color, variegation or the bold shape of *Chusquea*, *Aralia elata* or *Cornus controversa* might seem to pass the test. These are ingredients for extravagant contrasts and excitement but not for a restful garden. Some less extreme foliage colors are fully effective in the mixed border: for instance, if white and silver is the theme, it is not necessary to opt for the brightest variegation; gentle silvers, if accompanied by good texture and accurately scaled by appropriate pruning, are perfectly able to carry the theme. *Salix alba* var. *sericea* or *S. elaeagnos* subsp. *angustifolia*, pruned or stooled to keep them to the required size, and *Elaeagnus* 'Quicksilver' would all be excellent in a white or soft-colored scheme. Even the odd once-flowering rose or philadelphus could be permitted, perhaps draped with a late-flowering clematis such as 'Alba Luxurians'. However, there is great temptation to overdo the clematis trick and swathe every shrub the moment it passes out of flower, giving an effect that looks mannered, repetitive and annoying when it should appear unforced and casually charming. Of course, there are other climbers that can be used in the same way, perhaps especially annuals such as *Ipomoea* species.

At Kiftsgate Court in Gloucestershire, a sumptuous mixture of red Floribunda roses accompanies the purple foliage of Atriplex hortensis *var.* rubra *and smoke bush.*

If dazzle is required, then variegation has a role to play. Among the most striking variegated plants are the white- and gold-edged aralias, *Aralia elata* 'Variegata' and *A.* 'Aureovariegata', with an openly branched habit and moderate height, allowing them to form a canopy above the border. Dogwoods such as white-edged *Cornus alba* 'Elegantissima' and gold-variegated 'Spaethii' and 'Gouchaltii' are outstanding and can be stooled each spring if a height of 40in/1m is required. If taller variegation is needed, these dogwoods can be pruned on a two-year cycle, cutting out the half of the stems that are two years old and leaving one-year-old stems each year; for yet more height, a three-year cycle of cutting out one-third of the stems can be used, though the winter stems will be less brilliant. This same two- or three-year cycle can be used for variegated or purple elders.

The same principle of not necessarily opting for the most extreme forms applies to purple-flushed foliage, whether for use with hot colors or with gentler shades of blue to pink or crimson. Less strident combinations can be achieved using colored foliage that is not of the deepest purple, for example the dusky grey-purple *Prunus spinosa* 'Purpurea' or the purple-flushed (but not deep) *Cotinus coggygria* Rubrifolius Group. Such gentler tones avoid the harsh insistence of the most strongly colored forms and can prevent richly toned schemes seeming too cloying.

Strong purple foliage, for all its usefulness in the more artificial areas near the house, can easily be overdone and can look out of place in wilder parts of the garden. Where deep purple really is required, dark variants of plums, maples and filberts would be leaden and perhaps best avoided, though there are first-rate cultivars of *Cotinus coggygria* such as 'Royal Purple', berberis such as *Berberis* × *ottawensis* 'Superba' and *B. thunbergii* 'Atropurpurea Nana' and, if a small tree is needed, *Cercis canadensis* 'Forest Pansy'.

I have reservations about purple plums and maples, but I have seen a memorable combination of rose 'Climbing Masquerade' growing into a purple crab that might work even better with these same trees. Though this rose lacks subtlety and has a poor flower shape, the combination of dark

In this border the pale yellow of shrub rose Tall Story® *contrasts perfectly with blue cranesbills, though the anthemis and* Scabiosa ochroleuca *are too close in color to read distinctly.* Gillenia trifoliata, *silver pear, white cranesbills and mallows harmonize with the scheme. The Turkish red of the opium poppies makes an excellent contrast to the rose; however, it is not used in sufficient quantity to create a telling combination and is a slight distraction from the prevailing theme of yellow, blue and white.*

foliage with spangled swags of yellow, orange and red blooms was dazzling and worth repeating with any purple-leaved tree that, unlike the crab, retains good, dark foliage into the autumn. In this case, the purple sloe would be too soft and too grey to provide the necessary pizzazz.

Yellow-leaved plants can also play a valuable role in the mixed border with roses, whether it is to be a hot-colored design including purple foliage, yellow, orange and red flowers or a simple contrast with white, yellow and blue flowers and some glaucous foliage. Particularly useful shrubs for such schemes include *Philadelphus coronarius* 'Aurea' and *Sambucus racemosa* 'Plumosa Aurea', with *Cornus alba* 'Aurea' or *Choisya ternata* Sundance to furnish the front of the border and *Robinia pseudoacacia* 'Frisia' giving either height at the back or accents further forward, standing above the rest of the border. The golden honey locust, *Gleditsia triacanthos* 'Sunburst', can, with pruning, be limited in size or treated as a large shrub, as seen in the Long Border at Great Dixter. Perhaps *Catalpa bignonioides* 'Aurea' provides the boldest of all gold foliage: pruned to fork into several branches near ground level and cut back severely to about 40in/1m each spring when established, this produces enormous leaves of semi-tropical luxuriance, another effect seen at Great Dixter. The same trick can be used with ordinary green-leaved catalpa or the purple-flushed *Catalpa* × *erubescens* 'Purpurea' as well as the foxglove tree, *Paulownia tomentosa*.

The pink-tinged smoky blue-grey foliage of Rosa glauca *makes an effective background for* Kniphofia *'Sunningdale Yellow',* Anthemis tinctoria *'E.C. Buxton' and feverfew.*

Floribunda and Hybrid Tea roses are often found in mixed borders but generally poorly used. Besides the problem of scale already mentioned, not enough attention is paid to the roses' foliage: varieties with the least coarse leaves should always be chosen. Catalogues seldom give any indication of foliage quality, but a visit to a local nursery or trial ground will help. Patio and Ground Cover roses have immense potential in mixed borders but are scandalously underused. Part of the reluctance to use Ground Cover varieties stems from their being associated with roundabouts and supermarket car parks where the most sophisticated, highly colored and showy sorts can look vulgar and out of place. These varieties can be successful and appropriate in the mixed border. Those with a low arching habit are best not confined and should be used towards the front of the border surrounded by lower plants, not hemmed in by perennials of similar height. Roses with a tall arching habit, such as *Rosa moyesii* and *R. glauca*, are also best given some room, standing forward from other plants of the same height to show off their graceful form.

It is best not to pay too much attention to the reported height of varieties given in catalogues but to alter the pruning to fit the rose to its site. With light pruning, many Floribundas make impressive small shrub roses without any sacrifice to flowering, and are comparable in size to shrubs from the middle ranks of the border. To prevent their becoming woody and shy-flowering, at least in their second flush, a system of "restorative pruning" is needed, cutting out a quarter to a third of the older stems fairly low in the bush each year. Some pillar roses, the shorter Ramblers such as 'Maigold', can make impressive spreading shrubs if given room to mound up towards the front of large borders.

If borders are planted to last from spring to summer, the roses in them must be encouraged to be colorful for as long as possible. This requires not only choosing varieties that are thoroughly recurrent but pruning hard each spring and deadheading severely so that later flushes of growth are strong enough to produce plentiful bloom. (This applies equally to the other inhabitants of the border: plants such as *Campanula lactiflora* and *Salvia* × *superba* can be encouraged to flower right through from summer until fall with timely deadheading.) Light spring pruning tends to lead to a plentiful first flush but fewer flowers for late summer and autumn. The lower concentration of roses in a mixed border helps reduce rose infections but organic gardeners must avoid varieties whose later flushes might be minimized by blackspot, rust or other defoliating disease. Those who do not object to synthetic pesticides can spray susceptible varieties regularly with the appropriate fungicide. The chemical should be changed at least once a year to prevent resistance building up.

Although mixed borders differ from those where roses predominate, many of the same principles of rose borders apply here, relating to, for example, underplanting, the use of bulbs and contrasts of form and texture. With roses isolated from each other by varied planting, it is no longer crucial for each non-rose to play a key design role. Provided that there are no slabs of border with undifferentiated foliage and that plant architecture, textures and foliage effects are well handled, some plants that are decorative without having distinctive form (for instance, hardy geraniums or galegas) may be incorporated without diminishing the impact.

Climbing rose 'Maigold' grown as a shrub with Nectaroscordum siculum

Most gardeners will want their mixed borders to perform from spring to fall, and perhaps also to contain enough structure of foliage and twigs to look agreeable through the winter. Spring flowers will start the display, including bulbs whose space may be filled as later flowers spread their leaves. The likes of primroses, polyanthus, pulmonarias and epimediums will happily survive beneath the branches of deciduous shrubs and roses, even though they receive little light through the summer. The young foliage of roses, particularly if it is a rich red-purple, can be an effective feature to consider in composing plant associations; if it is to complement polyanthus, tulips or narcissi, the roses must be pruned fairly early so that they are not still too twiggy to be an asset when all else is at its peak.

Early-flowering biennials can also play a role in filling spring gaps, to be removed as the rest of the border fills out. Suitable sorts include wallflowers, forget-me-nots and honesty, though slightly later biennials such as *Smyrnium perfoliatum* and sweet rocket might be accommodated if late-leafing perennials can fill their space. Similarly, biennials can be used where summer bedding is to be planted, particularly towards the front of the border. However, if the biennials are as late as smyrnium, rocket and sweet Williams, bedding might need to be planted late (take care it does not suffer a check from becoming pot bound).

The same principles apply to an early summer scheme used at Sissinghurst for some years. Here the combination of foxgloves (*Digitalis purpurea* f. *albiflora* and *D.p.* 'Sutton's Apricot') with the elder 'Guincho Purple' and roses such as palest lemon 'Pax' and pale peach 'Penelope' is one of transcendent beauty. The foxgloves must be grown fat for the most imposing spikes and a good crop of secondary side-shoots. Used as bedding plants, they are removed as they pass their best to be replaced with tender perennials such as gentian blue *Salvia patens* mixed with silver *Helichrysum petiolare*.

The roses start to come into their own in late spring, when the first species and hybrids bloom. Many of these, for instance *Rosa primula*, *R. xanthina* and 'Helen Knight', are yellow. Those blessed with Z9 gardens or microclimates (Z7 in continental areas such as North America or southern Europe) can add *R. banksiae* to these and let it scramble into shrubs; ceanothus makes a classic combination, though perhaps the deepest blues are not as effective as those a shade lighter. Most early-flowering roses need to be pruned immediately after flowering if they are to make suitable wood in time for the next season, though *R. banksiae* needs only occasional pruning.

Other flowers of fairly long-lasting interest coinciding with these include spurges, especially *Euphorbia characias* subsp. *wulfenii* cultivars and *E. polychroma* 'Major' in chartreuse and *E. griffithii*; avoid the rampageous and now variable *E.g.* 'Fireglow' and plump for 'Fern Cottage', 'King's Caple' or 'Robert Poland', or 'Dixter' if bronze foliage is required. Cardoons and globe artichokes (*Cynara cardunculus* and *C.c.* Scolymus Group) are already showing handsome foliage, though they can become untidy by late summer, and there are many excellent violas that will flower for months, so long as they do not have to endure a hot, dry summer.

Early clematis such as *Clematis montana*, *C. alpina* and *C. macropetala* can be used both over adjacent walls and across shrubs, though the extreme vigor of *C. montana* can prove a problem; if space is limited, a realistic program of pruning to limit its size will be needed. There are few spring-flowering shrubs that remain attractive for long enough to be admitted to the long-season border, though several berberis species and cultivars will pass muster, among them glaucous *Berberis temolaica* and *B. dictyophylla*, purple-leaved *B.* × *ottawensis* 'Superba', *B. thunbergii* 'Atropurpurea' and 'Atropurpurea Nana'; also evergreens including *B. darwinii* and slightly recurrent *B.* × *stenophylla* and its sport 'Lemon Queen' (syn. Cream Showers™). The pink-splashed variegation of *B. thunbergii* 'Rose Glow' or *B.t.* 'Harlequin' might be thought messy but it provides a slightly lighter tone of purple foliage that may be an advantage for certain schemes. On a smaller scale, perennial wallflowers, especially 'Bowles' Mauve', flower profusely for many months and are excellent value, though they are short-lived, suffer from wind rock in open sites and are often killed in colder than average winters.

Of course, there are many shrubs that produce a stunning spring display but are dull for the rest of the year. In some of these, such as the brooms (*Cytisus* cultivars), *Spiraea* 'Arguta' and *Tamarix tetrandra* and the similar *T. parviflora*, the flowers emphasize a graceful habit of growth that is less apparent when there are only stems and leaves to see. Both tamarisk species are very fleeting in bloom and require careful timing if they are to coincide with early roses or other border flowers. In some, such as lilacs and *Viburnum opulus* 'Roseum' (syn. *V.o.* 'Sterile'), it is the bold shape of the inflorescence that creates the effect. Those living in areas too cold for the Banksian-rose-with-ceanothus trick can instead combine a yellow rose such as primrose *Rosa xanthina* f. *hugonis*, its unfurling buds borne upright like candles on a Christmas tree, or gold 'Helen Knight' with a rich purple lilac such as *Syringa* 'Andenken an Ludwig Späth' or 'Charles Joly'. One choice herbaceous peony, *Paeonia mlokosewitschii*, combines beautifully with the early small-flowered yellow roses, its greyish, pink-tinted leaves surrounding large goblets of butter yellow. None of these plants, for all their charms, can really be considered to earn its keep through the rest of the year. Such fleeting beauties suggest that those who are lucky enough to have room to spare should consider a late spring border to house them.

Rugosa rose 'Agnes'

A charmingly informal mixture of English roses, 'Sutton's Apricot' foxgloves and Geranium × oxonianium *at Chenies Manor in Buckinghamshire. Such gentle and understated harmonies, with the spikes of the foxgloves providing the only contrast, can be immensely soothing when all are in bloom, though there is a risk of dullness when the peak of flowering has passed.*

PAGES 128–129 *In the relatively small Cotswold garden of Pam Schwerdt and Sibylle Kreutzberger, there is no room for a host of separate color-themed areas; the vast majority of plants blend together happily provided the most disputatious colors, such as fierce orange and strong yellow, are segregated. Roses, with their supreme floral quality – as in the flat and formal blooms of Gallica 'Charles de Mills', on the right – are an important feature. On an arbor with a variegated cordyline as its focal point, clad also with claret and Japanese glory vines, the Rambler 'May Queen' displays its slightly nodding bunches of blossom.*

The combinations of just these few genera with early roses, perhaps overtopped with a delicate flowering cherry or *Malus floribunda*, are immensely appealing and seldom seen.

The next wave of roses, as spring passes into summer, includes yet more shrubs such as 'Nevada', the Frühlings series of Sweet-briar hybrids ('Frühlingsgold' is especially good), 'Agnes', *Rosa elegantula* 'Persetosa' (commonly known as Farrer's threepenny bit rose) and, if only lightly pruned and grown as a shrub, 'Maigold'. These coincide with columbines, a promiscuous lot that must be isolated and their seedlings rigorously selected if they are to be kept true to type yet allowed to self-sow. If different columbines are grown near to each other, they should be deadheaded to prevent seeding, though, even with occasional division and replanting, vigor declines as virus diseases accumulate. The traditional granny's bonnets (*Aquilegia vulgaris*) come in red, blue, pink and mauve, double or single, spurred or spurless. They are all charming and continue in flower long enough to combine with the old roses, whose colors blend agreeably. Soft yellow roses seem to be more common than rich gold at this season, but either of these will combine well with *A. canadensis* and *A. formosa* var. *truncata* in scarlet with yellow, and with some individuals from the long-spurred hybrids that also include these hues. Deadheading will prolong their flowering and encourage enough later bloom to earn them a place in the long-season border.

Other plants providing excellent value at this time of year include *Anthemis punctata* subsp. *cupaniana*, a carpet of silver foliage with abundant white daisies for the front of the border, geums and tree lupins and *Campanula glomerata* 'Superba', an excellent purple-blue for planting beneath early yellow roses. Each of these is sufficiently good for long enough to merit its place. Intermediate Bearded irises, though they have the bonus of fairly good foliage contrast, are not as effective in this respect as Tall Bearded varieties whose greater height helps their leaves slice into expanses of dull rose growth more effectively.

The intimate mixture of Rosa gallica *var.* officinalis *and* Allium cristophii *at Sudeley Castle works only because of the hard pruning of the rose. This ensures that enough light reaches the leaves of the allium in spring for the bulbs to achieve flowering size, keeps the stems of the rose no higher than the flowers of the onion, and also slightly delays the flowering of the rose so that the two bloom at exactly the same time.*

Oriental poppies come into their own at this time too but have the disadvantage of dying down after flowering and leaving a gap. Late-planted bedding plants can fill this, or adjacent dahlias, *Aster divaricatus* or gypsophila can be encouraged to grow into the space, as Miss Jekyll recommended. The poppies' round flower shape can match that of any roses near to them in the mixed border. If color and flower size of rose and poppy are too similar, the combination can be ineffective; placing a plant with contrasting foliage and flowers in between can overcome the problem. This same drawback affects the combination of peonies, both shrubby and herbaceous, with roses, though most are a little later than the poppies in flower. Herbaceous *Paeonia lactiflora* cultivars are a fairly close match to many of the old roses in color, floral form and even to some extent foliage, and should be used with discretion. In any event, peonies have a relatively short season; their space cannot be made to contribute to later display, so they are probably best used in a single-season border.

The onions are immensely valuable plants for combining with roses. Perhaps the most common is rosy mauve *Allium hollandicum*; at 3ft/90cm high, its spherical flowerheads are held aloft on vertical stems that point to them like exclamation marks. Starting into bloom in late spring, by the height of the rose season it bears green seedheads that remain attractive as they fade to parchment tints. 'Purple Sensation' and 'Purple Surprise' are two excellent richer-colored varieties. Perhaps even more useful is *A. aflatunense*, less rosy in color and taller at 5ft/1.5m but otherwise similar. The true species is rare, most nurseries selling *A. hollandicum* under its name. These two species will readily hybridize to give swarms of indifferent seedlings and are, like the columbines, best kept apart.

Coinciding with the main rose season, *Allium cristophii* has much larger globes of flower, the florets spaced sufficiently to appear as separate stars. This also ages attractively to pale buff seedheads by late summer. *A. cernuum* 'Hidcote' is a charming clumper for the front of the border in a color between dusky mauve and magenta. Among the best of the larger mauve onions

Onions such as Allium *'Gladiator' (top left),* A. hollandicum *(bottom right), and the rarer, similar but taller* A. aflatunense *are immensely useful for mixing with shrub roses of moderate height. Their globes of bloom are borne on stems long enough to display them against the flowers of roses such as, here, the English rose* Gertrude Jekyll®.

are 'Rien Poortvliet', 'Lucy Ball' and 'Gladiator', while 'Globemaster' and 'Globus' have the advantage of huge flowerheads and a long succession of flower derived from their parent, the slightly tender *A. giganteum*. All these onions have the disadvantage that their leaves start to become untidy and die back from the tips as the flowers reach their peak. There are three principal ways of overcoming this defect: plant the onions through an herbaceous perennial that spreads its leaves just as those of the onion start to fade; plant something in front of the onions that becomes tall enough to hide their dying foliage but not their flowers; or interplant with bedding plants that will decently screen the leaves, for example the tender silvery subshrub *Senecio viravira* with *Allium cristophii*.

Among those shrubs that earn a place in the long-season border, yet are at their peak at the same time as most roses, are lavateras such as 'Barnsley' (pale pink with a near-red eye) and deeper 'Rosea' which are long-flowering and excellent, though florally similar to many roses; 'Barnsley' can revert to 'Rosea' if cut back by frost. *Phlomis fruticosa* and *Brachyglottis* (*Senecio*) 'Sunshine' are useful for greyish foliage towards the front of the border, both with golden-yellow flowers; it is easy to cut off the senecio's flowers if they spoil the color scheme. The phlomis commonly called *Phlomis anatolica* or 'Lloyd's Variety', a cultivar or hybrid of *P. grandiflora*, has excellent silvery foliage but few flowers; its leaves are good enough on their own. A few hypericums merit inclusion towards the front: these include *Hypericum kouytchense*, *H.* 'Hidcote' and *H.* × *moserianum*, though their gold flowers can clash with many roses. For the larger border, where it has room to achieve its characteristic layered habit, *Viburnum plicatum* 'Mariesii' is excellent. Yuccas and phormiums can play a useful role as focal points and exclamation marks, the latter in a wide range of colored-leaved and variegated cultivars, though the brightest run the risk of overwhelming the roses they are intended to flatter. For West Coast gardens there are hebes, for example, 'Midsummer Beauty', 'Watson's Pink' and, for the front of the border, 'Mrs Winder', 'Youngii' and 'Blue Gem'.

Phlomis fruticosa *and Hybrid Musk 'Buff Beauty'*

The roses themselves need not be restricted to the traditional old or modern shrub sorts: there are some first-rate roses for foliage effect, such as *Rosa soulieana* in pale grey-green, *R. glauca* in grey flushed with red and its hardier hybrid 'Carmenetta'. The larger bush roses can be excellent if bold color effect is needed and many Ground Cover sorts – particularly if their flowers are brightly colored and intricately double – are much better suited to the sophisticated mixed border than to ground cover in some outer and semi-wild part of the garden. Among David Austin's English roses are many that are invaluable here.

Herbaceous perennials blooming at the peak of rose time but sufficiently long-flowering for the long-season border include hybrid achilleas, now available in many "in between" colors of apricot, orange, terracotta, peach and cream as well as the traditional white, pink, red and yellow. Those that combine yellow from, say, *Achillea* 'Taygetea' of gardens with pink or red from *A. millefolium* parents usually lose the red as the flowers age. Many fade from rich terracotta to pale biscuity yellow, making it difficult to compose harmonies with the entire range of their chameleon color range and almost impossible to achieve effective contrasts. Nevertheless, there are some bush roses that will flatter such varieties, usually in the warm part of the spectrum, for instance soft orange. Strong yellow achilleas such as 'Coronation Gold' blend well with hot colors; taller varieties derived from *A. filipendulina* with large, slightly domed heads of rich gold provide a telling contrast of form with shrub roses. Softer yellows such as 'Taygetea' of gardens, 'Moonshine', 'Credo', 'Hella Glashoff', 'Martina' or 'Lucky Break' can be mixed with slightly gentler tones, rich, deep red or even some pink roses, provided they are neither shocking pink, fuchsia nor carmine, and not so pale that a dash of yellow will overwhelm them. There are also some good pink, carmine and deep red cultivars of *A. millefolium* including 'Cerise Queen' and the sumptuous 'Sommerwein' that are easy to blend successfully with many roses.

Russell lupins make an excellent contrast of form with

summer roses and are available in many colors. Perhaps the best varieties are the clones raised by Woodfield Bros of Stratford-on-Avon, Warwickshire. These are fairly new and still scarce. However, seed-raised strains are an acceptable substitute, though they embrace variation in habit and flower color. Perfectionists can raise a packet of seed of each color they want and select the best seedlings, favoring long, dense flower spikes, good color and plentiful branching to give secondary spikes. As for many herbaceous plants, deadheading is well worth while, giving some bloom almost continually until late fall.

Larger vertical accents are useful to provide focal points or a unifying rhythm to the mixed border. They can be supplied by pillars of roses or clematis, or by fastigiate conifers. In the British Isles, where common yew (*Taxus baccata*) is native, the Irish yew (*T.b.* 'Fastigiata') seems to "belong" more than North American or less-than-hardy Italian cypresses. Like all of us, it has a tendency to become broader as it ages, losing its effectiveness as a vertical accent. Clipping robs it of its interesting texture, and though spiralling wires might restrain it, they look hideous. It can be severely cut back and will regrow, but this produces a fuzz of competing new verticals that never stiffen and lean drunkenly away from the prevailing wind. The solution seems to be never to allow more than a handful of vertical stems to develop and to remove the least robust periodically from the base of the plant. Thus air and light can reach every stem, each of which should remain stiffly upright, distinctly seen and casting an individual shadow, to give texture and form to the whole.

For the front of the border, *Alchemilla mollis* is such a classic plant that many gardeners have become blasé about it. Nevertheless, the piquancy of its yellow-green flowers can save gently colored schemes from suffocating softness, as well as lifting somber colors, and create bright contrasts with, for example, orange or scarlet roses. Magenta flowers can pep up the border in a similar way: one of the best foreground plants is *Geranium × riversleaianum* 'Russell Prichard', a charming and long-flowering sprawler able to weave itself through the front ranks of the border. *G.* 'Ann Folkard', its magenta blooms clashing agreeably with yellow-green leaves, is so vigorous that it demands a larger scale of planting. This can scramble up to a height of about 40in/1m and can be grown as an upright perennial with the support of peasticks, as a brighter-leaved alternative to *G. psilostemon*. *G. malviflorum* is very valuable in the southern United States, where it has good foliage in winter and spring and then goes dormant in the summer

Those who find magenta a little fierce can opt for the gentler *Geranium* 'Patricia', a sprawling plant of intermediate vigor, or soft satin-pink *G. × riversleaianum* 'Mavis Simpson', a slightly miffy but exquisite cousin of 'Russell Prichard' that is well worth the risk. Other front-line cranesbills include 'Kashmir Blue', *G. clarkei* 'Kashmir Purple' and 'Kashmir White', plus the admirable 'Johnson's Blue' (named for the eponymous Arthur Tysilio). The variants of *G. pratense* are also useful with roses, particularly silver-blue 'Mrs Kendall Clark', the dainty double 'Plenum Violaceum' and the dark-leaved Victor Reiter Strain.

Other long-flowering perennials that merit their place towards the front of the border include acanthus, for its handsome foliage and the vertical accents of its flower spikes, golden *Coreopsis verticillata* and its primrose cultivar 'Moonbeam' (though this can be short-lived), *Dictamnus albus* in mauve-pink or white and, where conditions suit them, hostas, always remembering that their leaves

Geranium psilostemon *(top) and* G. clarkei *'Kashmir Purple'*

PAGES 134–135 *At Alderley Grange in Gloucestershire, a border with Bourbon roses 'Prince Charles' and striped 'Ferdinand Pichard' is furnished in front with* Geranium × oxonianium, Nepeta *'Six Hills Giant', cotton lavender (*Santolina chamaecyparissus*) and variegated applemint (*Mentha × suaveolens *'Variegata'). The acid-yellow Welsh poppies add a note of cottage garden informality.*

will scorch in hot, dry summers. I find the fairly upright 'Krossa Regal' and 'Snowden' particularly effective, their bold lines making an effective contrast to relatively amorphous roses.

Aster amellus cultivars will flower from the height of the rose season until fall, while sedums related to *Sedum telephium* and *S. spectabile* are handsome long before their flowers color in late summer or early fall and useful in front of bush roses. The handsome hybrid 'Herbstfreude' (Autumn Joy) is pink enough in flower to be used with pink roses but ages by autumn to a brick red that can require quite different color associations. Deeper-colored flowers age most gracefully: white-flowered sedums such as *S. spectabile* 'Iceberg' are pretty for the first week of their floraison but are soon marred by dying brown blooms. Nevertheless, most of the larger sedums retain attractive seedheads through fall and winter.

Some useful greys and silvers for the front of the border include perennials such as catmints (*Nepeta racemosa, N.* × *faassenii* and the much bigger – often too big – hybrid 'Six Hills Giant') and *Stachys byzantina*, including 'Cotton Boll' bearing spikes without flowers, 'Silver Carpet' (just foliage, without flower spikes) and large-leaved, shy-flowering 'Big Ears'. Anaphalis, *Artemisia* 'Powis Castle' and *Helichrysum italicum* are yet more hardies, but there are also tender perennials such as feathery *Artemisia arborescens* and *Senecio viravira*, while *Helichrysum petiolare* will meander agreeably through the front ranks of the border. For those who want flowers with their silver foliage, *Lychnis coronaria* in magenta, white ('Alba') or white with a pink eye (Oculata Group) are easy and charming. *Ruta graveolens* 'Jackman's Blue' is another classic plant to furnish the front row, hiding ugly rose stems and softening the edge of the border if it adjoins paving.

Lavenders are also indispensable, the cultivars of *Lavandula angustifolia* such as 'Hidcote' and 'Munstead' being more useful for small gardens than *L.* × *intermedia* Old English Group or the more silvery Dutch Group, which can reach a height and spread of 40in/1m or more. However, avoid seed-raised 'Hidcote' and 'Munstead' which are more common in nurseries than plants from cuttings of the originals; they are very variable and usually inferior.

There are few herbaceous plants that can supply silver or glaucous foliage in the tallest and backmost ranks of the border. Macleayas, such as cream-flowered *Macleaya cordata* or coral *M. microcarpa* and *M.* × *kewensis*, are perhaps the most handsome, though biennial cotton thistle *Onopordum nervosum* is dazzlingly effective at breaking up expanses of dull foliage with its jagged candelabra of bright silver stems.

The daylilies are precious both at the front of the border and in its middle ranks, the earliest sorts such as lemon-yellow *Hemerocallis lilioasphodelus* flowering with the late spring roses, *Geranium sylvaticum* 'Mayflower' and the first flush of *G.* 'Johnson's Blue'. Most of the many thousands of cultivars start to flower before the end of the roses' first flush, the best of them continuing until fall. Their usefulness for mixing with roses derives from two main characteristics: the contrast provided by their foliage, and the bold outline of their flowers. Clarity and beauty of line, a quality readily appreciated in art, is too often overlooked in planting, both in flowers and in foliage. The contribution of line quality to floral beauty is perhaps best demonstrated in the flower studies of Charles Rennie Mackintosh or the plates of Redouté's *Les liliacées*. Gardeners who ignore it and include too few plants that possess it in good measure

Tall Floribunda 'Chinatown', sometimes classified as a Grandiflora rose, with Hosta montana *'Aureomarginata', at Hardwick Hall, Derbyshire*

The center of the walled garden at Arley Hall, Cheshire, is ringed with beds of Floribunda rose Iceberg, *edged with catmint and* Alchemilla mollis. *Though* Iceberg *is now old enough to need some protection from disease, its appearance is graceful and timeless, devoid of the stiffly sculptural petals and thick unbending stems of other Floribundas of the 1950s and 1960s.*

in their borders cannot achieve thoroughly pleasing effects.

It is sad, therefore, that perhaps 80 per cent of modern daylilies have been bred to have a flower of more or less round outline. These are utterly graceless and will not flatter roses, which themselves provide as many circular flowers as we need. Such varieties should be eschewed and we should make our selection from those long-flowering sorts of good shape such as 'Marion Vaughn', 'Corky', 'Golden Chimes', 'Hyperion' and the repeat-flowering 'Stella de Oro'. Even the old 'Stafford', considered passé by daylily buffs, is far more telling than most modern red cultivars when combined with roses. Most varieties are of the right stature to be used at the front or in the second rank of the border, where their height approximates to that of the bush roses. Taller varieties such as the pale lemon and fragrant 'Tetrina's Daughter' (5ft/1.5m) are excellent used with shrub roses of middling size such as Hybrid Musks or many of David Austin's English roses.

Rosa *'Fantin-Latour'*

Several other genera have flowers of such exquisite line that they are able to lift even the dullest and most amorphous border planting. Lilies come high on the list, though their foliage is generally indifferent. There are many that flower at the peak of the rose season, perhaps most notably *Lilium regale*, its white cultivar 'Album' and the Madonna lily, *L. candidum*. However, the latter has leaves that begin an unsightly death as their flowering approaches; the foliage must be screened by low planting in front, or perhaps annuals between the bulbs.

For late summer and fall, crinums (*Crinum* × *powellii* and *C.* × *p.* 'Album') have flowers that are equally telling, though marred by rather poor foliage that is too tall to be effectively hidden; their flowers still earn them a place in many schemes.

Many Tall Bearded irises also have flowers of superlative line quality. This is true particularly of the older sorts, including *Iris pallida* subsp. *pallida*, with fragrant light lavender-blue flowers and glaucous leaves, and *I. germanica*. Unfortunately, the breeders have been at work with these too, imposing on them what William Robinson called the florists' "standards of ugliness," so that most recent varieties are too stiff and round in outline to add grace to the mixed border. It is far better to use an old sort of good shape, as long as it is not disproportionately large, even if its color is slightly impure, than to deaden the beauty of the border by imposing graceless blobs where what is required is elegant shape.

Many other perennials can flatter roses at the peak of their season. Among campanulas, *Campanula lactiflora*, its white cultivar 'Alba' and the superb *C.l.* 'Prichard's Variety', plus the varieties of *C. persicifolia* and *C. latiloba* are perhaps especially good; all can be persuaded to flower longer if deadheaded. Other useful bell-flowers include *C. takesimana*, *C. punctata* 'Alba' and the hybrids 'Elizabeth' in dusky reddish pink, 'Kent Belle' in violet-blue and 'Burghaltii' in greyish mauve, all of them with large long bells. The repeated vertical accents of their nodding flowers give a pleasing "grain" to the display.

Alstroemerias are available in many more colors now than the familiar orange, though salmon-pink *Alstroemeria ligtu* hybrids remain immensely useful.

The flowering sea kale *Crambe cordifolia* offers clouds of white flowers that provide a delightful contrast of form and texture to roses such as 'Fantin-Latour'. Even after the blooms fade, the flowerheads remain attractive as they age from green to parchment. Other airy flowers that combine well with roses include *Verbena corymbosa* and *Gaura lindheimeri*. The latter has flowers in white with a touch of blush pink but the recent variety 'Siskiyou Pink' is much more definite, approaching carmine, and good in combination with white, pale pink or crimson roses.

Some of the salvias have a similarly light-textured effect, such as the forms of *Salvia pratensis* (Haematodes Group and 'Indigo' are first-rate). *S. forsskaolii*, though dull in isolation, makes a pretty foil for sugar-pink roses. *S. nemorosa*, *S.* × *superba* and *S.* × *sylvestris* have bolder vertical spikes that make a more definite impact in shades of blue-purple, dusky pink or white; the blue-purple sorts have near-blue florets set off by plum calyces. All these salvias need regular deadheading to keep them in flower until the fall.

A number of bedding plants combine excellently with roses, provided they have not been turned by the breeders into graceless dwarfs with disproportionately large flowers. Nicotianas are a case in point: cultivars of *Nicotiana* × *sanderae* shorter than about 10in/25cm are stiff, ugly and incapable of grading into the border and blending with the surrounding plants. Varieties larger than this are exceptionally useful, though they can easily succumb to fatal tobacco blue mould in cool moist weather if too many are grown together and if they do not have good circulation of air around the plants. *N. alata* 'Dwarf White Bedder' remains tall enough to retain its grace without being as uncontrollably lanky as the parent species and *N.* 'Lime Green' is charming, pacific with hot colors, and piquant with pinks and mauves. Their fragrance is a bonus, though most cultivars are scented only in the evening. Tall, white and handsome *N. sylvestris* and curious *N. langsdorffii* with nodding, round-lipped green trumpets are excellent companions for roses and not quite so susceptible to mould.

It is not always easy to coax bedding plants into bloom for the start of the rose season unless plants can be grown early and planted out in late spring in frost-free areas or in parts of the garden with good frost drainage. Penstemons have enough frost resistance to be hardened off and planted in time to flower with the roses. Most are tolerably hardy in Z8 gardens and need only be repropagated and replanted every few years. For those in colder climates, cuttings can easily be overwintered under frost-free glass. Argyranthemums are usually hardy only to Z9 but are equally easy to use as bedding plants, often having attractive glaucous foliage with white, yellow or pink daisy flowers – excellent to use in front of roses.

Annuals such as *Cosmos bipinnatus* and *Verbena bonariensis* should not be overlooked. Many cultivars of cosmos are available and will flower until the frosts; the shortest sorts have little use in the mixed border but full-sized cultivars at 5ft/1.5m and the Sonata Series at 2ft/60cm can flatter shrub or bush roses with their abundant flowers and feathery foliage. The airy stems of the verbena with their clouds of violet flowers can be threaded through the border from the middle ranks towards the front, helping prevent a monotonously even-banked effect. Though usually grown as an annual, the verbena is hardy in Z9 and will regrow in future years from self-sown seed, though this gives rather delayed flowering.

The long-season mixed border containing perpetual-flowering bush and shrub roses will need plenty of flowers that continue after the roses' first flush. For the cool part of the spectrum (with roses in white, pink, crimson and purple), agapanthus, *Phlox maculata* and *P. paniculata*, Japanese anemones, *Aster* × *frikartii* and eryngiums are invaluable. Hot-colored roses can be accompanied by heleniums, kniphofias, crocosmias and the feathery foliage and flowers of fennel in both its green and bronze forms.

Buddleja davidii cultivars come into their own as the roses approach the end of their first flush and remain attractive for a couple of months, their form contrasting well with roses. However, they do not shed their dead florets cleanly and so look better after deadheading, particularly in the case of the white-flowered varieties. The immensely broad panicles of *B.d.* 'Dartmoor' are perhaps the most showy, 'Nanho Blue', 'Nanho Purple' and var. *nanhoensis* 'Alba' the most graceful. The hybrids 'Lochinch', 'West Hill' and 'Malvern Blue' are also useful, their foliage inheriting some of the greyness of *B. fallowiana*, an attractive species for those with a favored climate, as is *B. crispa*. The dwarf *B.* 'White Ball' is good for smaller beds and borders.

The cultivars of *Hibiscus syriacus* are invaluable for late summer and autumn color in the border. Used as a large shrub or even a small tree, the best varieties include violet-blue 'Oiseau Bleu', white 'Diana', crimson-eyed white 'Red Heart', 'Hamabo' (blush pink with a red eye) and Pink Giant™ and 'Woodbridge' in rich deep pink. They can be trained as standards for repeated accents .

The most useful hardy fuchsias are perhaps the elegant variants of *Fuchsia magellanica* and the tall and showy 'Checkerboard', though Triphylla varieties such as 'Koralle', 'Mary', 'Thalia' and the similar 'Gartenmeister Bonstedt' can be bedded out in front of hot-colored roses. Most of the highly bred hybrids are a little small and fussy to use with roses and do not have a sufficiently graceful habit of growth; however, they generally remain attractive until the first frosts when many other hardier plants are looking untidy.

Whereas fuchsias can be small and twee, Hortensia hydrangeas can be large and vulgar. Those with smaller florets such as *Hydrangea macrophylla* 'Générale Vicomtesse de Vibraye' seem more in scale with shrub roses, although even this variety can overpower

most Hybrid Teas and Floribundas. The Lacecaps are daintier and mix much more easily with roses: the Teller Series, most of them with German bird names, such as 'Möwe', 'Blaumeise' and 'Rotdrossel', are especially worthy, in addition to the old favorites 'Mariesii Perfecta' (Blue Wave) and 'White Wave'. Cultivars of *H. serrata* and the hybrid 'Preziosa' also have lacecap flowers and, being rather smaller, are suited to the front of the border. The purest hydrangea blue is not, I feel, a color that mixes well with pink, salmon or scarlet roses, though it is effective with white or yellow; nor do mauve, pink or red hydrangeas assort well with hot-colored roses.

Hydrangea paniculata is usually pruned severely each year to produce massive conical panicles of white or pale pink flowers. Unless these contain many sterile florets to give a lacier effect, they seem too solid and out of scale with roses and most other flowers. Less severe pruning results in a larger shrub but inflorescences more in scale with other border plants. *H. quercifolia* is grown for its bold leaf shape as much as its flowers but its main glory comes in autumn when its foliage takes on reddish tints. All hydrangea flowers develop muted tones of green and brown in autumn; with frosts their chameleon colors change to parchment. The strong shape of the flowerheads still gives structure to the winter border.

The most serious and most frequent criticism made by the great German plantsman Karl Foerster (1874–1970) was "ghastly – a garden without grasses!" It is perhaps in autumn that grasses come into their own, with airy flowerheads in subtle tints of gold, pink and fawn. However, they add essential texture to the mixed border throughout the year. Only narrowly upright sorts such as some of the *Miscanthus* cultivars (*M. sinensis* 'Strictus', *M.s.* 'Gracillimus', *M.s.* 'Variegatus' and *M.s.* 'Silberfeder') will grade fully into the border; grasses with a more arching habit such as *Stipa gigantea*, pennisetums, the true *Miscanthus sinensis* 'Zebrinus' and pampas grasses must be used towards the front surrounded by lower plants so that they can express their natural beauty to the full.

Variegation in grasses at its most subtle can be regarded as a means of lightening tone and drawing attention to texture without appearing unduly strident: the narrowness of the pale banding in variegated cortaderias and some miscanthus could never be considered brash, though the likes of *Miscanthus sinensis* 'Cabaret' and tender *Arundo donax* var. *versicolor* are distinctly flashy and suited to planting that is meant to dazzle rather than pacify. *Miscanthus sinensis* 'Morning Light' has more subtle variegation. Those grasses with longitudinal gold variegation such as *Hakonechloa macra* 'Aureola' and *Cortaderia selloana* 'Aureolineata' are excellent in hot schemes with roses and other flowers in yellow, orange and scarlet. Though most pampas grasses do not perform until fall, *C. richardii* begins its display in high summer and lasts into winter, its parchment plumes playing in the slightest breeze, bringing movement to the garden as effectively as a grand fountain. The bold shape of the pampas grasses allows them to be used as focal points or as repeated and unifying accents along the border's length.

There are enough autumn flowers to devote a border to these alone, mixing them with roses that have a prolific late flush of bloom, such as some of the Chinas and Polyanthas, or attractive fall foliage and hips. There would be lots of asters including 'Little Carlow', dark-stemmed 'Calliope', *Aster turbinellus*, *A. lateriflorus* 'Horizontalis' and *A. amellus* 'Veilchenkönigin', associated as at Great Dixter with pink nerines. Other composites would include chrysanthemums, tall white *Leucanthemella serotina* and gloriosa daisies, with autumn-coloring shrubs aplenty. Here could be salmon and red schizostylis, towering and skilfully staked boltonias, Japanese maples and crimson spindlebushes; there would be seedheads of clematis lit by the low sun, and swags of Virginia creeper and Japanese glory vine in scarlet, gold and russet draped across the largest shrubs and small trees.

In the long-season border, some of these will still earn their space. A few of the asters are indispensable, especially the long-flowering cultivars of *Aster amellus*. *A.* × *frikartii* varieties such as 'Mönch' also perform from high summer until the frosts, and colored-foliage shrubs contribute to carefully planned associations throughout the year before their final autumnal blaze of glory. Some late-flowering shrubs have good foliage and neat habit that make them creditable before they bloom. Notable among those not so far considered are perovskias and caryopteris with greyish foliage and flowers of precious sapphire blue, both exquisite in front of white or yellow roses. *Caryopteris* × *clandonensis*

In Pam Schwerdt and Sibylle Kreutzberger's Cotswold garden, Climbing rose Constance Spry *is sufficiently early flowering to be used as a background to late spring biennials such as sweet rocket (*Hesperis matronalis*). The softly colored purple foliage of* Cotinus *'Grace' completes the picture.*

flowers are followed in late autumn by seedheads of an extraordinary turquoise; the new cultivar 'Pershore' has perhaps the most intense blue flowers and promises to be among the best. Though hardy to Z6, small plants of this hybrid do not always overwinter well even in Z8, especially if they are in poorly drained ground or suffer from wind rock; the original cultivar 'Arthur Simmonds' seems to be the easiest to establish.

It is in fall that dahlias really come into their own: most have colors that are autumnal and there are now many with dark foliage that makes a splendid foil to bright flowers. These might derive from the old *Dahlia laciniata* 'Atropurpurea', a delightful, dusky plant but so dark in leaf and flower it can scarcely be seen from a distance and thus of limited usefulness. The well-known and excellent 'Bishop of Llandaff' shows its influence in finely divided foliage, an improvement on the usually coarse green dahlia leaves. 'Tally Ho' is like the Bishop, handsome and with small, dark leaves but taller, single and brighter in vermilion, while 'David Howard' is fully double, golden orange with bronze leaves. Single 'Moonfire' has amber-yellow flowers with a red eye, a color scheme that restricts it to flashy plantings, though it is undeniably effective.

Among Dwarf Bedding dahlias with deep foliage, 'Yellow Hammer' is a good yellow shaded red and 'Bednall Beauty' is among the best with small leaflets and rich red fully double flowers. One of the few that will blend with the pink-to-purple part of the spectrum, and thus with asters, is single 'Mount Noddy' in two-tone bright pink and magenta, not subtle but undoubtedly effective. Larger green-leaved dahlias in autumnal tints include scarlet Small Cactus 'Doris Day' and its richer and less brash variant 'Alva's Doris'. 'Glorie van Heemstede' is a butter-yellow Small Waterlily, a fewer-petalled class that seems agreeably informal compared with some of the manically geometrical, multipetalled Pompons and Decoratives. Also in this class, 'Autumn Lustre' is tall, of open habit without being gawky with flowers of a soft, rich orange, a rare yet useful tint for this time of year and not brash.

Pyracanthas have a role in the mixed border, grown vigorously and pruned to encourage boldly arching sprays of flower, followed in fall by fruits in gold, orange or scarlet. Like the more spreading grasses, such a habit of growth requires them to be given some room and brought forward in the border to be fully effective. Though their foliage is relatively amorphous, their dramatic curved stems make a bold statement in autumn when smothered by bright berries. During their dull period between flowering and fruiting, they can be clad with annual climbers such as *Ipomoea lobata*.

Most Hybrid Musk roses perform well in late summer and autumn but soft buff-yellow 'Autumn Delight' is especially esteemed for this season; carmine 'Vanity' becomes a less strident color with the onset of cooler weather and the pale peach flowers of 'Penelope' are followed in late fall by coral-pink hips. The immense usefulness of this class of rose and their long and generous blooming have resulted in their widespread use in National Trust gardens, almost to excess: a double border of them at Gunby Hall in Lincolnshire demonstrates their merits. Among Polyanthas, 'Mevrouw Nathalie Nypels' is very floriferous in autumn, while from the Floribundas Iceberg is as dazzling as in early summer. For fall color, Rugosas offer butter-yellow foliage and scarlet hips, though these do not flatter remaining pink flowers. Among border roses with attractive hips, *Rosa moyesii* and its hybrids are perhaps supreme. The hips of *R. glauca* are a duller red and not so showy, though its pink-flushed pewter foliage takes on attractive scarlet tints.

Mixed borders offer the richest synthesis of shrubs, perennials, bedding plants and bulbs, giving the opportunity for many months of display. In them, roses are an essential element: they have the most beautiful blooms and the longest season of any hardy flowering shrub. Their companion plants can compensate for whatever deficiencies they have in foliage and form, to create a style of planting that will flatter almost every garden.

In this border, Rosa nutkana *'Plena' (syn.* R. californica *'Plena') and a sumptuous deep crimson* Paeonia lactiflora *cultivar are sufficiently distinct in size and color to avoid the visual confusion that can arise from juxtaposing similar flowers. Lavenders, including* Lavandula stoechas *subsp.* pedunculata *in the foreground, furnish the path, with an airy clump of* Stipa gigantea *balancing the bulk of the rose. Spikes of Foxy Group foxgloves spear into the view of distant fields; taller foxgloves would be unacceptably lanky here.*

Roses for Wild Gardens

It is paradoxical that in past ages gardening has been a sign of man's dominion over the natural world, an attempt to control nature and improve it in an environment where nature has had the upper hand. Today, we rarely see natural landscapes, and long for them so much that our prime objective in gardening is often not to control nature but to recreate it.

It was William Robinson who first tackled the subject of roses for the wildest and most informal settings in *The Wild Garden* (1870 and subsequent editions), though William Paul had mentioned the use of roses in semi-wild settings in 1848. Robinson's suggestions were taken up by a number of eminent authors including the Revd Henry Ellacombe (in 1895) and Gertrude Jekyll (in 1902). As we have seen, Shirley Hibberd also commented on the use of "hedgerow and wilderness roses" to create "the *négligé* style" and "to clothe the stems of decrepit trees and associate with ivy on ruins." In the early 1900s plantsman Reginald Farrer enjoyed using species roses in the wilder parts of his garden. Robinson complained that although everyone knew how beautiful native roses could be growing free in hedgerows, gardeners seldom tried to use them in the garden; nor did they plant any of the hundreds of unimproved species from other countries.

Robinson did not advocate using anything more fancy than species roses and the simpler Ramblers or Noisettes of looser and more abundant growth, and he owned that it was hard for gardeners to find from nurseries the range of species that he recommended. Nevertheless, he wrote that the likes of *Rosa multiflora*, *R.* 'Splendens', *R.* 'Dundee Rambler' and *R.* 'Aimée Vibert' could be grown into trees to produce fountains of bloom; *R. rugosa, R. foetida* and *R.* 'Wolley-Dod', planted in grass, would make agreeable large shrubs relating in size to neighbouring small trees; even smaller sorts such as *R. nitida* and Scotch briars would thrive and look attractive grown as mounds in grass. He stressed that it was no use planting roses in the depths of a gloomy wood: they must have enough light to bloom well. He did not restrict the planting he recommended to native wildflowers and included many exotic species, often of strikingly architectural form and sometimes even coarse, but never with the fat, complex and overbred form of the flowers most favored by florists of the time.

The style survives most notably in what British gardeners call the "Cornish garden," though there are many examples throughout Devon and Scotland, in Wales at Bodnant, in Sussex at Leonardslee and Wakehurst, and in a few famous Irish gardens, such as Mount Stewart, Rowallane and Glenveagh. However, these differ subtly from Robinson's original proposals: Chinese plants tend to predominate, particularly rhododendrons; there is usually little (not enough) bold herbaceous planting and there are few roses.

Today most of us are familiar with this style of planting in its adaptation to roses, especially Ramblers. However, we also know that it is not quite as easy as Robinson made it seem. It is difficult to achieve a long-lasting balance with the most ebulliently vigorous roses. We see the failures more often than the successes: too-large varieties such as 'Kiftsgate', capable of swamping a fairly large oak, smothering and even killing or toppling a smaller tree; roses in a glade that becomes overgrown and dark before they reach maturity, so that moribund rose twigs poke out all around and not a bloom is seen; excessively gorgeous and highly bred blooms proliferating where more natural simplicity would be preferable; or clumps of roses grown in grass but throttled by bindweed and other perennial weeds. All these pitfalls can be avoided. And today's gardeners have access to a far greater range of species and varieties than were available in Robinson's day.

In spite of the popularity of wild gardening today, the successes of the style are relatively few. Perhaps the most common mistake is to force wildness on a setting that is patently not wild, such as a relatively small and rectangular garden. Not only does the unnaturalness of the setting obtrude, with all-too-visible straight boundaries, assorted buildings and the noises of human activity, but the roses rarely have the space to achieve their characteristic habit. The illusion of nature is achieved not by pruning but by letting plants take on their natural form, usually a wide-spreading mound. If the soil is in good heart and the rose has sufficient light, the mound can be well furnished and attractive. However, most species and many hybrids will prove too large for the small garden; any attempt to restrain them by pruning is likely to destroy the natural effect. Sadly for those of us with small gardens, wild gardening with roses demands a substantial area – I would estimate a minimum of half an acre. One hesitates to make such pronouncements, being reminded of the probably apocryphal dictum of a Rothschild gardener that "every garden, no matter how small, should have at least fifteen acres of rough woodland." (The acreage increases each time the story is told.) Nevertheless, it is a fact that to achieve and perpetuate wild exuberance, our roses must have the room to sprawl and express themselves.

Many attempts at wild gardening with roses seem to belong to a style that might more accurately be termed non-gardening or anti-gardening, whereby a perfunctory attempt is made to clear pernicious weeds and improve the ground before planting the most unsuitably rampageous roses. After about three years, a tolerably attractive wilderness is achieved. After five years the decline starts: large shrubs and small trees are swamped by the roses and start to die in patches; each free-standing rose, by this time usually much too large for its site, begins to look like the hideous nest of some gigantic roc, bristling with dead and spiny stems; the weeds, quack grass, bindweed and ground elder invade once more and cannot be extricated from the thorny tangle. For a few years, the gardener pretends that this is the desired effect. This delusion is almost believable when in late spring there is a little fresh foliage and even one or two flowers; it is simply untenable for the rest of the year when all is ugliness. There is only one solution: sell up and move; someone else can sort out the mess.

We all know such gardens. We have seen photographs of them, the faults concealed by the photographer's art. They have been praised in books and the gardening press, proof of their creators' poetic spirit and their bravery in refusing to bow to the tyranny of horticultural best practice. Is the praise lavished on these gardens just the hypocrisy of those admiring the emperor's new clothes? It suggests a preference for lazy and ignorant gardening, an inability to tell the difference between beauty and ugliness, or a selective vision that sees a few tiny spots of loveliness and ignores the mess in between. This is not good gardening, which should be sustainable for as many years as the gardener wants, to give long-lasting pleasure.

The best gardeners will be sufficiently critical never to fall into such traps; they will realize that chaotic ugliness cannot be enjoyed, cannot be excused by euphemisms such as "pleasing informality" and should not be tolerated. Wild gardening, to achieve a harmonious and long-lasting equilibrium, is not a totally trouble-free option. It requires meticulous preparation and planning, a good deal of expertise, much care in the selection of plants and just enough labor to maintain balance, plant health and an absence of rank weeds. Miss Jekyll triumphed with the style and made such planting last in beauty for several decades. Few others have succeeded.

There is nothing inherently wrong with gardens that are as natural as possible, with the minimum of formality and horticultural interference and that do not rely on complex pruning and cultural techniques. These were the essence of Robinson's style. But for beauty to be achieved, the roses must be ideally suited

Exuberant roses mask a boundary fence, beside a perimeter path which separates the garden from the meadow and gives views to the countryside beyond.

PAGES 144–145 *Rugosa rose 'Fru Dagmar Hastrup'*

to their environment. Light levels, soil acidity, humus content and drainage should suit them perfectly, they must have room to grow and they must have precisely chosen companion plants, including natives that we might elsewhere call weeds – which have the potential to wreck the effect. If the conditions are not perfect to start with, they must be corrected. Above all, the choice of roses is crucial to the success of the scheme.

The essence of wild gardening is that it should look natural and should use plants that look as though they might well be found in the countryside beyond the garden gate. The effect can be enhanced by using the "borrowed landscape" of fields, hedgerows and trees outside the garden, separated perhaps by only a low hedge of roses or other plants to act as a *clairvoyée* and frame the view. Obviously alien and gaudy exotics should be rigorously excluded. Inevitably I have a perspective on the subject that is based on the climate and flora of northern cool-temperate areas, where there are few limitations on the vast variety of roses, and other herbaceous plants and shrubs, that will thrive. Gardeners in hotter areas or the southern hemisphere will have to adapt the plant content of their wild garden to their local flora if it is to look at all wild. They must incorporate a large proportion of native plants and varieties that look like natives and eschew many of the traditional garden plants of the north. The advantages of this approach are not just aesthetic but practical: a garden made with plants that are not suited to local conditions and climate not only looks out of place; it is hard work and a waste of effort too.

The first step is the choice of the site. There should be enough room for roses to sprawl. If there is insufficient light, some pruning of trees may be needed, or at least limbing up or thinning of their canopy. Perennial weeds that could spoil the effect should be eliminated. This includes the likes of brambles but also herbaceous weeds such as ground elder, common yarrow and docks. Herbaceous weeds in grass can be eliminated within a couple of years by close mowing. This is also a means of killing rhizomatous grasses such as quack grass that could mar the effect, especially if smaller shrub roses like Scotch briars or *Rosa nitida* are being used. However, for those who are not committed to organic techniques, spraying with a herbicide might be the quickest and most effective means, repeating the treatment until there is absolutely no regrowth of weeds.

If the ground is poor and it is assumed that wild gardening does not require good cultivation, the roses will achieve only their full potential for moribund hideousness. Though wildflower meadows demand impoverished soil if the flowers are to be able to compete with the grasses (well-nourished grasses easily overwhelm wildflowers), roses demand fertile ground. This might necessitate soil improvement, in effect cultivating a bed wherever a clump of roses is to be planted. Of course, we would not expect to see beds scattered throughout the wild garden but their shapes will disappear once the roses have filled their space and their under-planting has merged imperceptibly with the surrounding grass.

With a few exceptions, I do not like to see highly colored roses or roses with unnaturally shaped flowers in the wild garden. It is true that the old roses can be used to make the romantic suggestion that they are the remnants of an ancient and splendid garden. It is just this effect that the old roses in the walled garden at Elsing Hall, Norfolk, give. A few bushes of vermilion 'Fred Loads' would not have the same effect, nor would a white rose of formal shape, even Iceberg, look quite at home. Though many Ground Cover roses have a fairly loose form, those in orange, scarlet or vibrant salmon look out of place in temperate-zone wild gardens. With the exception of the cornfield poppy, wildflowers in these colors are rare, presumably because they are not attractive to pollinators, though they are common enough among bird-pollinated flowers of the tropics. The same applies to larger shrubs and Ramblers in these colors, though a little more latitude can be allowed in an old orchard, which is, after all, long cultivated and not entirely wild. I would not mind if my apple trees dripped with 'Albéric Barbier', or even 'Phyllis Bide' or 'François Juranville', but though it would be hard to beat 'Félicité Perpétue' or 'Adélaïde d'Orléans', I might draw the line at 'Crimson Shower'. Yellow is such a common color in wildflowers, particularly in spring, that it looks more natural and can, I think, be permitted.

In most cases, gardeners will want to grow Ramblers to drape larger shrubs and to cascade from surrounding trees. The roses should be planted to grow on the sunny side of a tree or shrub and should be positioned at least a yard or so away from their support,

Vigorous Rambler 'Rambling Rector', let loose over a pergola in Mirabel Osler's Shropshire garden, has created a dark tunnel, a place of gothic mystery that, like the subterranean passages of late-eighteenth-century gardens, provides a telling contrast with flowers, foliage and sunlight beyond.

Even a solitary rose is enough to provide an accent of floral beauty in the landscape. At Elsing Hall in Norfolk, 'Paul's Himalyan Musk' Rambler forms a wide-spreading mound smothered with delicate pink blooms, creating fragrant enclosure for an alfresco sitting place by the lake. The gentle color of the table and chairs and their curving lines blend agreeably with the surroundings without being so similar that they disappear. Cranesbills, feverfew and oxeye daisies ornament the water's edge, with bold spears of flag iris for foliage contrast. When seen from elsewhere in the garden, the rose's display is doubled by its reflection in the water.

to which they can be guided by a pole or string. Any string should not be gaudily colored and should be durable enough to last until the rose has hooked itself securely on to its support. The shady side of any supporting tree is likely to reveal a mass of tangled rose stems that is not attractive and best kept out of view.

The choice of Ramblers depends on whether they are to be periodically pruned or not. If they are not to be pruned, they must be suited in size to their support. The most vigorous species such as *Rosa filipes* and related *Synstylae* Ramblers will suppress and eventually kill any shrub and even trees less than, say, about 50ft/15m high. Such Ramblers cannot realistically be regularly pruned once they become entangled in their support. Roses of more moderate vigor, making only a relatively small number of stems of more manageable growth, for instance *R. arvensis* hybrids such as 'Splendens', can have any elderly shy-flowering stems removed from time to time, and middle-aged stems can be shortened to enhance flowering.

There are so many pitfalls in the choice of exactly the right Rambler for the wild garden that it is perhaps worth examining the range available. *Rosa filipes*, usually seen as the improved cultivar 'Kiftsgate', is among the most vigorous Ramblers, reaching 50ft/15m, with large trusses of scented single white flowers. It is easily capable of engulfing a house or a moderate-sized tree and is so unmanageable it should be used only where it can romp in perpetuity without the need for pruning and where it cannot smother choice trees and shrubs. Its vigor is inherited by its two hybrid offspring, single pale pink 'Brenda Colvin' and semi-double creamy apricot 'Treasure Trove'. There must be at least half a dozen gardeners in the world who are lucky enough to have a deep quarry garden or a cliff, from the top of which could tumble spectacular cascades of such roses. The trick could be used with more restrained varieties to furnish less dramatic falls or even the face of a retaining wall.

Rambler 'Phyllis Bide'

Several other species resemble *Rosa filipes* closely in vigor and flower, including unscented *R. longicuspis*, as tall as the former but not quite so coarse in growth. *R.l.* var. *sinowilsonii* is much less rampant at only 12ft/3.5m, hardy perhaps only to Z7 and a most handsome-leaved rose, though it does not excel in bloom. Its hybrid, prolific single creamy white and richly scented 'Wedding Day', is another beautiful thug, though it ages unattractively to pink and spots badly in rainy weather. Most plants in cultivation as *R. longicuspis* are in fact *R. mulliganii*, a choice and sweetly scented species attaining about 23ft/7m. 'Sir Cedric Morris' is a little more vigorous, a putative hybrid of this and *R. glauca*, from which perhaps it has acquired the purple flush to its young leaves.

Rosa multiflora is important as a parent of many Ramblers, Polyanthas and Floribundas which inherit its bunches of flowers. Its delicious fruity fragrance carries well and it can be grown as a mounding shrub or up into a tree to a height of 20ft/6m. The flowers open cream and fade to white, and are followed by a generous display of hips; it has an exquisite fully double blush-pink cultivar, *R.m.* 'Carnea'. Some of its hybrids link its scent and natural grace to gentle coloring and are excellent in the wild garden. 'Paul's Himalayan Musk', a fairly vigorous blush-pink double, reaches the same height. Profuse semi-double 'The Garland' (15ft/4.5m) has upright bunches of white blooms from creamy salmon buds and was a favorite of Miss Jekyll. 'Rambling Rector' (20ft/6m) is similar but with more lax inflorescences and more vigor; the rose grower Peter Beales considers this the best Rambler for growing into trees, though Graham Thomas notes that it is slightly marred by anthers that darken with age, looking like a plague of pollen beetles. 'Seagull' is a similar semi-double, a little more vigorous at 25ft/7.5m, while 'Bobbie James', also semi-double, can reach 30ft/9m. 'Francis E. Lester' (15ft/4.5m) has single flowers of palest blush deepening to pink at the edges, superlative in form and each with an exquisite sunburst of anthers at the center.

Rosa helenae (20ft/6m) differs from *R. multiflora* in its dark foliage setting off the compact bunches of flowers, borne upright but drooping by autumn under the weight of a generous display of hips. *R. rubus* (30ft/9m) is closely related and has deep cream blooms with orange anthers opening from pinkish buds and a rich fragrance like *R. multiflora*. The vigorous greyish-leaved *R. brunonii* (25ft/7.5m) is reputedly not quite hardy in British gardens but its sport or hybrid 'La Mortola' is, according to Peter Beales, hardy in Norfolk (Z8 but occasionally Z5 when the wind comes direct from Siberia). Its leaves are even more grey, suiting it to contrasts against a background of dark foliage, and its delicate-textured flowers are perhaps even more abundant.

Rambler 'Belvedere' growing over hollies at Warwick Castle

Most of the above are too vigorous and produce too many stems to be used where just a few swags and sprays are needed, though this suits them to hiding unsightly structures under a blanket of growth. The hybrids of *Rosa sempervirens* include a few that are less intractable, approaching manageability and indispensable for the wild garden. 'Flora' (12ft/3.5m) produces clusters of very double pink blooms and provides a memorable display grown up a tree at Sissinghurst with a carpet of pink astrantias beneath. 'Princesse Louise' (15ft/4.5m) opens blush white and double from pink buds. 'Adélaïde d'Orléans' is similar but a little taller and only semi-double, with nodding bunches of blooms, while 'Félicité Perpétue' matches 'Adélaïde' in height but has very double blooms with a particularly rich scent. It produces plentiful shoots that can suffocate supporting shrubs and make it difficult to thin or prune. 'Aimée Vibert' (15ft/4.5m) is an old hybrid, the product of a Noisette crossed with *R. sempervirens* and the first perpetual-flowering Rambler to be raised, blooming from early summer until autumn. The blooms are pure white showing yellow stamens. Graham Thomas considers that this variety and *R. longicuspis* var. *sinowilsonii* have "the most beautiful of all rose foliage." 'Princesse Marie' was a fully double rich pink. I am not sure whether it still exists but in England plants under that name are usually 'Belvedere', a superlative Irish variety capable of reaching 40ft/12m. It is a memorable sight in the Warwick Castle rose garden where it rampages across the encircling hollies.

The hybrids of *Rosa wichurana* and the related *R. luciae* (the two species are considered by some to be synonymous) are for the most part manageable, though they are often too sophisticated for the wild garden. However, a few are sufficiently informal to merit a place there. 'Blushing Lucy' is a free-growing hybrid with glossy leaves and pink flowers with a white eye, flowering until autumn. 'Sander's White Rambler' is, at 12ft/3.5m, a little too short to drape a tree, though it could scramble over large shrubs. 'Elisa Robichon' is one of the most vigorous Wichurana Ramblers (15ft/4.5m) and has loosely double pale flesh-pink flowers.

The Ayrshire roses are hybrids of the sweet-scented British native field rose, *Rosa arvensis,* and inherit its hardiness and habit of producing long stems, making them effective for trailing through trees. Perhaps the most useful is the loosely double myrrh-scented rose 'Splendens' (20ft/6m) in white with a touch of pink; it is obligingly tolerant of shade and the only one of its kin to inherit the fragrance of its parent. 'Ruga' (30ft/9m) is pale pink and semi-double, while 'Venusta Pendula' (18ft/5.5m) has prolific small clusters of white blooms with a pink flush. 'Dundee Rambler' (20ft/6m) has small double white flowers. 'Bennett's Seedling' is also a double white of similar height.

Wherever Ramblers are used in the wild garden, they may be combined with other climbers, chosen preferably to flower at the same time as the roses. Much the most useful of these are the

Rambler 'Francis E. Lester'

honeysuckles and species clematis, many of them having a delicious fragrance to enhance that of the roses. The vigor of any companion climbers should roughly match the Rambler's and, because they are likely to become inextricably intertwined, varieties should be chosen that will flower well without regular pruning.

All the Ramblers mentioned so far may be grown as free-standing shrubs and will in time form mounds with a spread almost twice their potential height, a severe limitation in gardens of modest size. The problem of how to treat the surrounding ground affects all roses in the wild garden but is perhaps more acute for these, for there is a period of several years when they provide only gappy cover across their ultimate domain. The first requirement is that the area they will in time occupy should not contain any weeds that could mar their effect. Though they can be started in a small cleared area, this will need to be widened as the roses grow and perhaps mulched to keep it free of incursions from

Multiflora Rambler 'Seagull'

surrounding herbage. A rotary mower can be run round under the skirts of each rose clump to prevent grasses growing up through the fringes.

Ground cover prevents a bed looking unnaturally bald, but it should be related in scale to the roses themselves: if only compact roses are being used, some ground covers can be too invasive and might make large and monotonous expanses of foliage. Comfreys are among the worst offenders. Cranesbills include many excellent candidates, some of which are sufficiently well behaved to create a charming tapestry of foliage and flower capable of remaining in equilibrium with neighbouring herbaceous plants for many years.

Many of the earliest-flowering shrub roses have blooms in shades of yellow, making attractive harmonies with deciduous azaleas, buttercups, globeflowers or doronicums and contrasts with bluebells (English or Spanish), early geraniums such as 'Johnson's Blue' or azure *Symphytum caucasicum*. The incense rose, *Rosa primula*,

is one such, its common name referring to the scent of its young leaves and its Latin name to both its earliness and its primrose-yellow blooms. *R. xanthina* has bright yellow blooms on arching stems while *R. x.* f. *hugonis* is a little paler, approaching primrose yellow, with furled buds, which never open wide, borne almost upright along the stems. The hybrid between these two, *R.x.* 'Canary Bird', has bright yellow blooms but, like *hugonis*, is subject to die-back and is best grown on its own roots. These flower with the lilacs and are effective with deep purple or white, also supplied at the same time by the snowball tree, *Viburnum opulus* 'Roseum'.

Rosa 'Cantabrigiensis' makes an excellent and trouble-free erect bush about 6½ft/2m high with pale yellow flowers, while 'Headleyensis' is a little taller and creamy yellow. Both are fragrant and are, in Graham Thomas's opinion, "the most satisfactory of the species-like yellow roses." 'Helen Knight' is an early bright yellow hybrid of *R. ecae*, while *R. pimpinellifolia* 'Grandiflora' is an early suckering burnet rose (known too as Scotch briar) with buds opening pale yellow and ageing to cream, also flowering at the same time as lilacs. *R.p.* 'Dunwichensis' is a more compact version.

Rosa pimpinellifolia crossed with *R. foetida* has produced *R.* × *harisonii*, of which there are three useful early-flowering clones: 'Harison's Yellow' is the yellow rose of Texas and is fairly upright-growing to almost 6½ft/2m; 'Lutea Maxima' is shorter, suckering and well clad with tiny rich green leaves; 'Williams' Double Yellow' was used by Wilhelm Kordes as the parent of a useful range of late-spring-flowering roses of which pale yellow 'Frühlingsgold' is the most spectacular. In 1968, Colin Pritchard, then the foreman of the park where I worked and later head gardener at Tatton Park, Cheshire, took me to a nearby garden to see a bush of this that he considered to be the horticultural marvel of north Leeds. It was 8ft/2.5m high by almost 12ft/3.5m across and smothered in fragrant blooms; like his kindness it was unforgettable, and an object lesson in giving a good plant the room it needs to achieve its potential.

This overgrown doorway at Elsing Hall evokes the mystery of the secret garden in Frances Hodgson Burnett's book. Inside, where fruit and vegetables bordered with flowers might once have grown, sprawling bushes of gorgeous old roses hint at a romantic past. The surrounding wall is clad with the classic combination of historic 'Rambling Rector' rose with honeysuckle, giving exquisite blends of flower shapes and fragrances.

Another excellent rose of species parentage, 'Nevada' has yellow-cream buds opening to white and becoming pink-flushed as they age; it also produces a few flowers in late summer. A bush near my home is seldom pruned and so flowers in late spring rather than early summer. Planted in front of golden *Chamaecyparis lawsoniana* 'Lanei', it looks a picture for two weeks but hideous when it flushes pink, showing how difficult such changeable flowers can be to place. Nevertheless, the offspring of a tetraploid variant of *Rosa moyesii* and a Hybrid Tea, it suggests that such species have great and virtually untapped potential as parents of more informal shrub roses.

Most of the shrub roses discussed so far are species or their primary hybrids and have an arching habit and relatively few main stems. In this they differ from many of the highly bred varieties, both old and new, that form a denser bush. On the whole, they have an attractive shape, though the very base of the shrub tends to look ugly and benefits from furnishing with a herbaceous plant of about 1ft/30cm or a little more. I would not normally recommend regular pruning of roses in the wild garden, usually too large an area for such detailed work. However, these varieties have so few main stems and are so greatly improved by a modicum of restorative pruning that the effort is well worth while. Their vase-shaped habit does not lend itself to pruning halfway down the main stems. A bush with only ten main stems, half of them arching gracefully to their full height, the other half kinking almost at right angles where pruned at their midpoint, makes for an ugly effect. Pruning out one or two of the oldest stems towards the base of the bush each year helps maintain vigor and floriferousness without marring the bush's natural habit.

Other shrub roses with this arching form include *Rosa glauca*, its hybrid 'Carmenetta', and 'Doncasteri', a hybrid of *R. macrophylla* noted for its autumn display of orange hips; all have single carmine flowers. *R. moyesii* and its hybrids are also renowned for their show of flagon-shaped hips, borne in sufficient profusion to create a distinct effect. 'Geranium' is perhaps the most famous, though I am not sure I have seen the true plant: supposed to have been a hybrid seedling of *R. moyesii*, 'Geranium' was said by A.T. Johnson to have had flowers the color of *Pelargonium* 'Paul Crampel', a rich scarlet quite unlike the soft cherry red of the plant usually seen in English gardens, which appears to be pure *R. moyesii*. 'Geranium', being at most 10ft/3m high, is more useful where space is limited than *R. moyesii* itself; Graham Thomas describes the latter as "a gawky tree-like shrub creating overhead shade," disadvantageous characteristics in most gardens but useful where wildness is wanted. Similar hybrids include 'Wintoniensis', 'Highdownensis', and 'Hillieri'. *R. setipoda* is a comparable species with large bunches of single pale pink flowers.

Rosa × harisonii *'Harison's Yellow'*

Several species and hybrids retain the simple charm of the briar rose allied to single pink flowers. 'Andersonii' is a neater, less thorny version of its parent *Rosa canina*, the dog rose. *R.* × *hibernica* is a naturally occurring hybrid (*R. canina* × *pimpinellifolia*) found in scattered locations throughout the British Isles but, as its name suggests, originally described from an Irish plant; the clone usually cultivated has a bright pink flower. 'Complicata' is a large-flowered, similarly bright pink cultivar, capable of scrambling to about 10ft/3m and also useful as a showy and informal hedge. The sweet-briar or eglantine, *R. rubiginosa* (syn. *R. eglanteria*), is another species with single pink flowers but has the advantage of sweetly scented foliage (especially after a summer shower) and a generous display of hips. A little sparse in growth, it can be roughly clipped to make an excellent, dense and informal hedge. In the 1890s Lord Penzance raised from it a series of hybrids, most of them vigorous and inheriting fragrant foliage. All but a couple are named after characters in Scott's novels and most are semi-double. I am not fond of these semi-doubles, which seem to sacrifice the beauty of the single species, but 'Lord Penzance' is an attractive single in pink shading to a lemon center that would be at home in the wild garden.

Two enchanting species with greyish leaves and white flowers for the wild garden are *Rosa soulieana* and *R. fedtschenkoana*. The former makes a large sprawling shrub about 10ft/3m high and a little more across. Its hybrid 'Kew Rambler' (18ft/5.5m) retains some of *soulieana*'s greyness but has plentiful bunches of rich pink single flowers. 'Wickwar' (12ft/3.5m) is a hybrid of the same species with greyish-green leaves and creamy white flowers. The plant grown as *R. fedtschenkoana* seems not to be the true species, flowering throughout the summer instead of for just one short burst; it makes an upright bush of 10ft/3m and spreads by suckers.

Modern Shrub rose 'Nevada'

The sophistication of most of the old garden roses does not suit them to wildness. I would not mind 'Alba Maxima' or 'Alba Semiplena', though these suffer badly from rust. We could always spray them regularly with fungicide or prune and thin them each year but these are jobs we might justifiably prefer not to do in the wild garden. The hemp-leaved rose 'Cymbifolia', an upright Alba with narrow leaflets and slightly muddled but charming double white flowers, is seen fairly often in France and seems to be less prone to rust. It might be thought a little coarse but it is full of character and ideal for the wild garden. I wish it were more widely grown. One mitigating feature of the Albas is their relative tolerance of shade; they are perhaps more shade-tolerant than any other class of old roses.

Some of the Damasks have loosely shaped flowers and sufficiently soft coloring to belong here, perhaps especially 'Professeur Emile Perrot', grown in British gardens as 'Kazanlik', or 'Trigintipetala', a different cultivar not found in Britain. Semi-double *Rosa nutkana* 'Plena' (syn. *R. californica* 'Plena') makes an upright and floriferous bush and would be good here too. The Wichurana Rambler 'Goldfinch' also makes an excellent and spreading shrub in the wild garden, with abundant fragrant flowers in soft yellowish cream. *R. villosa* and its semi-double hybrid 'Wolley-Dod' have downy grey-green leaves and pink flowers, followed by hips that age from orange to deep crimson. Graham Thomas considers that *R. villosa* "is not eclipsed in beauty by any other species" at flowering time.

The burnet roses or Scotch briars, hybrids or cultivars of *Rosa pimpinellifolia,* are immensely useful where a suckering, lower-growing rose is needed. Most flower in late spring only. Miss Jekyll used them often, especially to clothe banks. 'Double White' is perhaps my favorite, with its neat globular blooms and a penetrating lily-of-the-valley scent; its leaflets darken as autumn approaches, many of them turning a dazzling scarlet before they are shed. Double blush-pink 'Stanwell Perpetual' is another old favorite, perhaps owing its long flowering to an Autumn Damask parent.

Rugosa roses are indispensable for the wild garden, especially in colder climates, and will sucker if grown on their own roots. It is worth considering whether suckers are required or not and checking what rootstock is used when buying: they can be an advantage when an impenetrable barrier or hedge is needed but are a nuisance if roses have to stay within bounds.

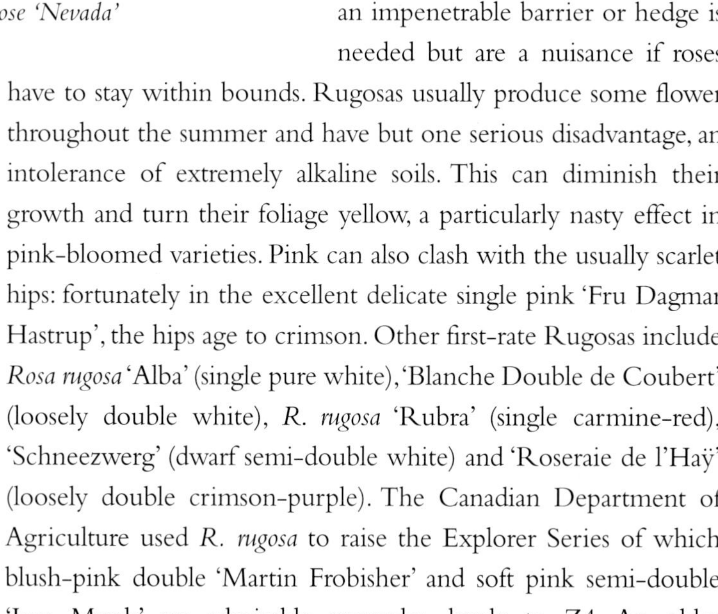

Rugosas usually produce some flower throughout the summer and have but one serious disadvantage, an intolerance of extremely alkaline soils. This can diminish their growth and turn their foliage yellow, a particularly nasty effect in pink-bloomed varieties. Pink can also clash with the usually scarlet hips: fortunately in the excellent delicate single pink 'Fru Dagmar Hastrup', the hips age to crimson. Other first-rate Rugosas include *Rosa rugosa* 'Alba' (single pure white), 'Blanche Double de Coubert' (loosely double white), *R. rugosa* 'Rubra' (single carmine-red), 'Schneezwerg' (dwarf semi-double white) and 'Roseraie de l'Haÿ' (loosely double crimson-purple). The Canadian Department of Agriculture used *R. rugosa* to raise the Explorer Series of which blush-pink double 'Martin Frobisher' and soft pink semi-double 'Jens Munk' are admirable examples, hardy to Z4. An older Canadian hybrid (*R. rugosa* × *foetida* 'Persiana'), 'Agnes' is an outstanding fully double light yellow, flowering in late spring, with some later blooms.

Rosa rugosa has also been used in the parentage of some useful Ground Cover roses such as single pink *R.* × *jacksonii* 'Max Graf', single white 'White Max Graf' and 'Paulii', and single pink 'Paulii Rosea'. Among other Ground Cover varieties that do not look too unnaturally fancy for the wild garden are Grouse and Partridge (both single white blushed pink), Kent® (compact semi-double white), Rosy Cushion® (semi-double pale pink) and Simon Robinson (single pale pink).

In the wild garden, it can be difficult to keep a balance between these if more than one Ground Cover variety is being planted in the same area, and they will suppress any herbaceous ground cover in adjoining areas. It is usually important to keep a balance between Ground Cover and other roses, herbaceous planting and meadow or mown grass, so some control of the most rampant varieties is usually needed. Their spread can be limited by an annual spring trim around their perimeter with a clearing saw, though it is worth pulling a few shoots out of the way before cutting; these can then be put back in place after trimming to break any abnormally hard line.

A display of hips on the sweet-briar, Rosa rubiginosa, *in autumn*

Many new Ground Cover roses are released each year, so it is difficult to keep up with the best of the latest varieties. Many more will be worthy and appropriate than the few mentioned here. The arrival of so many Ground Cover cultivars is one of the most significant developments affecting the potential for wild gardening, though they seem to be used to the full in very few gardens. William Robinson would have welcomed them.

Fall color offers exciting opportunities for wild gardening, numerous roses having a sufficiently showy display of hips or autumn leaves to compete with the brightest of other shrubs and trees. For foliage color, *Rosa* × *kochiana*, *R. nitida*, *R. virginiana* and *R. woodsii* plus the Rugosa varieties are among the best. The Rugosas generally also produce showy hips, as do *R. rubiginosa*, *R. helenae*, *R.* 'Highdownensis', *R. moyesii* and its hybrids and *R. multiflora*. The list of fall-coloring and -fruiting shrubs that could be used with roses in the wild garden is long and includes deciduous azaleas, maples, amelanchiers, aronias, berberis, clethras, *Cornus alba* cultivars, cotinus, enkianthus, euonymus, fothergillas, pyracanthas, stephanandras, sumacs, *Vaccinium corymbosum*, *Viburnum opulus* and witch-hazels. The same shrubs and trees that support Ramblers could also carry autumn-coloring climbers such as *Ampelopsis*, *Celastrus*, *Parthenocissus* and *Vitis* species and cultivars, including *V. belaii*, *V. coignetiae*, *V. pulchra* and *V. vinifera* 'Purpurea'.

Even the most ardent rosarian will probably want to include some shrubs other than roses in the wild garden. Stridently colored or variegated foliage should be avoided, and extreme forms, weeping or fastigiate, should be sparingly used and only where a telling accent is needed. Some evergreens, such as hollies, yews or laurels, might be needed to define areas within the garden and to give winter structure, the largest of them being able in time to support Ramblers. Junipers are perhaps the most useful of the conifers here, providing texture, shape and subtle variation of foliage color to the front of planted areas and matching the scale of the roses, though some may need to be planted in groups. It is worth noting that shade-loving evergreens, once they are a substantial size and age, will tolerate a blanket of roses better than most shrubs or trees, being able to survive low light levels and getting a chance to recuperate through winter while the roses are without leaves.

Flowering shrubs should be chosen to coincide in season with the roses and should match them in scale and informality. This is not the place for the tight and tiny gems of the inner garden like the smaller daphnes. There is a role for philadelphus, weigela, deutzia, kolkwitzia and dipelta, though care should be taken that they do not present large expanses of dull foliage after flowering. This is also a risk with lilacs, though these can be spectacularly effective with early roses; their season can be extended by adding some of the later-flowering Preston hybrids as well as the usual

Syringa vulgaris and *S.* × *hyacinthiflora* cultivars. The latest flowering of the deciduous azaleas can be useful, provided they are not brightly colored, and the larger brooms (*Genista* species and *Spartium junceum*) can add both bloom and a change of texture. Other useful shrubs include *Elaeagnus* 'Quicksilver', *Viburnum opulus* 'Roseum', *V. plicatum* and the choicer elders such as *Sambucus nigra* f. *laciniata*.

Areas of grass need to be treated in a way that looks natural if they are to match in character the rest of the planting; closely cropped, striped lawns with crisp edges will not do. There are principally two alternatives: a wildflower meadow or a semi-natural scheme with cornfield weeds among the grass. If lawn areas are fairly impoverished – which can be achieved by constantly removing mowings for some years – a wildflower meadow is possible. Wildflowers and grasses will be able to remain in equilibrium on the poor soil and a flowery mead can be achieved, to which more natural-looking bulbs such as lent lilies, pheasant's-eye narcissi, camassias, meadow saffron and *Crocus tommasinianus* may be added. It is generally more successful to sow the area with fine grasses suitable for combining with wildflowers first and add young wildflower plants in the sward afterwards. If a combined wildflower and grass seed mix is sown, seedling wildflowers cannot generally compete with the grasses and the resultant sward will have too few flowers. The wildflowers are nowadays available cheaply as young plants grown as plugs, though gardeners can also raise them from seed themselves. Mowing should not take place until wildflowers have had the opportunity to seed and all bulb foliage has had time to die back, usually in mid- to late summer. (The clippings can be composted but the compost heap must reach a high temperature if grass and other seeds are to be killed.) Under this regime, native wildflowers not in the original mix and especially orchids may sow themselves into the sward from the surrounding countryside and may then be able to increase. One or two subsequent cuts – at as high a setting as the mower blades will take – may be needed before autumn-flowering naturalized bulbs emerge.

Hips on Rosa rugosa *'Rubra'*

One possible disadvantage of this scheme is that the wildflowers will still be tall enough to obscure the shorter Ground Cover roses and herbaceous plants at their flowering time. Unless a strip is mown around the edge of bed areas, not a very natural-looking effect, roses and other ground cover will need to match the meadow in height at flowering time and will have to be, say, 20in/50cm or more high.

Paths can be mown through the longer meadow areas and maintained by frequent mowing but the impoverished nature of the soil and the slow growth of grasses in the path might mean that the paths are not able to withstand frequent heavy wear. If this is the case, it is perhaps best to sow the paths from the start with a hard-wearing grass seed mix containing bluegrasses. The lines of the paths are an important element of the design and need to be related to the contours of the site and the way any planted areas are to be viewed. For the most natural effect, absolutely straight paths with sharply angled junctions between them should be avoided.

If the ground is too rich, late cutting to give a natural effect will allow coarse grasses and rank broad-leaved weeds such as docks, thistles and nettles to predominate and wildflowers will not be able to compete. However, naturalized bulbs can still be grown and the first cut should be made as soon as their leaves have died back. Thereafter, the grass can be cut periodically at as high a setting as the mower will allow. Again, any paths can be cut lower to keep feet dry. As for wildflower meadows, the grass clippings should be removed, so that after a few years the fertility of the turf will have been reduced. This will allow fine grasses to take over from coarse ones, so that any wildflowers planted into the sward will be able to compete.

An alternative semi-natural effect for fairly fertile ground is to cultivate in autumn and sow with cornfield weeds such as poppies, larkspur, cornflowers, corncockles, quaking grass, chamomile and corn marigolds. The best forms of Queen Anne's lace (*Daucus carota*) have immensely decorative broad and lacy white umbels and are worth seeking for such mixtures. Such a scheme can give a spectacular display in summer with the roses, though there will be less color by late summer. Plants must be permitted to shed seed before cultivating again in autumn to allow the cycle to repeat. There are disadvantages: the site looks bare for a time after cultivation; there is no opportunity for a display of spring or autumn naturalized bulbs, and some permanent turf paths might be needed that can get in the way of cultivation. Such a scheme can be adapted in countries such as South Africa, Australia and the United States using native annuals, though the even mixture found in a cornfield would look unnatural and intermingling swathes of different species would work better.

Biennials can add greatly to the beauty of the wild garden but need some bare areas to sow themselves, so are not an option where impenetrable and evergreen ground cover has been established. Where roses have been drastically pruned, as they are likely to be occasionally in wilder parts of the garden where yearly treatment is too fiddly and time-consuming, biennials are especially useful as fillers. Among the most effective with early roses are honesty, sweet rocket, angelica and *Smyrnium perfoliatum*, while for a little later in the season there are foxgloves (especially *Digitalis purpurea* 'Sutton's Apricot' and white *D.p.* f. *albiflora*), the giant thistle *Onopordum nervosum* and white *Ammi majus*. Old plants should be removed as soon as seed has been shed to give room for the next year's plants.

Many herbaceous perennials look at home in the wild garden but this is not the place for complicated yearly replanting or staking (here we can forgive the odd plant that flops). Nor do the more spectacular manifestations of the breeder's art – such as towering delphiniums – look appropriate. Because wild gardens tend to be big, with plant combinations seen from farther away, the darkest colors disappear into the background and are not so effective.

China rose R. × odorata mutabilis (*syn. 'Tipo Ideale'*)

Some native European plants that gardeners might not think to introduce to the garden can play a role in wilder areas, including white and red campion (*Silene latifolia* and *S. dioica*), cow parsley (*Anthriscus sylvestris* and its dark-leaved form 'Ravenswing'), common fennel (*Foeniculum vulgare*) and mallows (*Malva crispa*, *M.c.* f. *alba* and *M. sylvestris*). A more exotic pink version of Queen Anne's lace, *Chaerophyllum hirsutum* 'Roseum', is exceptionally pretty, flowering as spring passes into summer.

A few of the better forms of *Achillea millefolium* merit a place, as do some of the stiffer variants of the bigger, bolder species such as *A. filipendulina* 'Parker's Variety', *A. ptarmica* 'Major' and *A. tomentosa*. Many columbines will prove useful and will seed themselves around the garden, though if several sorts are grown near to each other, they will not breed true to type. There are many good selections of *Aquilegia vulgaris* available, though excessive doubleness is not expected in the wild garden and does not give a bold shape that is effective from a distance. In this respect, some of the fewer-petalled forms of *A.v.* var. *stellata* are perhaps the most telling of all, as are the long-spurred species in North American gardens.

The creamy plumes of *Aruncus dioicus* make an excellent combination with roses at the peak of their flowering, though male plants should be sought: the flowers of female plants quickly discolor to brown and produce copious quantities of seed that can sow itself all too freely. Larger astilbes in gentler colors can provide the same effect in moister areas. *Astilbe rivularis* and the hybrids of *A. thunbergii* are perhaps the most useful. Asters tend to be too labor-intensive for the wild garden, preferring regular replanting, spraying against pests and diseases, and staking. However, some of the North American species merit a little extra effort to give an authentic native touch in gardens here. *Aster macrophyllus* is a wild-looking species that performs before the roses are past their peak, while others such as *A. turbinellus* are graceful and relatively trouble-free, at their best when roses are showing fall color and a display of hips. Like asters, many monardas need mildew control and too frequent replanting to be fully commendable, though several are mildew-resistant and are worth the effort in moist soils in their native North America.

I have professed my general indifference to the combination of campanula blue with rose pink, but I think these colors are immensely useful in the wild garden. The soft blue of *Campanula lactiflora* is exquisite with pale yellow or white roses; some cranesbills and *Salvia pratensis* Haematodes Group share the same blue. The true pure white clone of *Campanula lactiflora* 'Alba' (not its grey and grubby impostors) looks equally good with rose pink; the rich blue-purple of the deepest bellflowers such as *C.* 'Elizabeth', *C. glomerata* 'Superba', *C. latifolia* 'Brantwood' and *C. latiloba* 'Highcliffe Variety' is especially good with strong yellow. Other useful species include creamy *C. alliariifolia*, blue or white *C. persicifolia*, *C. punctata* and *C. takesimana.*

We expect to see grasses in wild gardens and they provide a welcome change of texture when used with roses. Arching sorts need to be given some room to display their habit to the full and should not be used in close planting, pushed up against roses and other plants, but should be set among low ground cover that does not hide their form. There are now many cultivars of genera such as deschampsia, miscanthus and molinia that could be used, though I would not want to see bright variegation or gold foliage in the wild garden. However, with these provisos, the faint white stripe in the leaf of *Miscanthus sinensis* 'Gracillimus' does not look in the least strident or unnatural and merely provides a soft greyish tone that is both useful and attractive. Narrowly upright growing varieties such as this can be mixed closely with other plants without marring their effect.

The biggest grasses such as cortaderias and the larger miscanthus can even be set in the surrounding sward – never, I think, as self-conscious singletons but in loosely clustered, unevenly spaced colonies with odd plants set away from the group. One slight drawback of many of the grasses is that they do not reach their full size until after the roses have flowered and are perhaps at their most attractive in autumn when plumes of flowers appear and their foliage turns to parchment tints. It is perhaps best to associate such grasses with roses that also have some autumn interest from fall color or a display of hips.

Crambe cordifolia is not too unnatural for wild gardening and one of few plants that produce a widely spreading cloud of tiny white flowers at rose time. The globe thistles, especially *Echinops ritro*, *E. bannaticus* 'Taplow Blue' and the fairly new *E. sphaerocephalus* 'Arctic Glow', though a little coarse for the herbaceous border, are perfectly appropriate here, their foliage providing a good contrast. Some of the larger spurges are also effective with roses, such as summer-flowering chartreuse *Euphorbia cornigera* and *E. schillingii*, as well as late-spring-blooming *E. griffithii* 'Dixter', with bronze leaves and vermilion bracts followed by brilliant scarlet fall color. A number of filipendulas have elegant flowers in sugar pink or white, good foliage and are useful where soil is not too dry. Among the most effective are *Filipendula camtschatica*, *F. palmata*, *F. purpurea* and, taller and bolder than the rest, the queen of the prairies, *F. rubra*.

Daylilies can be used in the wild garden, especially those that have the grace of the "unimproved" species, providing, like the grasses, good foliage contrast. Few are more lovely than lemon-yellow *Hemerocallis lilioasphodelus,* flowering in late spring. Some hybrids, such as yellow 'Hyperion', 'Corky' and 'Golden Chimes', still possess reasonable foliage and flowers with the elegant lines of the species, but many modern hybrids have round flowers that are so lacking in line quality they are best avoided.

As in the border, perennial peas such as *Lathyrus grandiflorus*, *L. latifolius* and *L. rotundifolius* can be useful for draping across shrub roses and also mounds of Ramblers, though the larger scale of the wild garden will often require several plants of the peas to be used. This scale allows even the thuggish golden hops (*Humulus lupulus* 'Aureus') to mingle with large shrub and Rambler roses (especially white or pale yellow varieties) without overwhelming them.

Of course, the choice of plants for the wild garden will need to respect the native flora if it is to look truly wild. For instance, a Mediterranean garden would have more drought-loving plants, labiates such as lavenders, sages, phlomis and rosemary; there would be cistus and bearded irises, plus other typical maquis flora. The roses themselves would need to be tolerant of drier conditions and hotter weather, perhaps including *Rosa stellata* var. *myrifica* and hybrids of *R. persica* such as Euphrates® and Tigris®, the latter with

flowers like the halimiums that thrive in the same conditions. This sort of planting has elements of the gravel gardening championed by Beth Chatto for the driest parts of England.

Similarly a North American wild garden would use native species, perhaps including the likes of thermopsis, baptisias, *Veronicastrum virginicum*, *Phlox maculata* and *Sanguisorba canadensis* in Z6, more tender penstemons, yuccas and romneyas in the warmer south-west. It is admittedly harder to find roses that flower for many months in the hottest climates, though the simpler hybrids of the China rose, especially the singles if they are to look truly wild, will perform as well as any.

There is of course a "halfway house," a garden that is utterly informal, has loosely arranged plants and beds without neatly trimmed edges set in roughly mown grass, yet uses a more vibrant range of colors and more sophisticated and complex flowers. This might be nearer to the house and the high-maintenance areas of the garden and less closely linked visually to the countryside beyond the garden fence. Just such planting can be seen at Bagatelle in Paris, where a trial ground of mostly new Ground Cover roses has been planted to assess their merits and performance. Planted areas are informally shaped and not edged, the grass just being cut beneath the outer edges of the roses to prevent its growing through and marring the effect. The roses can have brighter and more formally shaped blooms and, though there are only roses in the Bagatelle example, can be accompanied by more showy shrubs and perennials that have not the least relation to the native flora. This sort of planting does not demand the space of the true wild garden and could fit in to quite modest suburban plots, provided the informality is not compromised by too-visible straight boundaries.

The wild garden offers wonderful opportunities for filling large areas with natural-looking flowers and roses so that they look as though they belong. Elements of this sort of planting can be seen at Elsing Hall in East Anglia and in the spectacularly romantic garden at Ninfa in Italy. Although I have seen no garden that combines all the sorts of planting described above, I hope this chapter will serve as a challenge to rosarians to blend the beauty of nature with the charm of the rose.

ABOVE *An informal area of the garden at Bagatelle is planted mainly with Ground Cover roses grown for trial, most of them new. A few larger shrub roses are included for variety, some, such as 'Oleander Rose' here, grown as single specimens.*

LEFT *Rugosa rose 'William Baffin', one of the hardy Explorer series raised in Canada, has a more loosely open habit than* Rosa rugosa *itself. This suits it admirably to use in the wild garden.*

PAGES 166–167 *At Lower Brook House in Shropshire, Mirabel Osler planted several 'Rambling Rector' roses, letting some of them sprawl to achieve a charmingly natural effect in a semi-wild part of the garden.*

Pick of the Bunch

Each rose variety in the following lists has some outstanding merits, whether of floriferousness, color, exquisite floral form, tolerance of climatic extremes, foliage or habit of growth. Few if any have all the virtues but each one, given the right setting, can play a beautiful and useful role in the garden. Roses in modern colors such as bright yellow or orange are not excluded, nor even those with striped or picotee flowers. Though these can rarely be blended convincingly with old roses, they are as capable of being used effectively and attractively as a striped tulip or a two-tone dahlia. We should not be deterred from using them through timidity or snobbish preconceptions of brashness; many gardens will have a role for their brilliance and complexity, provided they are placed where they do not upstage the rest of the planting.

I make no apology for including many roses that are hard to buy in some countries, including both the USA and Britain, and hope that nurseries will take up the challenge by obtaining and propagating them for their customers. Sources of roses world-wide are given in *The Combined Rose List*, published annually; for national suppliers, check your country's plantfinder. Some specialist rose nurseries are listed on page 184.

An explanation of the USDA system of hardiness zones, used throughout these lists, is given on page 185. Most of the roses listed here are for use in Zones 5–8. Roses also suitable for the colder parts of Z5 and chillier areas are marked C. Roses also suitable for Z8 and hotter climates are marked H. It should be noted, however, that many of the roses marked Z7 or Z8 will not prove absolutely hardy in areas with relatively cool summers; this is a result of the lack of summer heat and sun needed to ripen the wood thoroughly. In such areas, they can behave like Z9 plants and need a sunny microclimate if they are to thrive and flower well.

Code names and further synonyms are included in the Index. Roses with 🏆 have been given the Royal Horticultural Society's Award of Garden Merit as plants of excellence and easy culture.

Roses for General Use

Ground Cover Roses (Procumbent)

Variety		Color	Zone		Type
Alba Meidiland®		white	Z5		Shrub/Ground Cover
Aspen		yellow	Z5		Ground Cover
Avon		blush pink	Z5		Ground Cover/Patio
'Ayrshire Queen'		purplish crimson	Z4	C	Rambler/Ground Cover
Baby Blanket		pink	Z5		Ground Cover
Bassino®		deep scarlet	Z5		Ground Cover
Berkshire		cerise	Z5		Ground Cover
Blenheim (syn. Schneesturm®)		white	Z5		Ground Cover
Broadlands (syn.Sonnenschirm®)		yellow	Z5		Ground Cover
Douceur Normande®		coral pink	Z4	C	Shrub/Ground Cover
Essex		deep pink	Z5		Ground Cover
Eyeopener		red	Z5		Ground Cover
Fiona®		scarlet	Z5		Shrub/Ground Cover
Flower Carpet™		deep pink	Z5		Ground Cover
Glenshane		scarlet	Z5		Ground Cover
Grouse		white	Z5		Ground Cover
Grouse 2000		blush white	Z5		Ground Cover
Hampshire		scarlet	Z5		Ground Cover
Heideschnee®		white	Z5		Ground Cover
Hertfordshire		cerise	Z5		Ground Cover
x *jacksonii* 'Max Graf'		pink	Z5	C	Ground Cover/Rugosa
x *jacksonii* White Max Graf		white	Z5	C	Ground Cover/Rugosa
Kent®		white	Z5		Shrub/Ground Cover
Laura Ashley		cerise-pink	Z5		Climbing Miniature/ Ground Cover
Lovely Fairy®		pink	Z5		Polyantha/Ground Cover
Magic Carpet		magenta-pink	Z5		Shrub/Ground Cover
'Newry Pink' (syn. 'Paulii Rosea')		pink	Z4	C	Rugosa/Climbing/ Ground Cover
nitida		pink	Z4	C	Shrub/Ground Cover
Northamptonshire		pale salmon pink	Z5		Ground Cover
'Nozomi'	🏆	pale pink	Z5		Climbing Miniature/ Ground Cover
Our Molly		light red	Z5		Shrub/Ground Cover
Pathfinder		vermilion	Z5		Ground Cover
'Paulii'		white	Z4	C	Rugosa/Ground Cover
Pheasant (syn. Heidekönigin®)		pink	Z5		Climbing Miniature/ Ground Cover
Pink Bells®		pink	Z5		Ground Cover
Pink Meidiland®		deep pink	Z5		Ground Cover
Red Blanket®	🏆	red	Z5		Shrub/Ground Cover
Red Trail		red	Z5		Shrub/Ground Cover
Rosy Cushion®	🏆	pale pink	Z5		Shrub/Ground Cover
Snow Carpet®	🏆	white	Z5		Ground Cover
Suma	🏆	cerise	Z5		Ground Cover
Surrey	🏆	pink	Z5		Shrub/Ground Cover
Sussex		apricot	Z5		Ground Cover
Swany®	🏆	white	Z5		Miniature/Ground Cover
White Flower Carpet®		white	Z5		Ground Cover
White Meidiland®		white	Z5		Shrub/Ground Cover
Wiltshire		salmon pink	Z5		Shrub/Ground Cover

Bush Roses (Generally upright habit and shorter than about 4ft/1.2m)

Variety		Color	Zone		Type
Abbeyfield Rose	🏆	deep pink	Z5		Hybrid Tea
Acey Deucy™		deep carmine	Z5		Miniature
Alexander®	🏆	vermilion	Z5		Hybrid Tea
Amber Queen®	🏆	apricot	Z5		Floribunda
Angela Rippon®		salmon pink	Z5		Miniature
Anna Ford®	🏆	orange	Z5		Patio
Anna Livia	🏆	salmon pink	Z5		Floribunda
Anne Harkness		apricot	Z5		Floribunda
'Apricot Nectar'		apricot-pink	Z5		Floribunda
Apricot Summer®		peach-pink	Z5		Patio
'Arthur Bell'	🏆	yellow	Z5		Floribunda
Auckland Metro		white, flushed apricot	Z5	H	Hybrid Tea
Auguste Renoir®		deep pink	Z5		Hybrid Tea (Romantica® series)
'Baby Darling'		apricot	Z5		Miniature
Baby Love		yellow	Z5		Miniature/Patio
Benita®		deep yellow	Z5		Floribunda
'Betty Uprichard'		coppery salmon	Z5		Hybrid Tea
Big Purple® (Stephens' Big Purple)		purple	Z5		Hybrid Tea
Birthday Girl		cream edged salmon	Z5		Floribunda
Blue Moon®		mauve	Z5		Hybrid Tea
Brown Velvet		russet	Z5		Floribunda
Carrot Top		vermilion	Z5		Patio
Centenaire de Lourdes®		pink	Z5		Floribunda
'Chanelle'		pale peach	Z5		Floribunda
Cherry Brandy®		orange-salmon blend	Z5		Hybrid Tea
Cider Cup	🏆	deep apricot	Z5		Miniature/Patio
City of Belfast®		scarlet	Z5		Floribunda
City of London®		pale blush	Z5		Floribunda
Classic Sunblaze		rich pink	Z5		Miniature
Congratulations		salmon pink	Z5		Hybrid Tea
Cornsilk™		pale yellow	Z5		Miniature
'Crimson Glory'		crimson	Z5		Hybrid Tea
Cupcake™		salmon	Z5		Miniature
'Dainty Bess'		pale pink	Z5		Hybrid Tea
Dawn Chorus		deep orange	Z5		Hybrid Tea
Dicky®	🏆	orange-pink	Z5		Floribunda
Doris Tysterman		light orange	Z5		Hybrid Tea
Drummer Boy		scarlet	Z5		Floribunda/Patio

'Duet'		pink	Z5		Hybrid Tea
Dutch Gold®		soft yellow	Z5		Hybrid Tea
Electron®		carmine	Z5		Hybrid Tea
Elina®	🏆	pale yellow	Z5		Hybrid Tea
Elizabeth of Glamis®		salmon pink	Z5		Floribunda
'Ellen Willmott'		pale apricot	Z5		Hybrid Tea
'English Miss'		pink	Z5		Floribunda
Escapade®	🏆	mauve-pink	Z5		Floribunda
Especially for You		yellow	Z5		Hybrid Tea
Europeana®		deep red	Z5		Floribunda
Eurostar		golden yellow	Z5		Floribunda
Evelyn Fison		deep red	Z5		Floribunda
Fragrant Cloud		coral red	Z5		Hybrid Tea
Fragrant Delight®		salmon	Z5		Floribunda
Fragrant Dream		salmon	Z5		Hybrid Tea
Freedom®	🏆	yellow	Z5		Hybrid Tea
Gingernut		russet	Z5		Patio
Gold Badge™		yellow	Z5	H	Hybrid Tea
Gold Medal®		golden yellow	Z5	H	Hybrid Tea/Grandiflora
Golden Wedding		yellow	Z5		Floribunda
Grand Nord®		ivory white	Z5	H	Hybrid Tea
'Gruss an Aachen'		blush white	Z6	H	Polyantha/Floribunda
'Horstmanns Rosenresli'		white	Z5		Floribunda
Iceberg	🏆	white	Z5	H	Floribunda
Indian Summer	🏆	orange	Z5		Hybrid Tea
Ingrid Bergman®	🏆	red	Z5		Hybrid Tea
International Herald Tribune®		amaranth purple	Z5		Floribunda
'Irène Watts'	🏆	pale salmon pink	Z6	H	China
Just Joey®	🏆	peach	Z5		Hybrid Tea
'Katharina Zeimet'		white	Z5		Polyantha
Keepsake		carmine-pink	Z5		Hybrid Tea
L'Aimant		salmon pink	Z5		Floribunda
'Lady Sylvia'		pink	Z5		Hybrid Tea
'Lavender Jewel'		deep mauve-pink	Z5		Miniature
Lilli Marlene		deep red	Z5		Floribunda
Little Bo-Peep		pink	Z5		Miniature/Patio
Livin' Easy		orange-salmon	Z5		Floribunda
'Lovers' Meeting'		orange	Z5		Hybrid Tea
Loving Memory		deep red	Z5		Hybrid Tea
'Mme Abel Chatenay'		pink	Z6	H	Hybrid Tea
'Mme Butterfly'		pale peach	Z5		Hybrid Tea
'Mme Caroline Testout'		pink	Z5		Hybrid Tea
'Mme Louis Laperrière'		deep red	Z5		Hybrid Tea
'Magenta'		mauve-pink	Z5		Hybrid Tea
Mandarin®		orange ageing salmon	Z5		Miniature
Margaret Merril	🏆	blush pink	Z5		Floribunda/Hybrid Tea
Mariandel®	🏆	deep red	Z5		Floribunda
'Marlena'		deep red	Z5		Floribunda
Marry Me		pink	Z5		Patio
Memoire®		creamy white	Z5		Hybrid Tea
'Mevrouw Nathalie Nypels'	🏆	pink	Z5		Polyantha
'Michèle Meilland'		flesh pink	Z5		Hybrid Tea
Minnie Pearl®		pale pink	Z5		Miniature
Mischief		coral	Z5		Hybrid Tea
'Mister Lincoln'		deep red	Z5	H	Hybrid Tea
'Mrs Oakley Fisher'	🏆	apricot	Z5		Hybrid Tea
Mountbatten®	🏆	yellow	Z5		Floribunda
'National Trust'		red	Z5		Hybrid Tea
New Zealand		pale pink	Z5	H	Hybrid Tea
News®		purple	Z5		Floribunda
Octavia Hill		pink	Z5		Floribunda/Shrub
'Ophelia'		pink	Z5		Hybrid Tea
Orange Sunblaze®		vermilion	Z5		Patio
Pandemonium		vermilion striped pale yellow	Z5		Floribunda/Patio
Papa Meilland®		deep red	Z6	H	Hybrid Tea
Pascali®		creamy white	Z5		Hybrid Tea
Paul Shirville	🏆	salmon pink	Z5		Hybrid Tea
Peace	🏆	soft yellow edged pink	Z5		Hybrid Tea
'Piccadilly'		coral red/yellow	Z5		Hybrid Tea
Pink Symphony		pink	Z5		Miniature
Playboy®		orange-yellow	Z5		Floribunda
Playgirl™		cerise-pink	Z5		Floribunda
Polar Star		creamy white	Z5		Hybrid Tea
Princess Alice		yellow	Z5		Floribunda

Pristine®		blush white	Z5		Hybrid Tea
Queen Mother	🏆	pink	Z5		Patio
'Queen of Bedders'		cerise	Z5		Bourbon
Red Devil®	🏆	deep red	Z5		Hybrid Tea
Red Rascal		deep red	Z5		Patio
Regensberg®		cerise-pink edged blush	Z5		Floribunda/Patio
Remember Me®	🏆	copper	Z5		Hybrid Tea
Robin Redbreast®		deep scarlet, white eye	Z5		Miniature/Ground Cover/Patio
Rosemary Harkness		orange-salmon	Z5		Hybrid Tea
'Rosemary Rose'		cerise-crimson	Z5		Floribunda
'Royal Highness'		pale pink	Z5		Hybrid Tea
Royal Salute		deep pink	Z5		Miniature
Royal Dane®		vermilion	Z5		Hybrid Tea
Royal William (syn. Fragrant Charm)	🏆	deep crimson	Z5		Hybrid Tea
Savoy Hotel	🏆	pale pink	Z5		Hybrid Tea
Sexy Rexy®	🏆	pale pink	Z5		Floribunda
Sheila's Perfume		peach edged red	Z5		Floribunda
Shine On		orange-coral	Z5		Patio
Silver Jubilee®	🏆	salmon pink	Z5		Tea
'Southampton'	🏆	apricot	Z5		Floribunda
Sue Lawley		red edged pink	Z5		Floribunda
Summer Dream		peach-pink	Z5		Hybrid Tea
Sun Hit™		deep yellow	Z5		Patio
Sunset Boulevard		orange-apricot	Z5		Floribunda
Sunset Celebration		peach	Z5		Hybrid Tea
Sweet Dream	🏆	peachy apricot	Z5		Patio
Sweet Magic	🏆	orange	Z5		Miniature/Patio
Sweet Memories		pale yellow	Z5		Patio
Tequila Sunrise	🏆	yellow edged red	Z5		Hybrid Tea
The Lady	🏆	yellow blend	Z5		Hybrid Tea
The McCartney Rose		deep pink	Z5		Hybrid Tea
Tiger Cub		gold striped crimson	Z5		Patio
Tintinara		light red	Z5		Hybrid Tea
Tip Top®		coral	Z5		Floribunda/Patio
Top Marks		vermilion	Z5		Miniature/Patio
Tropicana		vermilion	Z5		Hybrid Tea
Trumpeter®	🏆	scarlet	Z5		Floribunda
Tynwald		cream	Z5		Hybrid Tea
'Typhoon'		coral	Z5		Hybrid Tea
Valencia®		apricot	Z5		Hybrid Tea
Valentine Heart		pink	Z5		Floribunda
Westerland™	🏆	apricot	Z5		Floribunda
Whisky Mac		apricot	Z5		Hybrid Tea
'White Pet'	🏆	white	Z5		Polyantha
'White Wings'		white	Z5		Hybrid Tea
Yesterday®	🏆	magenta-purple	Z5		Polyantha
'Yvonne Rabier'	🏆	white	Z5		Polyantha

Shrub Roses

Abraham Darby®		blush pink	Z5		Shrub (English rose)
'Agnes'		light yellow	Z3	C	Rugosa
'Alba Maxima'	🏆	white	Z4	C	Alba
'Alba Semiplena'	🏆	white	Z4	C	Alba
'Alexander MacKenzie'		red	Z4	C	Shrub
'Archiduc Charles'		cerise shaded pink	Z7	H	Tea
'Archiduc Joseph'		copper	Z7	H	Tea
'Assemblage des Beautés'		light crimson	Z4	C	Gallica
'Autumn Delight'		pale cream	Z5		Hybrid Musk
'Ballerina'	🏆	pink	Z5		Hybrid Musk/Polyantha
'Baron Girod de l'Ain'		deep red edged white	Z5		Hybrid Perpetual
'Baronne Henriette de Snoy'		coppery pink	Z7	H	Tea
'Beau Narcisse'		purplish mauve	Z4	C	Gallica
'Belle Isis'		pale pink	Z4	C	Gallica
'Belle Poitevine'		magenta-pink	Z3	C	Rugosa
Biddulph Grange		red	Z5		Shrub
'Blanche Double de Coubert'	🏆	white	Z3	C	Rugosa
'Bon Silène'		carmine	Z7	H	Tea
Bonica®	🏆	pink	Z5	C	Shrub/Ground Cover
'Boule de Neige'		white	Z5		Bourbon
'Bourbon Queen' (syn. 'Queen of Bourbons')		pink	Z5		Bourbon
Brother Cadfael		pink	Z5		(English rose)
'Buff Beauty'	🏆	pale apricot	Z5		Hybrid Musk
californica		pink	Z3	C	Shrub

'Camaïeux'		white striped magenta-pink, ageing slaty lilac	Z4	C	Gallica
'Cantabrigiensis'	🏆	pale yellow	Z4	C	Shrub
'Cardinal de Richelieu'	🏆	purple	Z4	C	Gallica
Cardinal Hume®		light purple	Z5		Shrub
Carefree Beauty™		cerise-pink	Z4	C	Shrub
'Cécile Brünner'	🏆	pink	Z5		Polyantha
'Céleste' (syn. 'Celestial')	🏆	pink	Z4	C	Alba
'Celsiana'		pink	Z4	C	Damask
× *centifolia* (cabbage rose)		pink	Z5		Centifolia
× *centifolia* 'Cristata' (crested Moss rose, syn. 'Chapeau de Napoléon')	🏆	pink	Z5		Centifolia
× *centifolia* 'Muscosa' (common Moss rose)	🏆	pink	Z5		Moss
'Cerise Bouquet'	🏆	cerise	Z5		Shrub
'Charles de Mills'	🏆	purplish crimson	Z4	C	Gallica
Charles Rennie Mackintosh®		pink	Z5		Shrub (English rose)
'Chianti'		purplish red	Z5		Shrub (English rose)
'Chloris'		pale pink	Z4	C	Alba
'Clotilde Soupert'		white with pale pink center	Z5	H	Polyantha
Cocktail®		scarlet	Z5		Shrub
'Commandant Beaurepaire'		pink striped crimson, ageing mauve/purple-pink	Z5		Bourbon
'Complicata'	🏆	pink	Z4	C	Gallica
'Comtesse Cécile de Chabrillant'		deep pink	Z5		Hybrid Perpetual
'Comtesse du Caÿla'		peach/copper blend	Z7	H	Tea
'Conrad Ferdinand Meyer'		pink	Z5	C	Rugosa
'Cornelia'	🏆	coppery pink	Z5		Hybrid Musk
Cottage Rose™		pink	Z5		Shrub (English rose)
'Country Dancer'		cerise-pink	Z4	C	Shrub
'Coupe d'Hébé'		pink	Z5		Bourbon
'Cramoisi Supérieur'		red	Z7	H	China
'Cymbifolia'		white	Z4	C	Alba
'D'Aguesseau'		crimson	Z4	C	Gallica
'De Meaux'		pink	Z5		Centifolia
'De Rescht'	🏆	purplish cerise	Z5		Portland Damask
'Declic'		lilac-pink	Z5		Shrub
'Dentelle de Malines'		pale pink	Z5		Shrub
'Directeur Alphand'		deep blackish red	Z5		Hybrid Perpetual
'Doncasteri'		deep pink	Z5		Shrub
Douceur Normande®		coral pink	Z5	C	Shrub/Ground Cover
'Duc de Guiche'	🏆	cerise-red ageing purplish	Z4	C	Gallica
'Duchesse d'Angoulême'		pale pink	Z4	C	Gallica
'Duchesse de Montebello'	🏆	pale pink	Z4	C	Gallica
'Duchesse de Verneuil'		pink	Z5		Moss
'Dupontii'		white with pink blush	Z4	C	Shrub
ecae		yellow	Z4	C	Shrub
elegantula 'Persetosa' (syn. *R. farreri* 'Persetosa')		pink	Z4	C	Shrub
'Etoile de Lyon'		soft yellow	Z7	H	Tea
Euphrates		salmon with maroon eye	Z7		*persica* hybrid
'Eva'		deep carmine	Z5		Shrub
Evelyn®		apricot	Z5		Shrub (English rose)
'Fantin-Latour'	🏆	pale pink	Z5		Centifolia
fedtschenkoana		white	Z4	C	Shrub
'Felicia'	🏆	pale pink	Z5		Hybrid Musk
'Félicité Parmentier'	🏆	pale pink	Z5		Alba × Damask
'Ferdinand Pichard'	🏆	pale pink striped carmine	Z5		Bourbon
'Fimbriata'		pink	Z5	C	Rugosa
'Francesca'		apricot	Z5		Hybrid Musk
Francine Austin®		white	Z5		Shrub (English rose)
× *francofurtana* 'Empress Josephine'	🏆	pink	Z4	C	Shrub
'Fritz Nobis'	🏆	pink	Z5		Shrub
'Fru Dagmar Hastrup'	🏆	pink	Z4	C	Rugosa
'Frühlingsgold'	🏆	pale yellow	Z4	C	Pimpinellifolia Hybrid
'Frühlingsmorgen'		pink blend	Z4	C	Pimpinellifolia Hybrid
gallica var. *officinalis*	🏆	cerise-red	Z4	C	Gallica
gallica 'Versicolor' (Rosa Mundi)	🏆	cerise-red striped white	Z4	C	Gallica
'Général Galiéni'		coral red	Z7	H	Tea
'Général Kléber'		pink	Z5		Moss
'Général Schablikine'		coral red	Z7	H	Tea
'Georges Vibert'		crimson striped pale pink	Z4	C	Gallica
'Geranium'	🏆	cherry red	Z4	C	*moyesii* hybrid
Gertrude Jekyll®		rich pink	Z5		Shrub (English rose)
Glamis Castle		white	Z5		Shrub (English rose)
glauca (syn. *R. rubrifolia*)	🏆	deep pink	Z4	C	Shrub
'Gloire de Ducher'		purplish crimson	Z5		Hybrid Perpetual
'Gloire des Mousseuses'		cerise-pink fading to pale pink	Z5		Moss
Golden Celebration™		golden yellow	Z5		Shrub (English rose)
Golden Chersonese		yellow	Z4	C	Shrub
'Golden Wings'	🏆	pale yellow	Z4	C	Shrub
Graham Thomas		amber yellow	Z5		Shrub (English rose)
'Great Maiden's Blush'		white with pink blush	Z4	C	Alba
'Great Western'		magenta-crimson	Z5		Bourbon
'Grootendorst Supreme'		deep crimson	Z4	C	Rugosa
'Hansa'		magenta-cerise	Z3	C	Rugosa
× *harisonii* 'Harison's Yellow'		yellow	Z4	C	Pimpinellifolia Hybrid
'Helen Knight'	🏆	yellow	Z4	C	*ecae* hybrid
'Henri Martin'	🏆	crimson	Z5		Moss
'Henry Hudson'		white	Z3	C	Rugosa
Heritage®		pale pink	Z5		Shrub (English rose)
'Hermosa'		pink	Z6	H	China
'Highdownensis'	🏆	pink	Z4	C	*moyesii* hybrid
'Honorine de Brabant'		pale pink striped cerise	Z5		Bourbon
'Hugh Dickson'		crimson	Z5		Hybrid Perpetual
'Indigo'		purple	Z5		Portland Damask
'Ipsilanté'		pink	Z5		Damask
'Ispahan'	🏆	pink	Z5		Damask
Jacqueline du Pré	🏆	pale blush ageing to creamy white	Z5		Shrub
'James Mason'		scarlet	Z5		Gallica
'James Veitch'		purple	Z5		Damask Portland Moss
Jayne Austin		apricot	Z5		Shrub (English rose)
'Jens Munk'		pink	Z2	C	Rugosa
John Keats		pink	Z5		Shrub (Romantica® series)
'Joseph's Coat'		yellow edged red	Z5		Shrub/Climber
'Kathleen'		pale pink	Z5		Hybrid Musk
'Kathleen Harrop'		pale magenta-pink	Z5		Bourbon
Kathryn Morley		pink	Z5		Shrub (English rose)
'Kazanlik' (syn. 'Trigintipetala')		pink	Z5		Damask
'Königin von Dänemark	🏆	pink	Z4	C	Alba
L.D. Braithwaite®		crimson	Z5		Shrub (English rose)
'La Ville de Bruxelles'		pink	Z5		Damask
'Lanei'		crimson	Z5		Moss
Lavender Dream®		mauve-pink	Z5		Shrub
'Lavender Lassie'	🏆	mauve-pink	Z5		Hybrid Musk
'Le Rire Niais'		pink	Z5		Centifolia
'Léon Lecomte'		pink	Z5		Damask
'Le Vésuve'		carmine-pink shading to coppery red	Z7	H	China
Leander®		apricot	Z5		Shrub (English rose)
'Leda'		white tipped red	Z4	C	Damask
Lilian Austin®		salmon	Z5		Shrub (English rose)
'Lillian Gibson'		pale pink	Z4	C	*blanda* hybrid
Linda Campbell		crimson	Z4	C	Rugosa
'Lord Penzance'		pale yellow edged pink	Z5		Hybrid Sweet-briar
'Louis Philippe'		crimson	Z6	H	China
'Louis van Houtte'		deep crimson	Z5		Hybrid Perpetual
'Louis XIV'		deep red	Z7	H	China
'Louise Odier'		pink	Z5		Bourbon
'Mabel Morrison'		white	Z5		Hybrid Perpetual
macrophylla 'Master Hugh'	🏆	pink	Z5		Shrub
'Mme Delaroche-Lambert'		crimson	Z5		Damask Portland Moss
'Mme Ernest Calvat'		pink	Z5	H	Bourbon
'Mme Georges Bruant'		white	Z5		Rugosa
'Mme Knorr' (syn. 'Comte de Chambord')	🏆	pink	Z4	C	Portland Damask
'Mme Lauriol de Barny'		pink	Z5		Bourbon
'Mme Legras de Saint Germain'	🏆	white	Z5		Alba × Noisette
'Mme Louis Lévêque'	🏆	pink	Z5		Damask Portland Moss
'Mme Pierre Oger'		pale pink	Z5		Bourbon
'Mme Plantier'	🏆	white	Z5		Alba × Noisette
'Mme Wagram, Comtesse de Turenne'		pink	Z7	H	Tea
'Mme Zöetmans'		white	Z5		Damask
'Magna Charta'		cerise	Z5		Hybrid Perpetual
'Maiden's Blush'		white with pink blush	Z4	C	Alba
'Maman Cochet'		pink	Z7	H	Tea

'Marchesa Boccella' (syn. 'Jacques Cartier')	🏆	pink	Z4	H	Portland Damask
'Marguerite Hilling'	🏆	pink	Z5		Shrub
'Marie-Jeanne'		white	Z5	H	Polyantha
'Marie Pavic'		blush white	Z5	H	Polyantha
'Marie van Houtte'		cream blushed pink	Z7	H	Tea
Marjorie Fair®		crimson with white eye	Z5		Polyantha/Shrub
'Martin Frobisher'		pink	Z3	C	Rugosa
Mary Rose®		pink	Z5		Shrub (English rose)
'Menja'		pale blush pink	Z5		Shrub
Moje Hammarberg®		magenta-pink	Z3	C	Rugosa
'Monsieur Tillier'		copper-cerise blend	Z7	H	Tea
'Moonlight'		pale yellow fading white	Z5		Hybrid Musk
'Morden Blush'		pale pink	Z3	C	Shrub
'Morden Centennial'		cerise-pink	Z4	C	Shrub
'Morden Ruby'		deep pink	Z4	C	Shrub
'Mousseline'		pale blush pink	Z5		Damask Portland Moss
moyesii		red	Z4	C	Shrub
'Mrs Anthony Waterer'		purplish crimson	Z5	C	Rugosa
'Mrs B.R. Cant'		deep salmon	Z7	H	Tea
Mrs Doreen Pike		pink	Z5	C	Rugosa (English rose)
'Mrs Dudley Cross'		apricot flushed pink	Z7	H	Tea
'Mrs John Laing'		rich pink	Z5		Hybrid Perpetual
'Nevada'		pale yellow ageing white flushed pink	Z4	C	Shrub
nitida		pink	Z4	C	Shrub/Ground Cover
'Nova Zembla'		blush white	Z5	C	Rugosa
'Nuits de Young'		purple	Z5		Moss
'Nur Mahal'		crimson	Z5		Hybrid Musk
nutkana 'Plena'	🏆	pink	Z4	C	Shrub
'Nyveldt's White'		white	Z4	C	Rugosa
× *odorata* 'Mutabilis' (syn. 'Tipo Ideale')	🏆	buff ageing through pink to red	Z7	H	China
× *odorata* 'Ochroleuca' (Parks's yellow tea-scented China)		pale yellow	Z7	H	China
× *odorata* 'Pallida' (old blush China)		pink	Z6	H	China
× *odorata* Sanguinea Group		red	Z7	H	China
'Oeillet Panaché'		pale pink striped cerise-red	Z5		Moss
'Oeillet Parfait'		pink	Z4	C	Gallica
'Ombrée Parfaite'		cerise shading through crimson to purple	Z4	C	Gallica
'Pax'		creamy white	Z5		Hybrid Musk
Pearl Drift®		pearly white	Z5		Shrub
'Penelope'	🏆	palest peach fading white	Z5		Hybrid Musk
Perdita®		pale peach	Z5		Shrub (English rose)
'Perle d'Or'	🏆	pale peach	Z5		Polyantha
'Petite de Hollande'		pink	Z5		Centifolia
pimpinellifolia 'Andrewsii'	🏆	pink	Z3	C	Shrub
pimpinellifolia 'Double White'		white	Z3	C	Shrub
pimpinellifolia 'Grandiflora'		pale yellow	Z3	C	Shrub
pimpinellifolia 'Mary, Queen of Scots'		pale lilac shaded plum	Z3	C	Shrub
pimpinellifolia 'William III'		crimson ageing plum to lilac-pink	Z3	C	Shrub
'Pink Grootendorst'	🏆	pink	Z4	C	Rugosa
'Pink Prosperity'		pink	Z5		Hybrid Musk
Pink Robusta®		pink	Z5		Shrub
Pleine de Grâce		white	Z5		Shrub
'Pompon Blanc Parfait'		blush white	Z4	C	Alba
'Pompon Panaché'		cream striped cerise-pink	Z4	C	Gallica
'Prairie Dawn'		pink	Z4	C	Shrub
'Président de Sèze'	🏆	lilac-pink with purplish cerise center	Z4	C	Gallica
Prima	🏆	blush pink	Z5		Shrub/Floribunda
primula	🏆	pale yellow	Z4	C	Shrub
'Prince Charles'		crimson ageing purplish	Z5		Bourbon
'Professeur Emile Perrot'		pink	Z5		Damask
'Prosperity'	🏆	blush white	Z5		Hybrid Musk
'Raubritter'		pink	Z4	C	Shrub/Rambler
Redouté		pale pink	Z5		Shrub (English rose)
'Reine des Centifeuilles'		pink	Z5		Centifolia
'Reine des Violettes'		magenta-purple ageing slaty purple	Z5		Hybrid Perpetual
'Reine Victoria'		pink	Z5		Bourbon
'Robin Hood'		cherry red	Z5		Hybrid Musk
Robusta®		scarlet	Z4	C	Rugosa
'Roger Lambelin'		deep red edged white	Z5		Hybrid Perpetual
'Rosa Zwerg' (syn. Dwarf Pavement)		pink	Z4	C	Rugosa
'Rose à Parfum de l'Haÿ'		purplish crimson	Z4	C	Rugosa
'Roseraie de l'Haÿ'	🏆	purplish crimson	Z4	C	Rugosa
'Rose d'Amour'	🏆	pink	Z5		Shrub
Roselina®		cerise-pink	Z4	C	Rugosa/Ground Cover
Rote Max Graf®		scarlet	Z4	C	Ground Cover/Rugosa
'Rotes Meer' (syn.Purple Pavement)		purplish crimson	Z4	C	Rugosa
rubiginosa	🏆	pink	Z4	C	Sweet-briar
rugosa 'Alba'	🏆	white	Z3	C	Rugosa
rugosa 'Rubra'	🏆	cerise-red	Z4	C	Rugosa
'Rugspin'		red	Z4	C	Rugosa
'Ruskin'		crimson	Z5	C	Rugosa
'Safrano'		apricot	Z7	H	Tea
Saint Cecilia®		pale blush pink	Z5		Shrub (English rose)
Saint Swithun		pink	Z5		Shrub (English rose)
Sally Holmes®		blush white	Z5		Shrub/Hybrid Musk
'Scabrosa'	🏆	magenta-pink	Z3	C	Rugosa
'Scharlachglut'	🏆	scarlet	Z5		Shrub
Schnee-Eule® (syns. Snowy Owl, White Pavement)		white	Z3	C	Rugosa/Ground Cover
'Schneekoppe'		white flushed pink	Z3	C	Rugosa
'Schneezwerg'	🏆	white	Z4	C	Rugosa
'Sealing Wax'		red	Z4	C	*moyesii* hybrid
'Shailer's White Moss'	🏆	white	Z5		Moss
Sharifa Asma®		pale pink	Z5		Shrub (English rose)
'Shropshire Lass'		blush pink	Z5		Shrub (English rose)
Skyrocket	🏆	deep red	Z5		Hybrid Musk
soulieana	🏆	white	Z4	C	Shrub/Rambler
'Sourire d'Orchidée'		pale flesh pink	Z5		Shrub
'Souvenir d'Elise Vardon'		pale peach blend	Z7	H	Tea
'Souvenir d'un Ami'		pale salmon pink	Z7	H	Tea
'Souvenir de la Malmaison'		blush pink	Z6	H	Bourbon
'Souvenir de Mme Auguste Charles'		pink	Z5		Bourbon
'Souvenir de Philémon Cochet'		white	Z4	C	Rugosa
'Souvenir de St Anne's'	🏆	pale blush pink	Z5		Bourbon
'Stanwell Perpetual'		pale blush pink	Z3	C	Pimpinellifolia Hybrid
Stretch Johnson		scarlet edged coral with yellow eye	Z5		Shrub
sweginzowii 'Macrocarpa'		pink	Z5		Shrub
The Alexandra Rose		peach blend	Z5		Shrub (English rose)
'The Bishop'		magenta-purple	Z5		Centifolia × Gallica
The Countryman®		deep pink	Z5		Shrub (English rose)
The Dark Lady		crimson	Z5		Shrub (English rose)
'The Fairy'	🏆	pink	Z5	H	Polyantha
The Pilgrim		apricot	Z5		Shrub (English rose)
The Prince®		deep crimson ageing purplish	Z5		Shrub (English rose)
'Thérèse Bugnet'		pink	Z3	C	Rugosa
'Thisbe'		pale yellow	Z5		Hybrid Musk
Tigris®		yellow with red eye	Z7	H	*persica* hybrid
Topaz Jewel		pale yellow	Z4	C	Rugosa
Toulouse-Lautrec®		yellow	Z5		Shrub (Romantica® series)
'Tricolore de Flandre'		pale pink striped cerise	Z4	C	Gallica
'Triomphe du Luxembourg'		salmon pink	Z7	H	Tea
Tumbling Waters		white	Z5		Shrub
'Tuscany Superb'	🏆	deep red ageing purplish	Z4	C	Gallica
'Unique Blanche'		white	Z5		Centifolia
'Vanguard'		salmon	Z5		Rugosa
'Vanity'		cerise	Z5	H	Hybrid Musk
'Variegata di Bologna'		white striped cerise crimson	Z5		Bourbon
'Vick's Caprice'		pink striped blush white	Z5		Bourbon
villosa		pink	Z4	C	Shrub
virginiana	🏆	pink	Z3	C	Shrub
'White Cécile Brünner'		white	Z5	H	Polyantha
'White Grootendorst'		white	Z4	C	Rugosa
'William Baffin'		pink	Z3	C	Rugosa/Climbing Rugosa
'William Lobb'	🏆	purple	Z5		Moss
'William R. Smith'		cream flushed pink	Z7	H	Tea
willmottiae		magenta-pink	Z3	C	Shrub
Winchester Cathedral®		white	Z5		Shrub
Windrush®		pale yellow	Z5		Shrub
'Winnipeg Parks'		red	Z4	C	Shrub
'Wolley-Dod'		pink	Z4	C	Shrub

woodsii		pink	Z3	C	Shrub
xanthina 'Canary Bird'	🏆	yellow	Z5		Shrub
xanthina f. *hugonis*	🏆	pale yellow	Z4	C	Shrub
'Zéphirine Drouhin'	🏆	cerise-pink	Z5		Bourbon
'Zigeunerknabe'	🏆	purplish crimson	Z5		Shrub

Climbing Roses

'Adélaïde d'Orléans'	🏆	white (light pink)	Z5		Rambler
'Aimée Vibert'		blush white	Z5		Noisette
'Albéric Barbier'	🏆	cream	Z6		Rambler
'Albertine'	🏆	coppery pink	Z5		Rambler
'Alchymist'		apricot-yellow	Z5		Climbing/Shrub
'Alexandre Girault'		cerise	Z5		Rambler
'Alexandre Tremouillet'		creamy white with pale yellow center	Z5		Rambler
'Alister Stella Grey'	🏆	light yellow	Z7	H	Noisette
Altissimo®	🏆	red	Z5		Climbing
Antique '89®		pale pink edged rose red	Z5		Climbing
'Auguste Gervais'		pale apricot	Z5		Rambler
'Aviateur Blériot'		pale apricot yellow	Z5		Rambler
Awakening		light pink	Z5		Rambler
'Ayrshire Queen'		purplish crimson	Z4		Rambler/Ground Cover
banksiae var. *banksiae*		white	Z8	H	Rambler
banksiae var. *lutea*	🏆	soft yellow	Z7	H	Rambler
Bantry Bay®		rich pink	Z5		Climbing Hybrid Tea
'Belvedere'		pink	Z5		Rambler
'Belle Portugaise'		light peach	Z7	H	Climbing
'Bennett's Seedling'		white	Z5		Rambler
'Black Boy'		crimson	Z7	H	Climbing
'Blairii Number Two	🏆	pink	Z5		Climbing Bourbon
'Bleu Magenta'		purple	Z5		Rambler
'Blossomtime'		pink	Z5		Climbing
'Blush Rambler'		pink	Z5		Rambler
'Blushing Lucy'		pink	Z5		Rambler
'Bobbie James'	🏆	white	Z5		Rambler
'Bougainville'		lilac-pink	Z7	H	Noisette
'Bouquet d'Or'		apricot-yellow	Z7	H	Noisette
bracteata		white	Z7	H	Climbing
Breath of Life		peach-pink	Z5		Climbing Hybrid Tea
'Brenda Colvin'		pale blush pink	Z5		Rambler
brunonii 'La Mortola'		creamy white	Z6		Rambler
'Captain Samuel Holland'		pink	Z3	C	Shrub/Climbing
Casino®		yellow	Z5	H	Climbing Hybrid Tea
'Céline Forestier'	🏆	pale yellow	Z7	H	Noisette
'Champneys' Pink Cluster'		pale blush	Z7	H	Noisette
'Chaplin's Pink Climber'		carmine-pink	Z5		Climbing
'Cherub'		salmon pink	Z7	H	Rambler
City of York		white	Z5		Climbing
Clair Matin®		pale pink	Z5		Climbing
'Claire Jacquier'		pale yellow	Z7	H	Noisette
'Climbing Blue Moon'		mauve	Z5	H	Climbing Hybrid Tea
'Climbing Cécile Brünner'	🏆	pink	Z5	H	Climbing Polyantha
'Climbing Devoniensis'		cream	Z7	H	Climbing Tea
'Climbing Ena Harkness'		red	Z5		Climbing Hybrid Tea
'Climbing Etoile de Hollande'	🏆	deep red	Z5		Climbing Hybrid Tea
Climbing Gold Badge		yellow	Z5	H	Climbing Hybrid Tea
'Climbing Iceberg'	🏆	white	Z5	H	Climbing Floribunda
'Climbing Josephine Bruce'		deep scarlet	Z5		Climbing Hybrid Tea
'Climbing Lady Hillingdon'	🏆	apricot	Z7	H	Climbing Tea
'Climbing Lady Sylvia'		pink	Z5		Climbing Hybrid Tea
'Climbing Mme Abel Chatenay'		pink	Z6	H	Climbing Hybrid Tea
'Climbing Mme Butterfly'		pale peach	Z5		Climbing Hybrid Tea
'Climbing Mme Caroline Testout'		pink	Z5		Climbing Hybrid Tea
'Climbing Masquerade'		yellow ageing to red	Z5		Climbing Floribunda
'Climbing McGredy's Yellow'		pale yellow	Z5		Climbing Hybrid Tea
'Climbing Mrs Herbert Stevens'		white	Z6	H	Climbing Hybrid Tea
'Climbing Mrs Sam McGredy'	🏆	coppery salmon	Z5		Climbing Hybrid Tea
'Climbing Niphetos'		white	Z7		Climbing Tea
'Climbing Ophelia'		pink	Z5		Climbing Hybrid Tea
'Climbing Paul Lédé'		peach-pink	Z7	H	Climbing Tea
'Climbing Pompon de Paris'		deep pink	Z6	H	Climbing China
'Climbing Shot Silk'	🏆	coral pink	Z5		Climbing Hybrid Tea
'Climbing Souvenir de la Malmaison'		pale pink	Z6	H	Climbing Bourbon
'Compassion'	🏆	pink	Z5		Climbing Hybrid Tea
Constance Spry®	🏆	pink	Z5		Climbing/Shrub (English rose)
'Cooperi'		white	Z7	H	Rambler
'Crépuscule'		apricot	Z7	H	Noisette
'Crimson Shower'	🏆	light crimson	Z5		Rambler
'Cupid'		pale peach-pink	Z5		Climbing Hybrid Tea
'Debutante'		pink	Z5		Rambler
'Desprez à Fleurs Jaune'	🏆	soft yellow	Z7	H	Noisette
'Dorothy Perkins'		pink	Z5	H	Rambler
'Dream Girl'	🏆	salmon pink	Z5		Climbing
Dublin Bay	🏆	scarlet	Z5		Climbing
'Dundee Rambler'		white	Z5		Rambler
'Easlea's Golden Rambler'		soft yellow	Z5		Rambler
'Edmond Proust'		light pink	Z5		Rambler
'Elisa Robichon'		pale blush	Z5		Rambler
'Emily Gray'		soft yellow	Z6		Rambler
'Félicité Perpétue'	🏆	white with pink blush	Z5	H	Rambler
filipes 'Kiftsgate'	🏆	white	Z5		Rambler
'Flora'		pink	Z5		Rambler
× *fortuneana*		white	Z7		Rambler
'Francis E. Lester'	🏆	pink	Z5		Rambler
'François Juranville'	🏆	salmon	Z5		Rambler
Galway Bay®		cerise-coral	Z5		Climbing Hybrid Tea
'Gardenia'		creamy white	Z7	H	Rambler
'Geschwinds Nordlandsrose'		pale pink	Z5	C	Rambler
'Geschwinds Orden'		cerise	Z5	C	Rambler/Rugosa
'Ghislaine de Féligonde'		pale apricot	Z6		Rambler
gigantea		creamy white	Z7	H	Climber
'Gloire de Dijon'	🏆	apricot-buff	Z7	H	Climbing Tea
Gloriana '97		cerise-pink	Z5		Climbing Miniature
Golden Showers®	🏆	soft yellow	Z5		Climbing
'Goldfinch'		cream	Z5		Rambler
Good as Gold		yellow	Z5		Climbing Miniature
'Grimpant Cramoisi Supérieur'		red	Z7	H	Climbing Tea
'Guinée'		deep red	Z5		Climbing Hybrid Tea
Handel®	🏆	pale pink edged cerise	Z5		Climbing
'Heideröslein'		pink	Z5		Rambler/Shrub
helenae		white	Z5		Rambler
'Henry Kelsey'		red	Z3	C	Climbing
High Hopes		pink	Z5		Climbing
Highfield		yellow	Z5		Climbing Hybrid Tea
'Jean Guichard'		deep pink	Z7	H	Rambler
'Jeanne Lajoie'		pink	Z5	C	Climbing Miniature
'John Cabot'		cerise	Z3	C	Climbing
'John Davies'		pale pink	Z3	C	Climbing
'Kew Rambler'		pink	Z5		Rambler
'La Follette'		pink ageing carmine	Z7	H	Climbing
laevigata		white	Z7	H	Rambler
'Lamarque'		white	Z7	H	Noisette
Laura Ford®	🏆	yellow ageing peach	Z5		Climbing Miniature
'Laure Davoust'		pink	Z5		Rambler
Lawinia®	🏆	rich pink	Z5		Climbing Hybrid Tea
Leaping Salmon		salmon pink	Z5		Climbing Hybrid Tea
'Léontine Gervais'		apricot-pink blend	Z5		Rambler
'Leverkusen'		pale yellow	Z5		Climbing
Little Rambler		pale pink	Z5		Climbing Miniature
longicuspis var. *sinowilsonii*		white	Z5		Rambler
'Lykkefund'		white, shaded pale apricot	Z5		Rambler
'Mme Alfred Carrière'		white	Z6	H	Noisette
'Mme de Sancy de Parabère'		pink	Z5		Boursault
'Mme Driout'		pink striped carmine	Z7	H	Climbing Tea
'Mme Grégoire Staechelin'	🏆	rich pink	Z5		Climbing Hybrid Tea
'Mme Hardy'	🏆	white	Z4	C	Climbing Damask
'Mme Isaac Pereire'	🏆	cerise	Z5		Climbing Bourbon
'Mme Jules Gravereaux'		apricot	Z7	H	Climbing Tea
'Mme Legras de Saint Germain'	🏆	white	Z5		Alba × Noisette
'Mme Plantier'	🏆	white	Z5		Alba × Noisette
'Maigold'	🏆	golden yellow	Z5		Pimpinellifolia Hybrid
'Maréchal Niel'		soft yellow	Z7	H	Noisette
'May Queen'		pink	Z5		Rambler
'Meg'		peach-pink	Z5		Climbing Hybrid Tea
'Mermaid'	🏆	pale yellow	Z6	H	Climbing
'Mrs F.W. Flight'		deep pink	Z5		Rambler
mulliganii	🏆	white	Z5		Rambler
multiflora		white	Z5		Rambler/Shrub

multiflora 'Carnea'		pink	Z5		Rambler
'Narrow Water'		pale pink	Z6		Noisette
'New Dawn'		pale pink	Z5		Climbing/Rambler
Nice Day		salmon pink	Z5		Climbing Miniature
Night Light®		golden yellow	Z5		Climbing
'Noisette Carnée' (Blush Noisette)		pink	Z6	H	Noisette
× *odorata* 'Pseudindica' (Fortune's double yellow)		peach	Z7	H	Climbing China
'Parade'	🏆	cerise	Z5		Climbing
Parure d'Or®		soft yellow, edges suffused deep pink	Z5		Climbing Hybrid Tea
'Paul Noël'		coppery salmon	Z5		Rambler
'Paul Transon'	🏆	coppery salmon	Z5		Rambler
'Paul's Himalayan Musk'	🏆	pale pink	Z5		Rambler
'Paul's Lemon Pillar'		pale lemon	Z5		Climbing Hybrid Tea
'Paul's Scarlet Climber'		light red	Z5		Climbing/Rambler
Penny Lane		blush, pale peach center	Z5		Climbing
'Phyllis Bide'	🏆	pale peach blend	Z5		Rambler
'Pink Perpétué'		pink	Z5		Climbing
Polka®		peach	Z5		Climbing (Romantica® series)
'Princesse de Nassau'		cream	Z6	H	Rambler
'Princesse Louise'		white	Z5		Rambler
'Princesse Marie'		pink	Z5		Rambler
'Rambling Rector'	🏆	white	Z5		Rambler
'Rêve d'Or'		buff-yellow	Z7	H	Noisette
Rosalie Coral		vermilion	Z5		Climbing Miniature
'Rose-Marie Viaud'		cerise-purple ageing grayish purple	Z5		Rambler
'Rosy Mantle'		deep pink	Z5		Climbing
'Royal Gold'		golden yellow	Z5	H	Climbing
rubus		white	Z7	H	Rambler
'Ruga'		blush white	Z5		Rambler
'Sander's White Rambler'	🏆	white	Z5		Rambler
'Schoolgirl'		apricot	Z5		Climbing
'Seagull'	🏆	white	Z5		Rambler
'Sombreuil'		white	Z7	H	Climbing Tea
'Souvenir d'Alphonse Lavallée'		deep red	Z5		Climbing Hybrid Perpetual
'Souvenir de Claudius Denoyel'		deep red	Z5		Climbing Hybrid Tea
'Souvenir de Mme Léonie Viennot'		coppery pink	Z7	H	Climbing Tea
'Souvenir du Docteur Jamain'		deep red	Z5		Climbing Hybrid Perpetual
Sparkling Scarlet		scarlet	Z5		Climbing Floribunda
'Splendens'		blush white	Z5		Rambler
Summer Wine	🏆	coral	Z5		Climbing
Super Dorothy®		pink	Z5		Rambler
Super Excelsa®		crimson	Z5		Rambler
Super Fairy		pink	Z5		Rambler
Super Sparkle		crimson	Z5		Rambler
'Swan Lake'		pale blush pink	Z5		Climbing
Sympathie®		crimson	Z5		Climbing
'Tausendschön'		peach blend	Z5	H	Rambler
'Tea Rambler'		pink	Z5		Rambler
'The Garland'	🏆	white	Z5		Rambler
'Toby Tristam'		cream	Z5		Rambler
'Treasure Trove'		pale apricot	Z5		Rambler
'Veilchenblau'	🏆	purple	Z5		Rambler
'Venusta Pendula'		blush white	Z5		Rambler
'Violette'		purple	Z5		Rambler
'Vicomtesse Pierre du Fou'		red ageing coral	Z6	H	Climbing Hybrid Tea
Warm Welcome	🏆	vermilion	Z5		Climbing Miniature
'Wedding Day'		white	Z5		Rambler
White Cloud		white	Z5		Climbing/Shrub
White Cockade®	🏆	white	Z5		Climbing
'Wickwar'		creamy white	Z5		Rambler
'William Allen Richardson'		apricot-yellow	Z7	H	Noisette

Roses for Arcades SEE *Roses for Pergolas, Arcades and Catenaries*

Roses for Autumn Color

f = flowers h = hips l = leaves

'Aimée Vibert'		blush white (f)	Z5		Noisette
'Autumn Delight'		pale cream (f)	Z5		Hybrid Musk
'Blanche Double de Coubert'	🏆	white (h, l)	Z3	C	Rugosa
californica		pink (h)	Z3	C	Shrub
'Dart's Dash'		red (h, l)	Z4	C	Rugosa
'Delicata'		carmine-pink (h, l)	Z4	C	Rugosa/Ground Cover
'Doncasteri'		deep pink (h)	Z5		Shrub
elegantula 'Persetosa'		pink (l)	Z4	C	Shrub
fedtschenkoana		white (f, h)	Z4	C	Shrub
filipes 'Kiftsgate'	🏆	white (h)	Z5		Rambler
Fiona®		scarlet(f, h)	Z5		Shrub/Ground Cover
Foxi®		deep pink (f, h)	Z4	C	Rugosa
'Geranium'	🏆	cherry red (h)	Z4	C	*moyesii* hybrid
glauca (syn. *R. rubrifolia*)	🏆	deep pink (h)	Z4	C	Shrub
helenae		yellow (h)	Z5		Shrub
'Herbstfeuer'		dark red (f, h, l)	Z5		Hybrid Sweet-briar
'Highdownensis'	🏆	pink (h)	Z4	C	*moyesii* hybrid
× *kochiana*		pink (h, l)	Z4	C	Shrub
'Lavender Lassie'	🏆	mauve-pink (f)	Z5		Hybrid Musk
'Mevrouw Nathalie Nypels'	🏆	pink (f)	Z5		Polyantha
Moje Hammarberg®		magenta-pink (f, h, l)	Z3		Rugosa
'Monte Cassino'		deep pink (l, h)	Z3		Rugosa
'Moonlight'		pale yellow fading white (f)	Z5		Hybrid Musk
moyesii		red (h)	Z4	C	Shrub
multiflora		white (h)	Z5		Rambler/Shrub
nitida		pink (h, l)	Z4	C	Shrub/Ground Cover
'Nyveldt's White'		white (h, l)	Z4	C	Rugosa
× *odorata* 'Mutabilis' (syn. 'Tipo Ideale')	🏆	buff ageing through pink to red (f)	Z7	H	China
× *odorata* Sanguinea Group		red (f)	Z7	H	China
pendulina		pink (h, l)	Z5		Shrub
'Penelope'	🏆	palest peach fading white (f, h)	Z5		Hybrid Musk
pimpinellifolia 'Double White'		white (f, l)	Z3	C	Shrub
Pink Robusta®		pink (f)	Z5		Shrub
'Rosa Zwerg'		pink (h, l)	Z4	C	Rugosa
'Rotes Meer' (syn. Purple Pavement)		purplish crimson (f, h, l)	Z4	C	Rugosa
rubiginosa	🏆	pink (h)	Z4	C	Sweet-briar
rugosa 'Alba'	🏆	white (h, l)	Z3	C	Rugosa
rugosa 'Rubra'	🏆	cerise-red (h, l)	Z4	C	Rugosa
'Scabrosa'	🏆	magenta-pink (h, l)	Z3	C	Rugosa
Schnee-Eule® (syns. Snowy Owl, White Pavement)		white (h, l)	Z3	C	Rugosa/Ground Cover
'Schneekoppe'		white flushed pink (h, l)	Z3	C	Rugosa
'Schneezwerg'	🏆	white (h, l)	Z4	C	Rugosa
'Sealing Wax'		red (h)	Z4	C	*moyesii* hybrid
soulieana	🏆	white (h)	Z4	C	Shrub/Rambler
sweginzowii 'Macrocarpa'		pink (h)	Z5		Shrub
Tequila Sunrise	🏆	yellow edged red (f)	Z5		Hybrid Tea
'Thérèse Bugnet'		pink (f, l)	Z3	C	Rugosa
'Thisbe'		pale yellow (f)	Z5		Hybrid Musk
'Vanguard'		salmon (f)	Z5		Rugosa
'Vanity'		cerise (f)	Z5	H	Hybrid Musk
villosa		pink (h)	Z4	C	Shrub
virginiana	🏆	pink (h, l)	Z3	C	Shrub
'Wickwar'		pale pink (h)	Z5		Rambler
'Winnipeg Parks'		red (f)	Z4	C	Shrub
'Wolley-Dod'		pink (h)	Z4	C	Shrub
woodsii		pink (h)	Z3	C	Shrub

Roses for Bedding

Ideally these should have an even and fairly dense habit of growth and should be long-flowering. However, though older varieties tend to be less recurrent-flowering, I have still included some of the best for gardens intended to show old-fashioned planting. Bedding is usually intended to make a long-range impact and coarse foliage is less of a problem than for roses used in small numbers and seen at close quarters.

Anna Livia	🏆	salmon pink	Z5	Floribunda
Birthday Girl		cream edged salmon	Z5	Floribunda
'Duet'		pink	Z5	Hybrid Tea
Elizabeth of Glamis®		salmon pink	Z5	Floribunda
Evelyn Fison		deep red	Z5	Floribunda
Fidélio®		orange-red	Z5	Hybrid Tea
French Lace		white blushed peach	Z5	Floribunda
'Irène Watts'	🏆	pale salmon pink	Z6	China
'Katharina Zeimet'		white	Z5	Polyantha
Keepsake		carmine-pink	Z5	Hybrid Tea
Lilli Marlene		deep red	Z5	Floribunda
Livin' Easy		orange-salmon	Z5	Floribunda

Variety		Color	Zone		Type
'Lovers' Meeting'		orange	Z5		Hybrid Tea
Mariandel®	🏆	deep red	Z5		Floribunda
'Marlena'		deep red	Z5		Floribunda
Mischief		coral	Z5		Hybrid Tea
'Piccadilly'		coral red, yellow reverse	Z5		Hybrid Tea
Playboy®		orange-yellow	Z5		Floribunda
Playgirl™		cerise-pink	Z5		Floribunda
Regensberg®		cerise-pink edged blush	Z5		Floribunda/Patio
Remember Me®	🏆	copper	Z5		Hybrid Tea
Royal Dane®		vermilion	Z5		Hybrid Tea
'Royal Highness'		pale pink	Z5		Hybrid Tea
Royal William	🏆	deep crimson	Z5		Hybrid Tea
Sexy Rexy®	🏆	pale pink	Z5		Floribunda
Sunset Boulevard		apricot-orange	Z5		Floribunda
Sunsprite		yellow	Z5		Floribunda
Susan Hampshire		pink	Z5		Hybrid Tea
Tip Top®		coral	Z5		Floribunda/Patio
Trumpeter®	🏆	scarlet	Z5		Floribunda
'Typhoon'		coral	Z5		Hybrid Tea

Roses for Catenaries SEE *Roses for Pergolas, Arcades and Catenaries*

Roses with Colored Foliage

g = glaucous/gray p = pink-flushed r = red/bronze

Variety		Color	Zone		Type
Basildon Bond		apricot (r)	Z5		Hybrid Tea
Blessings®		rich salmon (r)	Z5		Hybrid Tea
brunonii 'La Mortola'		creamy white (g)	Z6		Rambler
'Carmenetta'		deep pink (p)	Z4	C	Shrub
'Copper Gem'		copper (r)	Z5		Hybrid Tea
Dawn Chorus		deep orange (r)	Z5		Hybrid Tea
Europeana®		deep red (r)	Z5		Floribunda
fedtschenkoana		white (g)	Z4	C	Shrub
glauca (syn. *R. rubrifolia*	🏆	deep pink (g/p)	Z4	C	Shrub
Gordon's College		salmon (r)	Z5		Floribunda
Mariandel®	🏆	deep red (r)	Z5		Floribunda
soulieana	🏆	white (g)	Z4	C	Shrub/Rambler
'Wickwar'		creamy white (g)	Z5		Rambler

Roses for Conservatories

The following roses can be used to furnish the walls and roofs of conservatories. Most varieties recommended for pots and containers (page 178) may also be used in conservatories, as can many Teas, Chinas, Bourbons and Hybrid Perpetuals, though these require a good deal of training both to fit them to the usually limited space available and to make them look attractive.

Variety		Color	Zone		Type
'Climbing Devoniensis'		cream	Z7	H	Climbing Tea
'Climbing Mme Abel Chatenay'		pink	Z6	H	Climbing Hybrid Tea
'Climbing Niphetos'		white	Z7	H	Climbing Tea
'Climbing Ophelia'		pink	Z5		Climbing Hybrid Tea
'Climbing Pompon de Paris'		deep pink	Z6	H	Climbing China
'Gloire de Dijon'	🏆	apricot-buff	Z7	H	Climbing Tea
'Grimpant Cramoisi Supérieur'		red	Z7	H	Climbing Tea
'Lamarque'		white	Z7	H	Noisette
'Mme Driout'		pink striped carmine	Z7	H	Climbing Tea
'Mme Jules Gravereaux'		apricot	Z7	H	Climbing Tea
'Maréchal Niel'		soft yellow	Z7	H	Noisette
× *odorata* 'Pseudindica' (Fortune's double yellow)		peach	Z7	H	Climbing China
'Sombreuil'		white	Z7	H	Climbing Tea
'William Allen Richardson'		apricot-yellow	Z7	H	Noisette

Roses for Cutting

Ideally these should have graceful blooms borne on fairly long stems that are neither too stiff nor too weak-necked. However, a few shorter-stemmed sorts are included for posies and some stiffer varieties that produce blooms of exceptional quality. Few roses are unsuitable for cutting and the list could be very much longer. I have selected those that seem to me particularly suitable, including some older Hybrid Teas that have a grace lacking from some modern varieties.

Variety		Color	Zone		Type
Big Purple® (syn. Stephens' Big Purple)		purple	Z5		Hybrid Tea
Blue Moon®		mauve	Z5		Hybrid Tea
'Boule de Neige'		white	Z5		Bourbon
'Buff Beauty'	🏆	pale apricot	Z5		Hybrid Musk
'Camaïeux'		white striped magenta-pink, ageing slaty lilac	Z4	C	Gallica
'Cécile Brünner'	🏆	pink	Z5		Polyantha
'Charles de Mills'	🏆	purplish crimson	Z4	C	Gallica
'Commandant Beaurepaire'		pink, striped crimson, ageing mauve/purple	Z5		Bourbon
'Comtesse Cécile de Chabrillant'		deep pink	Z5		Hybrid Perpetual
Congratulations		salmon pink	Z5		Hybrid Tea
Dawn Chorus		deep orange	Z5		Hybrid Tea
'Directeur Alphand'		deep blackish red	Z5		Hybrid Perpetual
Elina®	🏆	pale yellow	Z5		Hybrid Tea
'Felicia'	🏆	pale pink	Z5		Hybrid Musk
'Ferdinand Pichard'	🏆	pale pink striped carmine	Z5		Bourbon
Fulton Mackay		apricot-yellow	Z5		Hybrid Tea
gallica 'Versicolor' (Rosa Mundi)	🏆	cerise-red striped white	Z4	C	Gallica
Glad Tidings		red	Z5		Hybrid Tea
Graham Thomas		amber yellow	Z5		Shrub
'Honorine de Brabant'		pale pink striped cerise	Z5		Bourbon
'Hugh Dickson'		crimson	Z5		Hybrid Perpetual
Ingrid Bergman®	🏆	red	Z5		Hybrid Tea
Kordes' Golden Times		yellow	Z5		Floribunda (H)
'Lady Sylvia'		pink	Z5		Hybrid Tea
'Louis van Houtte'		deep crimson	Z5		Hybrid Perpetual
'Louis XIV'		deep red	Z7	H	China
'Louise Odier'		pink	Z5		Bourbon
Loving Memory		deep red	Z5		Hybrid Tea
'Mabel Morrison'		white	Z5		Hybrid Perpetual
'Mme Butterfly'		pale peach	Z5		Hybrid Tea
'Mme Caroline Testout'		pink	Z5		Hybrid Tea
Mme Georges Delbard®		crimson	Z5		Hybrid Tea
'Mme Jules Gravereaux'		apricot	Z7	H	Climbing Tea
'Mme Louis Laperrière'		deep red	Z5		Hybrid Tea
'Mme Pierre Oger'		pale pink	Z5		Bourbon
'Mme Victor Verdier'		crimson	Z5		Hybrid Perpetual
'Maman Cochet'		pink	Z7		Tea
Memoire®		creamy white	Z5		Hybrid Tea
'Michèle Meilland'		flesh pink	Z5		Hybrid Tea
'Mrs Dudley Cross'		apricot flushed pink	Z7		Tea
'Mrs John Laing'		rich pink	Z5		Hybrid Perpetual
Octavia Hill		pink	Z5		Floribunda/Shrub
'Ophelia'		pink	Z5		Hybrid Tea
Papa Meilland®		deep red	Z6		Hybrid Tea
Pascali®		creamy white	Z5		Hybrid Tea
'Perle d'Or'	🏆	pale peach	Z5		Polyantha
Summer Dream		peach-pink	Z5		Hybrid Tea
Tynwald		cream	Z5		Hybrid Tea
'Typhoon'		coral	Z5		Hybrid Tea
Valencia®		apricot	Z5		Hybrid Tea

Roses for Fences

The following roses are suitable for fences and also for walls of about 4ft/1.2m to 6½ft/2m high. Taller climbing roses are not included here because they would cover a long stretch of fence out of scale with the vast majority of gardens. However, for larger gardens with long fences, many more vigorous varieties from the general list of climbing roses (pages 172–3) would be suitable. Some roses usually classed as shrubs, especially some of the Bourbons and Hybrid Perpetuals, are flexible enough to be trained in this way and will thrive on a fence, though they might be too susceptible to fungal disease for growing on a house wall. (Roses recommended for house walls may be found under Roses for Walls, pages 180–81.)

Variety		Color	Zone		Type
'Baron Girod de l'Ain'		deep red edged white	Z5		Hybrid Perpetual
'Boule de Neige'		white	Z5		Hybrid Perpetual
Clair Matin®		pale pink	Z5		Climbing
'Commandant Beaurepaire'		pink, striped crimson, ageing mauve/purple	Z5		Bourbon
'Declic'		lilac pink	Z5		Shrub
'Directeur Alphand'		deep blackish red	Z5		Hybrid Perpetual
'Dorothy Perkins'		pink	Z5	H	Rambler
'Edmond Proust'		light pink	Z5		Rambler
'Ferdinand Pichard'	🏆	pale pink striped carmine	Z5		Bourbon
'François Juranville'	🏆	salmon	Z5		Rambler
'Gloire de Ducher'		purplish crimson	Z5		Hybrid Perpetual
'Goldfinch'		cream	Z5		Rambler
Graham Thomas		amber yellow	Z5		Shrub
'Heideröslein'		pink	Z5		Rambler/Shrub
'Honorine de Brabant'		pale pink striped cerise	Z5		Bourbon
'Hugh Dickson'		crimson	Z5		Hybrid Perpetual
'Jeanne Lajoie'		pink	Z5	C	Climbing Miniature
'Joseph's Coat'		yellow edged red	Z5		Shrub/Climber

Laura Ford®	🏆	yellow ageing peach	Z5		Climbing Miniature
'Lavender Lassie'	🏆	mauve-pink	Z5		Hybrid Musk
'Leverkusen'		pale yellow	Z5		Climbing
Little Rambler		pale pink	Z5		Climbing Miniature
'Louis van Houtte'		deep crimson	Z5		Hybrid Perpetual
'Louise Odier'		pink	Z5		Bourbon
'Mme Ernest Calvat'		pink	Z5	H	Bourbon
'Mme Hardy'	🏆	white	Z4	C	Climbing Damask
'Mme Isaac Pereire'	🏆	cerise	Z5		Climbing Bourbon
'Mme Lauriol de Barny'		pink	Z5		Bourbon
'Mme Legras de Saint Germain'	🏆	white	Z5		Alba × Noisette
'Mme Pierre Oger'		pale pink	Z5		Bourbon
'Mme Plantier'	🏆	white	Z5		Alba × Noisette
'Mrs John Laing'		rich pink	Z5		Hybrid Perpetual
Nice Day		salmon pink	Z5		Climbing Miniature
'Noisette Carnée' (Blush Noisette)		pink	Z6	H	Noisette
'Paul Noël'		coppery salmon	Z5		Rambler
'Paul Transon'	🏆	coppery salmon	Z5		Rambler
'Phyllis Bide'	🏆	pale peach blend	Z5		Rambler
Polka®		peach	Z5		Climbing (Romantica® series)
'Raubritter'		pink	Z4	C	Shrub/Rambler
'Reine des Violettes'		magenta-purple ageing slaty purple	Z5		Hybrid Perpetual
'Reine Victoria'		pink	Z5		Bourbon
'Roger Lambelin'		deep red edged white	Z5		Hybrid Perpetual
'Sander's White Rambler'	🏆	white	Z5		Rambler
soulieana	🏆	white	Z4	C	Shrub/Rambler
'Souvenir d'Alphonse Lavallée'		deep red	Z5		Climbing Hybrid Perpetual
'Souvenir de Mme Auguste Charles'		pink	Z5		Bourbon
'Souvenir de St Anne's'	🏆	pale blush pink	Z5		Bourbon
'Souvenir du Docteur Jamain'		deep red	Z5		Climbing Hybrid Perpetual
Super Dorothy®		pink	Z5		Rambler
Super Excelsa®		crimson	Z5		Rambler
Super Fairy		pink	Z5		Rambler
Super Sparkle		crimson	Z5		Rambler
'Variegata di Bologna'		white striped cerise-crimson	Z5		Bourbon
Warm Welcome	🏆	vermilion	Z5		Climbing Miniature

Roses for Fragrance

All the following roses are strongly fragrant. However, roses that are only moderately scented but bear flowers in great profusion and/or have a fragrance that carries on the air without the need to bury one's nose in the blooms, such as the Hybrid Musks and Synstylae Ramblers, can be equally effective in perfuming the garden. Few of the smaller roses (Patios and Miniatures) are strongly scented; perhaps this should be a future objective for rose breeders.

Abraham Darby®		blush pink	Z5		Shrub
'Aimée Vibert'		blush white	Z5		Rambler
'Assemblage des Beautés'		light crimson	Z4	C	Gallica
Avon		blush pink	Z5		Ground Cover/Patio
'Belle Isis'		pale pink	Z4	C	Gallica
'Belvedere'		pink	Z5		Rambler
Big Purple® (Stephens' Big Purple)		purple	Z5		Hybrid Tea
'Blairii Number Two'	🏆	pink	Z5		Climbing Bourbon
'Blanche Double de Coubert'	🏆	white	Z3	C	Rugosa
Blue Moon®		mauve	Z5		Hybrid Tea
'Boule de Neige'		white	Z5		Hybrid Perpetual
'Bourbon Queen' (syn. 'Queen of Bourbons')		pink	Z5		Bourbon
'Brenda Colvin'		pale blush pink	Z5		Rambler
Brother Cadfael		pink	Z5		Shrub (English rose)
brunonii 'La Mortola'		creamy white	Z6		Rambler
'Camaïeux'		white striped magenta-pink, ageing slaty lilac	Z4	C	Gallica
'Céleste' (syn. 'Celestial')	🏆	pink	Z4	C	Alba
'Céline Forestier'	🏆	pale yellow	Z7	H	Noisette
× *centifolia* (cabbage rose)		pink	Z5		Centifolia
× *centifolia* 'Cristata' (Moss rose)	🏆	pink	Z5		Centifolia
× *centifolia* 'Muscosa' (common Moss rose)	🏆	pink	Z5		Moss
'Champneys' Pink Cluster'		pale blush	Z7	H	Noisette
'Charles de Mills'	🏆	purplish-crimson	Z4	C	Gallica
Charles Rennie Mackintosh®		pink	Z5		Shrub (English rose)
'Chianti'		purplish red	Z5		Shrub (English rose)
Chinatown®		yellow	Z5		Floribunda/Shrub
'Chloris'		pale pink	Z4	C	Alba
City of London®		pale blush	Z5		Floribunda
'Climbing Blue Moon'		mauve	Z5	H	Climbing Hybrid Tea
'Climbing Ena Harkness'		red	Z5		Climbing Hybrid Tea
'Climbing Etoile de Hollande'	🏆	deep red	Z5		Climbing Hybrid Tea
'Climbing Souvenir de la Malmaison'		pale pink	Z6	H	Climbing Bourbon
'Complicata'	🏆	pink	Z4	C	Gallica
'Conrad Ferdinand Meyer'		pink	Z5	C	Rugosa
Constance Spry®	🏆	pink	Z5		Climbing/Shrub (English rose)
'Cornelia'	🏆	coppery pink	Z5		Hybrid Musk
'Coupe d'Hébé'		pink	Z5		Bourbon
'Crimson Glory'		crimson	Z5		Hybrid Tea
'De Rescht'	🏆	purplish cerise	Z5		Portland Damask
'Directeur Alphand'		deep blackish red	Z5		Hybrid Perpetual
'Duc de Guiche'	🏆	cerise-red ageing purplish	Z4	C	Gallica
'Duchesse d'Angoulême'		pale pink	Z4	C	Gallica
'Duchesse de Montebello'	🏆	pale pink	Z4	C	Gallica
'Duchesse de Verneuil'		pink	Z5		Moss
'Dupontii'		white with pink blush	Z4	C	Shrub
Evelyn®		apricot	Z5		Shrub (English rose)
'Fantin-Latour'	🏆	pale pink	Z5		Centifolia
'Felicia'	🏆	pale pink	Z5		Hybrid Musk
'Félicité Parmentier'	🏆	pale pink	Z5		Alba × Damask
'Fimbriata'		pink	Z5	C	Rugosa
Fragrant Cloud		coral red	Z5		Hybrid Tea
Fragrant Delight®		salmon	Z5		Floribunda
Fragrant Dream		salmon	Z5		Hybrid Tea
'Fritz Nobis'	🏆	pink	Z5		Shrub
'Général Kléber'		pink	Z5		Moss
'Georges Vibert'		crimson striped pale pink	Z4	C	Gallica
gigantea		creamy white	Z7	H	Climber
Glamis Castle		white	Z5		Shrub
'Great Maiden's Blush'		white with pink blush	Z4	C	Alba
'Guinée'		deep red	Z5		Climbing Hybrid Tea
'Hansa'		magenta-cerise	Z3	C	Rugosa
'Henri Martin'	🏆	crimson	Z5		Moss
'Henry Hudson'		white	Z3	C	Rugosa
Heritage®		pale pink	Z5		Shrub (English rose)
Indian Summer	🏆	orange	Z5		Hybrid Tea
'Indigo'		purple	Z5		Portland Damask
'Ipsilanté'		pink	Z5		Damask
'Ispahan'	🏆	pink	Z5		Damask
'James Mason'		scarlet	Z5		Gallica
'Kazanlik' (syn. 'Trigintipetala')		pink	Z5		Damask
'Königin von Dänemark'	🏆	pink	Z4	C	Alba
L'Aimant		salmon pink	Z5		Floribunda
'La Ville de Bruxelles'		pink	Z5		Damask
'Lady Sylvia'		pink	Z5		Hybrid Tea
'Lamarque'		white	Z7	H	Noisette
'Lavender Lassie'	🏆	mauve-pink	Z5		Hybrid Musk
Little Rambler		pale pink	Z5		Climbing Miniature
'Louis van Houtte'		deep crimson	Z5		Hybrid Perpetual
'Lovers' Meeting'		orange	Z5		Hybrid Tea
'Lykkefund'		white shaded pale apricot	Z5		Rambler
'Mme Alfred Carrière'		white	Z6	H	Noisette
'Mme Butterfly'		pale peach	Z5		Hybrid Tea
'Mme Delaroche-Lambert'		crimson	Z5		Damask Portland Moss
'Mme Ernest Calvat'		pink	Z5	H	Bourbon
'Mme Hardy'	🏆	white	Z4	C	Climbing Damask
'Mme Isaac Pereire'	🏆	cerise	Z5		Climbing Bourbon
'Mme Knorr' (syn. 'Comte de Chambord')	🏆	pink	Z4	C	Portland Damask
'Mme Lauriol de Barny'		pink	Z5		Bourbon
'Mme Legras de Saint Germain'	🏆	white	Z5		Alba × Noisette
'Mme Louis Laperrière'		deep red	Z5		Hybrid Tea
'Mme Louis Lévêque'	🏆	pink	Z5		Damask Portland Moss
'Mme Plantier'	🏆	white	Z5		Alba × Noisette
'Magenta'		mauve-pink	Z5		Hybrid Tea
'Maiden's Blush'		white with pink blush	Z4	C	Alba
Margaret Merril	🏆	blush pink	Z5		Floribunda/Hybrid Tea
Mary Rose®		pink	Z5		Shrub (English rose)

'May Queen'		pink	Z5		Rambler
'Mister Lincoln'		deep red	Z5	H	Hybrid Tea
Moje Hammarberg®		magenta-pink	Z3	C	Rugosa
'Mrs Anthony Waterer'		purplish crimson	Z5	C	Rugosa
'Mrs John Laing'		rich pink	Z5		Hybrid Perpetual
mulliganii	🏆	white	Z5		Rambler
multiflora		white	Z5		Rambler/Shrub
New Zealand		pale pink	Z5	H	Hybrid Tea
'Nova Zembla'		blush white	Z5	C	Rugosa
'Nuits de Young'		purple	Z5		Moss
'Nur Mahal'		crimson	Z5		Hybrid Musk
'Nyveldt's White'		white	Z4	C	Rugosa
× *odorata* 'Pallida' (old blush China)		pink	Z6	H	China
'Ombrée Parfaite'		cerise shading through crimson to purple	Z4	C	Gallica
'Ophelia'		pink	Z5		Hybrid Tea
Papa Meilland®		deep red	Z6	H	Hybrid Tea
Paul Shirville	🏆	salmon pink	Z5		Hybrid Tea
'Paul's Lemon Pillar'		pale lemon	Z5		Climbing Hybrid Tea
Pleine de Grâce		white	Z5		Shrub
'Pompon Blanc Parfait'		blush white	Z4	C	Alba
'Président de Sèze'	🏆	lilac-pink with purplish cerise center	Z4	C	Gallica
primula (foliage)	🏆	pale yellow	Z4	C	Shrub
'Princesse de Nassau'		cream	Z6	H	Rambler
'Professeur Emile Perrot'		pink	Z5		Damask
'Rambling Rector'	🏆	white	Z5		Rambler
'Reine des Centifeuilles'		pink	Z5		Centifolia
'Reine Victoria'		pink	Z5		Bourbon
'Rose à Parfum de l'Haÿ'		purplish crimson	Z4	C	Rugosa
Rosemary Harkness		orange-salmon	Z5		Hybrid Tea
'Roseraie de l'Haÿ'	🏆	purplish crimson	Z4	C	Rugosa
Royal Dane®		vermilion	Z5		Hybrid Tea
rubiginosa (foliage)	🏆	pink	Z4	C	Sweet-briar
rugosa 'Alba'	🏆	white	Z3	C	Rugosa
rugosa 'Rubra'	🏆	cerise-red	Z4	C	Rugosa
'Ruskin'		crimson	Z5	C	Rugosa
Saint Swithun		pink	Z5		Shrub (English rose)
'Schoolgirl'		apricot	Z5		Climbing
'Shailer's White Moss	🏆	white	Z5		Moss
Sharifa Asma®		pale pink	Z5		Shrub (English rose)
Sheila's Perfume		peach edged red	Z5		Floribunda
'Sombreuil'		white	Z7	H	Climbing Tea
'Souvenir d'Alphonse Lavallée'		deep red	Z5		Climbing Hybrid Perpetual
'Souvenir de la Malmaison'		blush pink	Z6	H	Bourbon
'Souvenir de Philémon Cochet'		white	Z4	C	Rugosa
'Splendens'		blush white	Z5		Rambler
Susan Hampshire		pink	Z5		Hybrid Tea
Sympathie®		crimson	Z5		Climbing
The Compass Rose		white	Z5		Shrub (English rose)
The Countryman®		deep pink	Z5		Shrub (English rose)
The McCartney Rose		deep pink	Z5		Hybrid Tea
The Prince®		deep crimson ageing purplish	Z5		Shrub (English rose)
'Thisbe'		pale yellow	Z5		Hybrid Musk
Toulouse-Lautrec®		yellow	Z5		Shrub (Romantica® series)
'Treasure Trove'		pale apricot	Z5		Rambler
'Tuscany Superb'	🏆	deep red ageing purplish	Z4	C	Gallica
Tynwald		cream	Z5		Hybrid Tea
'Typhoon'		coral	Z5		Hybrid Tea
'Unique Blanche'		white	Z5		Centifolia
Valentine Heart		pink	Z5		Floribunda
'Vanity'		cerise	Z5	H	Hybrid Musk
'Wedding Day'		white	Z5		Rambler
Westerland™	🏆	apricot	Z5		Floribunda
'Wickwar'		creamy white	Z5		Rambler
'William Lobb'	🏆	purple	Z5		Moss
Windrush®		pale yellow	Z5		Shrub
'Zéphirine Drouhin'	🏆	cerise-pink	Z5		Bourbon

Roses for Hanging Baskets

The choice of variety is determined by the size of container and by the ability of the rose to clothe it attractively, preferably hiding the basket. A graceful, recumbent habit of growth, and fairly small leaves help. A fairly light soilless compost is generally preferable for hanging baskets, and so accurate feeding is important: the compost should include slow-release fertilizer, supplemented by liquid feed whenever the roses show signs of starvation. As with any container, moisture-retentive polymer granules incorporated in the compost can help regulate water availability.

Aspen		yellow	Z5	Ground Cover
Avon		blush pink	Z5	Ground Cover/Patio
Blenheim (syn. Schneesturm®)		white	Z5	Ground Cover
Hertfordshire		cerise	Z5	Ground Cover
Kent®		white	Z5	Shrub/Ground Cover
Magic Carpet		magenta-pink	Z5	Shrub/Ground Cover
Pathfinder		vermilion	Z5	Ground Cover
Queen Mother	🏆	pink	Z5	Patio
Wiltshire		salmon pink	Z5	Shrub/Ground Cover

Roses for Hedges

Here choice depends on the required height and the width of the available site. Narrowly upright roses often have poorly furnished bases and benefit from a planting of other roses, small shrubs, herbaceous plants or even annuals to hide ugly ankles. The overall appearance of the rose should be attractive, even when out of flower, with pleasing foliage and a fairly dense, not straggly habit. Pruning of individual bushes is likely to be too labor-intensive for a long hedge: ability to tolerate annual trimming with hedge-cutters or even a clearing saw is an advantage. Roses for even the largest hedges are included here, some of them suitable for the perimeter of the wild garden. Shorter varieties such as Miniatures and Patio roses, or, if more informality is required, Ground Cover varieties, can be used as an edging.

Abraham Darby®		blush pink	Z5		Shrub (English rose)
'Agnes'		light yellow	Z3	C	Rugosa
'Alba Maxima'	🏆	white	Z4	C	Alba
'Alba Semiplena'	🏆	white	Z4	C	Alba
Anne Harkness		apricot	Z5		Floribunda
'Ballerina'	🏆	pink	Z5		Hybrid Musk/Polyantha
'Belle Poitevine'		magenta-pink	Z3	C	Rugosa
'Blanche Double de Coubert'	🏆	white	Z3	C	Rugosa
Bonica®	🏆	pink	Z5	C	Shrub/Ground Cover
'Buff Beauty'	🏆	pale apricot	Z5		Hybrid Musk
Centenaire de Lourdes®		pink	Z5		Floribunda
'Charles de Mills'	🏆	purplish crimson	Z4	C	Gallica
'Cornelia'	🏆	coppery pink	Z5		Hybrid Musk
'De Meaux'		pink	Z5		Centifolia
Escapade®	🏆	mauve-pink	Z5		Floribunda
'Eutin'		deep carmine	Z5		Floribunda
'Excellenz von Schubert'		pink	Z5		Polyantha
'Fantin-Latour'	🏆	pale pink	Z5		Centifolia
'Felicia'	🏆	pale pink	Z5		Hybrid Musk
'Fervid'		scarlet	Z5		Floribunda
Freedom®	🏆	yellow	Z5		Hybrid Tea
'Fru Dagmar Hastrup'	🏆	pink	Z4	C	Rugosa
gallica var. *officinalis*	🏆	cerise-red	Z4	C	Gallica
gallica 'Versicolor' (Rosa Mundi)	🏆	cerise-red striped white	Z4	C	Gallica
Glamis Castle		white	Z5		Shrub (English rose)
'Hansa'		magenta-cerise	Z3	C	Rugosa
'Henry Hudson'		white	Z3	C	Rugosa
Iceberg	🏆	white	Z5	H	Floribunda
L.D. Braithwaite®		crimson	Z5		Shrub (English rose)
'Mabel Morrison'		white	Z5		Hybrid Perpetual
'Mme Caroline Testout'		pink	Z5		Hybrid Tea
'Marchesa Boccella' (syn. 'Jacques Cartier')	🏆	pink	Z4	H	Portland Damask
'Marguerite Hilling'	🏆	pink	Z5		Shrub
'Marie-Jeanne'		white	Z5		Polyantha
'Marie Pavic'		blush white	Z5		Polyantha
Marjorie Fair®		crimson with white eye	Z5		Polyantha/Shrub
'Martin Frobisher'		pink	Z3	C	Rugosa
'Mevrouw Nathalie Nypels'	🏆	pink	Z5		Polyantha
'Morden Blush'		pale pink	Z3	C	Shrub
'Nevada'		pale yellow ageing white flushed pink	Z4	C	Shrub
'Penelope'	🏆	palest peach fading white	Z5		Hybrid Musk
'Petite de Hollande'		pink	Z5		Centifolia
pimpinellifolia 'Double White'		white	Z3	C	Shrub
pimpinellifolia 'Grandiflora'		pale yellow	Z3	C	Shrub
Princess Alice		yellow	Z5		Floribunda
'Prosperity'	🏆	blush white	Z5		Hybrid Musk
'Rose à Parfum de l'Haÿ'		purplish crimson	Z4	C	Rugosa
'Rosa Zwerg' (syn. Dwarf Pavement)		pink	Z4	C	Rugosa

'Roseraie de l'Haÿ'	🏆	purplish crimson	Z4	C	Rugosa
'Rose d'Amour'	🏆	pink	Z5		Shrub
rubiginosa	🏆	pink	Z4	C	Sweet-briar
rugosa 'Alba'	🏆	white	Z3	C	Rugosa
rugosa 'Rubra'	🏆	cerise-red	Z4	C	Rugosa
Sally Holmes®		blush white	Z5		Shrub/Hybrid Musk
'Scabrosa'	🏆	magenta-pink	Z3	C	Rugosa
Schnee-Eule® (syns. Snowy Owl, White Pavement)		white	Z3	C	Rugosa/Ground Cover
'Schneezwerg'	🏆	white	Z4	C	Rugosa
'Souvenir de Philémon Cochet'		white	Z4	C	Rugosa
'The Fairy'	🏆	pink	Z5	H	Polyantha
The McCartney Rose		deep pink	Z5		Hybrid Tea
'Thisbe'		pale yellow	Z5		Hybrid Musk
Toulouse-Lautrec®		yellow	Z5		Shrub (Romantica® series)
'Vanity'		cerise	Z5	H	Hybrid Musk
'White Pet'	🏆	white	Z5		Polyantha
Windrush®		pale yellow	Z5		Shrub
'Zigeunerknabe'	🏆	purplish crimson	Z5		Shrub

Roses for Pergolas, Arcades and Catenaries

These should have a graceful habit of growth, a moderate number of lax (and so easily trained) shoots (not just one or two), foliage that is not too coarse and preferably pendulous flower stems. Few Climbing Hybrid Teas or Climbing Floribundas fulfil these criteria and they are thus excluded unless they have supreme floral quality. The roses should reach to the top of the pergola's or arcade's pier and at least halfway towards the adjacent pier, requiring an ideal height of about 13-16ft/4-5m; this excludes many favorite and otherwise excellent Ramblers. Some early and late varieties are identified to help synchronize the flowering of roses with that of their companion plants.

E = early L = late

'Adélaïde d'Orléans'	🏆	white (light pink)		Z5		Rambler
'Aimée Vibert'		blush white		Z5		Noisette
'Albéric Barbier'	🏆	cream	E	Z6		Rambler
'Albertine'	🏆	coppery pink	E	Z5		Rambler
'Alexandre Girault'		cerise		Z5		Rambler
'Alexandre Tremouillet'		creamy white with pale yellow center		Z5		Rambler
'Alister Stella Grey'	🏆	light yellow		Z7	H	Noisette
'Auguste Gervais'		pale apricot		Z5		Rambler
'Aviateur Blériot'		pale apricot yellow	E	Z5		Rambler
Awakening		light pink		Z5		Rambler
banksiae var. *banksiae*		white	E	Z8	H	Rambler
banksiae var. *lutea*	🏆	soft yellow	E	Z7	H	Rambler
'Black Boy'		crimson		Z7	H	Climbing
'Blairii Number Two'	🏆	pink		Z5		Climbing Bourbon
'Bleu Magenta'		purple		Z5		Rambler
'Blush Rambler'		pink		Z5		Rambler
'Céline Forestier'	🏆	pale yellow		Z7	H	Noisette
'Chaplin's Pink Climber'		carmine-pink		Z5		Climbing
City of York		white		Z5		Climbing
'Climbing Cécile Brünner'	🏆	pink		Z5	H	Climbing Polyantha
'Climbing Ena Harkness'		red		Z5		Climbing Hybrid Tea
'Climbing Iceberg'	🏆	white		Z5	H	Climbing Floribunda
'Climbing Mme Caroline Testout'		pink		Z5		Climbing Hybrid Tea
'Climbing Mrs Herbert Stevens'		white		Z6	H	Climbing Hybrid Tea
'Climbing Paul Lédé'		peach-pink		Z7	H	Climbing Tea
'Crépuscule'		apricot		Z7	H	Noisette
'Crimson Shower'	🏆	light crimson	L	Z5		Rambler
'Debutante'		pink	L	Z5		Rambler
'Desprez à Fleurs Jaunes'	🏆	soft yellow		Z7	H	Noisette
'Dorothy Perkins'		pink	L	Z5	H	Rambler
'Dundee Rambler'		white		Z5		Rambler
'Edmond Proust'		light pink		Z5		Rambler
'Elisa Robichon'		pale blush		Z5		Rambler
'Emily Gray'		soft yellow		Z6		Rambler
'Félicité Perpétue'	🏆	white with pink blush		Z5	H	Rambler
'Flora'		pink		Z5		Rambler
'Francis E. Lester'	🏆	pink		Z5		Rambler
'François Juranville'	🏆	salmon	E	Z5		Rambler
'Gardenia'		creamy white		Z7	H	Rambler
'Ghislaine de Féligonde'		pale apricot		Z6		Rambler
'Gloire de Dijon'	🏆	apricot-buff		Z7	H	Climbing Tea
'Jean Guichard'		deep pink		Z7	H	Rambler
'Kew Rambler'		pink		Z5		Rambler
'La Follette'		pink ageing carmine		Z7	H	Climbing

'Lamarque'		white		Z7	H	Noisette
'Laure Davoust'		pink		Z5		Rambler
Lawinia®	🏆	rich pink		Z5		Climbing Hybrid Tea
'Léontine Gervais'		apricot-pink blend	E	Z5		Rambler
'Mme Alfred Carrière'		white	E	Z6	H	Noisette
'Mme Driout'		pink striped carmine		Z7	H	Climbing Tea
'Mme Grégoire Staechelin'	🏆	rich pink		Z5		Climbing Hybrid Tea
'Maréchal Niel'		soft yellow		Z7	H	Noisette
'May Queen'		pink		Z5		Rambler
'Mermaid'	🏆	pale yellow		Z6	H	Climbing
mulliganii	🏆	white		Z5		Rambler
'Narrow Water'		pale pink		Z6		Noisette
'New Dawn'		pale pink		Z5		Climbing/Rambler
'Paul Noël'		coppery salmon	E	Z5		Rambler
'Paul Transon'	🏆	coppery salmon		Z5		Rambler
'Rêve d'Or'		buff-yellow		Z7	H	Noisette
'Rose-Marie Viaud'		cerise-purple ageing grayish purple	L	Z5		Rambler
'Seagull'	🏆	white		Z5		Rambler
'Sombreuil'		white		Z7	H	Climbing Tea
Summer Wine	🏆	coral		Z5		Climbing
Super Excelsa®		crimson		Z5		Rambler
Super Sparkle		crimson		Z5		Rambler
'Tausendschön'		peach blend		Z5	H	Rambler
'Tea Rambler'		pink		Z5		Rambler
'Treasure Trove'		pale apricot		Z5		Rambler
'Veilchenblau'	🏆	purple	E	Z5		Rambler
'Violette'		purple		Z5		Rambler
'William Allen Richardson'		apricot-yellow		Z7	H	Noisette

Roses for Pillars

Varieties listed here are suitable also for cones and obelisks. Such features are often used as exclamation marks in the garden and so the impact of strong color may be useful. Spiral training gives better flower production and therefore pliable stems are an advantage. Because the individual shoots and leaves are scarcely visible, the rose's habit and foliage are less important than usual.

'Albéric Barbier'	🏆	cream	Z6		Rambler
'Albertine'	🏆	coppery pink	Z5		Rambler
'Alchymist'		apricot-yellow	Z5		Climbing/Shrub
'Alexandre Tremouillet'		creamy white with pale yellow center	Z5		Rambler
Altissimo®	🏆	red	Z5		Climbing
Antique '89®		pale pink edged rose red	Z5		Climbing
'Auguste Gervais'		pale apricot	Z5		Rambler
'Aviateur Blériot'		pale apricot-yellow	Z5		Rambler
Awakening		light pink	Z5		Rambler
'Black Boy'		crimson	Z7	H	Climbing
'Blairii Number Two'	🏆	pink	Z5		Climbing Bourbon
'Bleu Magenta'		purple	Z5		Rambler
'Blossomtime'		pink	Z5		Climbing
'Blush Rambler'		pink	Z5		Rambler
'Blushing Lucy'		pink	Z5		Rambler
'Bougainville'		lilac-pink	Z7	H	Noisette
'Captain Samuel Holland'		pink	Z3	C	Shrub/Climbing
Casino®		yellow	Z5	H	Climbing Hybrid Tea
'Champneys' Pink Cluster'		pale blush	Z7	H	Noisette
'Chaplin's Pink Climber'		carmine-pink	Z5		Climbing
'Cherub'		salmon pink	Z7	H	Rambler
City of York		white	Z5		Climbing
Clair Matin®		pale pink	Z5		Climbing
'Climbing Blue Moon'		mauve	Z5	H	Climbing Hybrid Tea
'Climbing Ena Harkness'		red	Z5		Climbing Hybrid Tea
'Climbing Etoile de Hollande'	🏆	deep red	Z5		Climbing Hybrid Tea
Climbing Gold Badge		yellow	Z5	H	Climbing Hybrid Tea
'Climbing Iceberg'	🏆	white	Z5	H	Climbing Floribunda
'Climbing Masquerade'		yellow ageing to red	Z5		Climbing Floribunda
'Climbing McGredy's Yellow'		pale yellow	Z5		Climbing Hybrid Tea
'Climbing Mrs Herbert Stevens'		white	Z6	H	Climbing Hybrid Tea
'Crépuscule'		apricot	Z7	H	Noisette
'Crimson Shower'	🏆	light crimson	Z5		Rambler
'Debutante'		pink	Z5		Rambler
'Dorothy Perkins'		pink	Z5	H	Rambler
'Dream Girl'	🏆	salmon pink	Z5		Climbing
'Easlea's Golden Rambler'		soft yellow	Z5		Rambler
'Edmond Proust'		light pink	Z5		Rambler

'Emily Gray'		soft yellow	Z6		Rambler
'François Juranville'	🏆	salmon	Z5		Rambler
Galway Bay®		cerise-coral	Z5		Climbing Hybrid Tea
'Gardenia'		creamy white	Z7	H	Rambler
'Ghislaine de Féligonde'		pale apricot	Z6		Rambler
Gloriana '97		cerise-pink	Z5		Climbing Miniature
Golden Showers®	🏆	soft yellow	Z5		Climbing
'Goldfinch'		cream	Z5		Rambler
Good as Gold		yellow	Z5		Climbing Miniature
Handel®	🏆	pale pink edged cerise	Z5		Climbing
'Heideröslein'		pink	Z5		Rambler/Shrub
High Hopes		pink	Z5		Climbing
'Jeanne Lajoie'		pink	Z5	C	Climbing Miniature
'Kew Rambler'		pink	Z5		Rambler
'Laure Davoust'		pink	Z5		Rambler
Lawinia®	🏆	rich pink	Z5		Climbing Hybrid Tea
Leaping Salmon		salmon pink	Z5		Climbing Hybrid Tea
'Léontine Gervais'		apricot-pink blend	Z5		Rambler
'Leverkusen'		pale yellow	Z5		Climbing
'Mme de Sancy de Parabère'		pink	Z5		Boursault
'Mme Driout'		pink striped carmine	Z7	H	Climbing Tea
'Mme Grégoire Staechelin'	🏆	rich pink	Z5		Climbing Hybrid Tea
'Mme Hardy'	🏆	white	Z4	C	Climbing Damask
'Mme Isaac Pereire'	🏆	cerise	Z5		Climbing Bourbon
'Mme Lauriol de Barny'		pink	Z		Bourbon
'Mme Legras de Saint Germain'	🏆	white	Z5		Alba × Noisette
'Mme Plantier'	🏆	white	Z5		Alba × Noisette
'Maigold'	🏆	golden yellow	Z5		Pimpinellifolia Hybrid
'Mary Wallace'		pink	Z		Climbing
'May Queen'		pink	Z5		Rambler
'Mrs F.W. Flight'		deep pink	Z5		Rambler
multiflora 'Carnea'		pink	Z5		Rambler
'New Dawn'		pale pink	Z5		Climbing/Rambler
Night Light®		golden yellow	Z5		Climbing
'Noisette Carnée' (Blush Noisette)		pink	Z6	H	Noisette
'Parade'	🏆	cerise	Z5		Climbing
Parure d'Or®		soft yellow, edges suffused deep pink	Z5		Climbing Hybrid Tea
'Paul Noël'		coppery salmon	Z5		Rambler
'Paul Transon'	🏆	coppery salmon	Z5		Rambler
'Paul's Lemon Pillar'		pale lemon	Z5		Climbing Hybrid Tea
'Paul's Scarlet Climber'		light red	Z5		Climbing/Rambler
Penny Lane		blush, pale peach center	Z5		Climbing
Pheasant (syn. Heidekönigin®)		pink	Z5		Climbing Miniature/ Ground Cover
'Phyllis Bide'	🏆	pale peach blend	Z5		Rambler
'Pink Perpétué'		pink	Z5		Climbing
Polka®		peach	Z5		Climbing (Romantica® series)
'Rose-Marie Viaud'		cerise-purple ageing grayish purple	Z5		Rambler
'Rosy Mantle'		deep pink	Z5		Climbing
'Royal Gold'		golden yellow	Z5	H	Climbing
'Sander's White Rambler'	🏆	white	Z5		Rambler
'Schoolgirl'		apricot	Z5		Climbing
'Souvenir de Claudius Denoyel'		deep red	Z5		Climbing Hybrid Tea
'Souvenir de Mme Léonie Viennot'		coppery pink	Z7	H	Climbing Tea
Sparkling Scarlet		scarlet	Z5		Climbing Floribunda
Summer Wine	🏆	coral	Z5		Climbing
Super Dorothy®		pink	Z5		Rambler
Super Excelsa®		crimson	Z5		Rambler
Super Fairy		pink	Z5		Rambler
Super Sparkle		crimson	Z5		Rambler
'Swan Lake'		pale blush pink	Z5		Climbing
'Tausendschön'		peach blend	Z5	H	Rambler
'Veilchenblau'	🏆	purple	Z5		Rambler
'Venusta Pendula'		blush white	Z5		Rambler
'Violette'		purple	Z5		Rambler
Warm Welcome	🏆	vermilion	Z5		Climbing Miniature

Roses for Pots or Containers

A graceful habit of growth and reasonably good foliage are advantages for these; recumbent Ground Cover varieties that arch over the edge of the container can often be extremely effective. The flower color should not clash with a container: terracotta can clash hideously with carmine- or mauve-pink roses. I have not included the Hybrid Perpetuals, Teas and old Hybrid Teas that were popularly grown in pots a hundred years ago: these demand careful attention to training and disbudding, more labor than most gardeners would want to devote to them, though they could doubtless still provide a *tour de force* for fanatical gardeners. Climbing Miniatures are suitable for cones or pyramids placed in large pots or containers.

Apricot Summer®		peach-pink	Z5		Patio
Aspen		yellow	Z5		Ground Cover
Avon		blush pink	Z5		Ground Cover/Patio
Blenheim		white	Z5		Ground Cover
Brass Ring		peach-orange blend	Z5		Miniature/Patio
Bush Baby		pale salmon	Z5		Miniature
Cider Cup	🏆	deep apricot	Z5		Miniature/Patio
Gingernut		russet	Z5		Patio
Gloriana '97		cerise-pink	Z5		Climbing Miniature
Golden Jewel		yellow	Z5		Patio
Good as Gold		yellow	Z5		Climbing Miniature
Hertfordshire		cerise	Z5		Ground Cover
'Jeanne Lajoie'		pink	Z5	C	Climbing Miniature
Kent®		white	Z5		Shrub/Ground Cover
Laura Ford®	🏆	yellow ageing peach	Z5		Climbing Miniature
Little Bo-Peep		pink	Z5		Miniature/Patio
Little Rambler		pale pink	Z5		Climbing Miniature
Lovely Fairy®		pink	Z5		Polyantha/Ground Cover
Magic Carpet		magenta-pink	Z5		Shrub/Ground Cover
Marry Me		pink	Z5		Patio
Nice Day		salmon pink	Z5		Climbing Miniature
Orange Sunblaze®		orange	Z5		Miniature
Pathfinder		vermilion	Z5		Ground Cover
Pink Symphony		pink	Z5		Miniature
Queen Mother	🏆	pink	Z5		Patio
Robin Redbreast®		deep scarlet with white eye	Z5		Miniature/Ground Cover/Patio
Rosalie Coral		vermilion	Z5		Climbing Miniature
Shine On		orange-coral	Z5		Patio
Suma	🏆	cerise	Z5		Ground Cover
Sun Hit™		deep yellow	Z5		Patio
Sweet Dream	🏆	peachy apricot	Z5		Patio
Sweet Magic	🏆	orange	Z5		Miniature/Patio
Sweet Memories		pale yellow	Z5		Patio
Tiger Cub		gold striped crimson	Z5		Patio
Top Marks		vermilion	Z5		Miniature/Patio
Warm Welcome	🏆	vermilion	Z5		Climbing Miniature
'White Pet'	🏆	white	Z5		Polyantha
Wiltshire		salmon pink	Z5		Shrub/Ground Cover

Roses for Shade and for Walls Facing Away From the Sun

Gardeners in cool temperate regions tend to assume that roses prefer full sun, though many will tolerate an open aspect without sun or sites where they are only in the sun for a part of the day. In hotter climates, roses will tolerate more shade and the range of varieties that will thrive in part shade is much greater. Albas, Rugosas and Hybrid Musks are among the classes of roses that perform tolerably in part shade.

'Alba Maxima'	🏆	white	Z4	C	Alba
Alba Meidiland®		white	Z5		Shrub/Ground Cover
'Alba Semiplena'	🏆	white	Z4	C	Alba
'Albéric Barbier'	🏆	cream	Z6		Rambler
Awakening		light pink	Z5		Rambler
'Belle Poitevine'		magenta-pink	Z3	C	Rugosa
'Belvedere'		pink	Z5		Rambler
'Blanche Double de Coubert'	🏆	white	Z3	C	Rugosa
'Bourbon Queen'		pink	Z5		Bourbon
'Buff Beauty'	🏆	pale apricot	Z5		Hybrid Musk
californica		pink	Z3	C	Shrub
Casino®		yellow	Z5	H	Climbing Hybrid Tea
'Céleste' (syn. 'Celestial')	🏆	pink	Z4	C	Alba
'Cerise Bouquet'	🏆	cerise	Z5		Shrub
'Chloris'		pale pink	Z4	C	Alba
City of York		white	Z5		Climbing
'Climbing Paul Lédé'		peach-pink	Z7	H	Climbing Tea
'Complicata'	🏆	pink	Z4	C	Gallica
'Conrad Ferdinand Meyer'		pink	Z5	C	Rugosa
'Cornelia'	🏆	coppery pink	Z5		Hybrid Musk
'Dentelle de Malines'		pale pink	Z5		Shrub
'Dundee Rambler'		white	Z5		Rambler
'Emily Gray'		soft yellow	Z6		Rambler

Name		Color	Zone		Type
'Felicia'	🏆	pale pink	Z5		Hybrid Musk
'Félicité Parmentier'	🏆	pale pink	Z5		Alba × Damask
'Félicité Perpétue'	🏆	white with pink blush	Z5	H	Rambler
'Fimbriata'		pink	Z5	C	Rugosa
'Flora'		pink	Z5		Rambler
Francine Austin®		white	Z5		Shrub (English rose)
'Fred Loads'		vermilion	Z5		Floribunda
'Fru Dagmar Hastrup'	🏆	pink	Z4	C	Rugosa
gallica var. *officinalis*	🏆	cerise-red	Z4	C	Gallica
glauca (syn. *R. rubrifolia*)	🏆	deep pink	Z4	C	Shrub
'Gloire de Dijon'	🏆	apricot-buff	Z7	H	Climbing Tea
Golden Showers®	🏆	soft yellow	Z5		Climbing
'Goldfinch'		cream	Z5		Rambler
'Great Maiden's Blush'		white with pink blush	Z4	C	Alba
'Grootendorst Supreme'		deep crimson	Z4	C	Rugosa
'Hansa'		magenta-cerise	Z3	C	Rugosa
× *harisonii* 'Harison's Yellow'		yellow	Z4	C	Pimpinellifolia Hybrid
'Henry Hudson'		white	Z3	C	Rugosa
'Henry Kelsey'		red	Z3	C	Climbing
'Honorine de Brabant'		pale pink striped cerise	Z5		Bourbon
'Jens Munk'		pink	Z2	C	Rugosa
'Kathleen Harrop'		pale magenta-pink	Z5		Bourbon
'Königin von Dänemark'	🏆	pink	Z4	C	Alba
'Lavender Lassie'	🏆	mauve-pink	Z5		Hybrid Musk
'Leverkusen'		pale yellow	Z5		Climbing
Linda Campbell		crimson	Z4	C	Rugosa
'Louise Odier'		pink	Z5		Bourbon
'Mme Alfred Carrière'		white	Z6	H	Noisette
'Mme Alice Garnier'		pink	Z		Rambler
'Mme de Sancy de Parabère'		pink	Z		Boursault
'Mme Ernest Calvat'		pink	Z5	H	Bourbon
'Mme Grégoire Staechelin'	🏆	rich pink	Z5		Climbing Hybrid Tea
'Mme Hardy'	🏆	white	Z4	C	Climbing Damask
'Mme Isaac Pereire'	🏆	cerise	Z5		Climbing Bourbon
'Mme Lauriol de Barny'		pink	Z		Bourbon
'Mme Plantier'	🏆	white	Z5		Alba × Noisette
'Maiden's Blush'		white with pink blush	Z4	C	Alba
'Maigold'	🏆	golden yellow	Z5		Pimpinellifolia Hybrid
'Martin Frobisher'		pink	Z3	C	Rugosa
'May Queen'		pink	Z5		Rambler
'Mermaid'	🏆	pale yellow	Z6	H	Climbing
Moje Hammarberg®		magenta-pink	Z3	C	Rugosa
'Moonlight'		pale yellow fading white	Z5		Hybrid Musk
'Morden Blush'		pale pink	Z3	C	Shrub
'Morden Centennial'		cerise-pink	Z4	C	Shrub
'Morden Ruby'		deep pink	Z4	C	Shrub
'Mrs Anthony Waterer'		purplish crimson	Z5	C	Rugosa
Mrs Doreen Pike		pink	Z5	C	Rugosa (English rose)
'Nevada'		pale yellow ageing white flushed pink	Z4	C	Shrub
'New Dawn'		pale pink	Z5		Climbing/Rambler
nitida		pink	Z4	C	Shrub/Ground Cover
'Nova Zembla'		blush white	Z5	C	Rugosa
nutkana 'Plena'	🏆	pink	Z4	C	Shrub
'Nyveldt's White'		white	Z4	C	Rugosa
'Parade'	🏆	cerise	Z5		Climbing
'Paul's Lemon Pillar'		pale lemon	Z5		Climbing Hybrid Tea
'Paul's Scarlet Climber'		light red	Z5		Climbing/Rambler
Pearl Drift®		pearly white	Z5		Shrub
'Penelope'	🏆	palest peach fading white	Z5		Hybrid Musk
pimpinellifolia 'Grandiflora'		pale yellow	Z3	C	Shrub
pimpinellifolia 'Mary, Queen of Scots'		pale lilac shaded plum	Z3	C	Shrub
'Pink Grootendorst'	🏆	pink	Z4	C	Rugosa
Pink Robusta®		pink	Z5		Shrub
Pleine de Grâce		white	Z5		Shrub
'Pompon Blanc Parfait'		blush white	Z4	C	Alba
'Prosperity'	🏆	blush white	Z5		Hybrid Musk
'Raubritter'		pink	Z4	C	Shrub/Rambler
Robusta®		scarlet	Z4	C	Rugosa
Roselina®		cerise-pink	Z4	C	Rugosa/Ground Cover
'Rosa Zwerg' (syn. Dwarf Pavement)		pink	Z4	C	Rugosa
'Rose à Parfum de l'Haÿ'		purplish crimson	Z4	C	Rugosa
'Roseraie de l'Haÿ'	🏆	purplish crimson	Z4	C	Rugosa
Rote Max Graf®		scarlet	Z4	C	Ground Cover/Rugosa

Name		Color	Zone		Type
'Rotes Meer' (syn. Purple Pavement)		purplish crimson	Z4	C	Rugosa
rugosa 'Alba'	🏆	white	Z3	C	Rugosa
rugosa 'Rubra'	🏆	cerise-red	Z4	C	Rugosa
'Rugspin'		red	Z4	C	Rugosa
'Ruskin'		crimson	Z5	C	Rugosa
Sally Holmes®		blush white	Z5		Shrub/Hybrid Musk
'Scabrosa'	🏆	magenta-pink	Z3	C	Rugosa
'Scharlachglut'	🏆	scarlet	Z5		Shrub
Schnee-Eule® (syns. Snowy Owl, White Pavement)		white	Z3	C	Rugosa/Ground Cover
'Schneekoppe'		white flushed pink	Z3	C	Rugosa
'Schneezwerg'	🏆	white	Z4	C	Rugosa
'Souvenir de Claudius Denoyel'		deep red	Z5		Climbing Hybrid Tea
'Souvenir de Philémon Cochet'		white	Z4	C	Rugosa
'Splendens'		blush white	Z5		Rambler
'Stanwell Perpetual'		pale blush pink	Z3	C	Pimpinellifolia Hybrid
Sympathie®		crimson	Z5		Climbing
'The Fairy'	🏆	pink	Z5	H	Polyantha
'Thérèse Bugnet'		pink	Z3	C	Rugosa
'Thisbe'		pale yellow	Z5		Hybrid Musk
Topaz Jewel		pale yellow	Z4	C	Rugosa
'Treasure Trove'		pale apricot	Z5		Rambler
'Veilchenblau'	🏆	purple	Z5		Rambler
villosa		pink	Z4	C	Shrub
virginiana	🏆	pink	Z3	C	Shrub
Westerland™	🏆	apricot	Z5		Floribunda
'White Grootendorst'		white	Z4	C	Rugosa
'William Baffin'		pink	Z3	C	Rugosa/Climbing Rugosa
'Wolley-Dod'		pink	Z4	C	Shrub
woodsii		pink	Z3	C	Shrub
'Zéphirine Drouhin'	🏆	cerise-pink	Z5		Bourbon

Roses for Standards

I have already expressed my dislike for roses with a stiff habit of growth and coarse foliage when used as standards. Thus I have excluded most Hybrid Teas and Floribundas that show poor leaves and hold up the ugly base of the head of the standard and prefer weeping or recumbent varieties.

Name		Color	Zone		Type
Alba Meidiland®		white	Z5		Shrub/Ground Cover
'Albéric Barbier'	🏆	cream	Z6		Rambler
'Albertine'	🏆	coppery pink	Z5		Rambler
'Alexandre Tremouillet'		creamy white with pale yellow center	Z5		Rambler
Aspen		yellow	Z5		Ground Cover
'Auguste Gervais'		pale apricot	Z5		Rambler
'Aviateur Blériot'		pale apricot-yellow	Z5		Rambler
Avon		blush pink	Z5		Ground Cover/Patio
Awakening		light pink	Z5		Rambler
'Ballerina'	🏆	pink	Z5		Hybrid Musk/Polyantha
Blenheim (syn. Schneesturm®)		white	Z5		Ground Cover
Centenaire de Lourdes®		pink	Z5		Floribunda
'Climbing Pompon de Paris'		deep pink	Z6	H	Climbing China
'Crimson Shower'	🏆	light crimson	Z5		Rambler
'Debutante'		pink	Z5		Rambler
'Dorothy Perkins'		pink	Z5	H	Rambler
Douceur Normande®		coral pink	Z5	C	Shrub/Ground Cover
Eyeopener		red	Z5		Ground Cover
'Félicité Perpétue'	🏆	white with pink blush	Z5	H	Rambler
Flower Carpet™		deep pink	Z5		Ground Cover
'François Juranville'	🏆	salmon	Z5		Rambler
'Gardenia'		creamy white	Z7	H	Rambler
Grouse		white	Z5		Ground Cover
Grouse 2000		blush white	Z5		Ground Cover
'Heideröslein'		pink	Z5		Rambler/Shrub
Heideschnee®		white	Z5		Ground Cover
Hertfordshire		cerise	Z5		Ground Cover
'Jeanne Lajoie'		pink	Z5	C	Climbing Miniature
'Katharina Zeimet'		white	Z5		Polyantha
Kent®		white	Z5		Shrub/Ground Cover
'Laure Davoust'		pink	Z5		Rambler
'Léontine Gervais'		apricot-pink blend	Z5		Rambler
Lovely Fairy®		pink	Z5		Polyantha/Ground Cover
'Mme Caroline Testout'		pink	Z5		Hybrid Tea
'May Queen'		pink	Z5		Rambler
'Neige d'Avril'		white	Z5		Rambler
'New Dawn'		pale pink	Z5		Climbing/Rambler

Name		Color		Zone		Type
Nice Day		salmon pink		Z5		Climbing Miniature
'Paul Noël'		coppery salmon		Z5		Rambler
'Paul Transon'	🏆	coppery salmon		Z5		Rambler
Pheasant (syn. Heidekönigin®)		pink		Z5		Climbing Miniature/ Ground Cover
'Phyllis Bide'	🏆	pale peach blend		Z5		Rambler
Pink Bells®		pink		Z5		Ground Cover
Red Blanket®	🏆	red		Z5		Shrub/Ground Cover
Red Trail		red		Z5		Shrub/Ground Cover
Rosalie Coral		vermilion		Z5		Climbing Miniature
'Sander's White Rambler'	🏆	white		Z5		Rambler
Snow Carpet®	🏆	white		Z5		Ground Cover
Super Dorothy®		pink		Z5		Rambler
Super Excelsa®		crimson		Z5		Rambler
Super Fairy		pink		Z5		Rambler
Super Sparkle		crimson		Z5		Rambler
Surrey	🏆	pink		Z5		Shrub/Ground Cover
Sussex		apricot		Z5		Ground Cover
Swany®	🏆	white		Z5		Miniature/Ground Cover
Tumbling Waters		white		Z5		Shrub
'Veilchenblau'	🏆	purple		Z5		Rambler
Warm Welcome	🏆	vermilion		Z5		Climbing Miniature
'White Pet'	🏆	white		Z5		Polyantha

Roses for Training into Trees

These are discussed more fully in the chapter on Roses for Wild Gardens. Those that are too vigorous to be grown over shrubs or into small trees and are impractical to prune once entangled with their support are annotated with a V for vigorous.

Name		Color		Zone		Type
'Adélaïde d'Orléans'	🏆	white (light pink)		Z5		Rambler
'Aimée Vibert'		blush white		Z5		Noisette
'Albéric Barbier'	🏆	cream		Z6		Rambler
'Alexandre Girault'		cerise		Z5		Rambler
'Alexandre Tremouillet'		creamy white with pale yellow center		Z		Rambler
'Auguste Gervais'		pale apricot		Z5		Rambler
Awakening		light pink		Z5		Rambler
banksiae var. *banksiae*		white		Z8	H	Rambler
banksiae var. *lutea*	🏆	soft yellow		Z7	H	Rambler
'Belvedere'		pink	V	Z5		Rambler
'Bennett's Seedling'		white		Z5		Rambler
'Bobbie James'	🏆	white	V	Z5		Rambler
'Brenda Colvin'		pale blush pink	V	Z5		Rambler
brunonii 'La Mortola'		creamy white	V	Z6		Rambler
'Claire Jacquier'		pale yellow		Z7	H	Noisette
'Climbing Masquerade'		yellow ageing to red		Z5		Climbing Floribunda
Constance Spry®	🏆	pink		Z5		Climbing/Shrub English rose)
'Debutante'		pink		Z5		Rambler
'Desprez à Fleurs Jaunes'	🏆	soft yellow		Z7	H	Noisette
'Dundee Rambler'		white		Z5		Rambler
'Edmond Proust'		light pink		Z5		Rambler
'Elisa Robichon'		pale blush		Z5		Rambler
'Emily Gray'		soft yellow		Z6		Rambler
'Félicité Perpétue'	🏆	white with pink blush		Z5	H	Rambler
filipes 'Kiftsgate'	🏆	white	V	Z5		Rambler
'Flora'		pink	V	Z5		Rambler
'Francis E. Lester'	🏆	pink		Z5		Rambler
'François Juranville'	🏆	salmon		Z5		Rambler
'Gardenia'		creamy white		Z7	H	Rambler
helenae		white	V	Z5		Rambler
'Jean Guichard'		deep pink		Z7	H	Rambler
'Kew Rambler'		pink		Z5		Rambler
'Lamarque'		white		Z7	H	Noisette
'Léontine Gervais'		apricot pink blend		Z5		Rambler
longicuspis var. *sinowilsonii*		white	V	Z5		Rambler
'Lykkefund'		white, shaded pale apricot	V	Z5		Rambler
mulliganii	🏆	white	V	Z5		Rambler
'New Dawn'		pale pink		Z5		Climbing/Rambler
'Paul Transon'	🏆	coppery salmon		Z5		Rambler
'Paul's Himalayan Musk'	🏆	pale pink	V	Z5		Rambler
'Princesse de Nassau'		cream		Z6	H	Rambler
'Princesse Louise'		white		Z5		Rambler
'Princesse Marie'		pink		Z5		Rambler
'Rambling Rector'	🏆	white	V	Z5		Rambler
'Rêve d'Or'		buff-yellow		Z7	H	Noisette
'Rose-Marie Viaud'		cerise-purple ageing grayish purple		Z5		Rambler
rubus		white	V	Z7	H	Rambler
'Ruga'		blush white		Z5		Rambler
'Seagull'	🏆	white		Z5		Rambler
'Splendens'		blush white		Z5		Rambler
'The Garland'	🏆	white	V	Z5		Rambler
'Toby Tristam'		cream		Z5		Rambler
'Treasure Trove'		pale apricot	V	Z5		Rambler
'Veilchenblau'	🏆	purple		Z5		Rambler
'Venusta Pendula'		blush white		Z5		Rambler
'Violette'		purple		Z5		Rambler
'Wedding Day'		white	V	Z5		Rambler
'Wickwar'		creamy white	V	Z5		Rambler

Roses for Walls

Here foliage and habit are less noticeable than when roses are grown on a pergola or similar structure and so coarse leaves and stiff stems are less disadvantageous. When choosing the variety, the background color of the wall should be borne in mind. For a fuller discussion of choice of varieties, see the chapter on Roses for Structure.

Name		Color	Zone		Type
'Albéric Barbier'	🏆	cream	Z6		Rambler
'Albertine'	🏆	coppery pink	Z5		Rambler
'Alchymist'		apricot-yellow	Z5		Climbing/Shrub
'Alister Stella Grey'	🏆	light yellow	Z7	H	Noisette
Altissimo®	🏆	red	Z5		Climbing
Antique '89®		pale pink edged rose red	Z5		Climbing
'Auguste Gervais'		pale apricot	Z5		Rambler
Awakening		light pink	Z5		Rambler
banksiae var. *banksiae*		white	Z8	H	Rambler
banksiae var. *lutea*	🏆	soft yellow	Z7	H	Rambler
Bantry Bay®		rich pink	Z5		Climbing Hybrid Tea
'Belle Portugaise'		light peach	Z7	H	Climbing
'Black Boy'		crimson	Z7	H	Climbing
'Blairii Number Two'	🏆	pink	Z5		Climbing Bourbon
'Bleu Magenta'		purple	Z5		Rambler
'Blossomtime'		pink	Z5		Climbing
'Bougainville'		lilac-pink	Z7	H	Noisette
'Bouquet d'Or'		apricot-yellow	Z7	H	Noisette
bracteata		white	Z7	H	Climbing
Breath of Life		peach-pink	Z5		Climbing Hybrid Tea
Casino®		yellow	Z5	H	Climbing Hybrid Tea
'Céline Forestier'	🏆	pale yellow	Z7	H	Noisette
'Chaplin's Pink Climber'		carmine-pink	Z5		Climbing
City of York		white	Z5		Climbing
Clair Matin®		pale pink	Z5		Climbing
'Claire Jacquier'		pale yellow	Z7	H	Noisette
'Climbing Blue Moon'		mauve	Z5	H	Climbing Hybrid Tea
'Climbing Cécile Brünner	🏆	pink	Z5	H	Climbing Polyantha
'Climbing Etoile de Hollande'	🏆	deep red	Z5		Climbing Hybrid Tea
Climbing Gold Badge		yellow	Z5	H	Climbing Hybrid Tea
'Climbing Iceberg'	🏆	white	Z5	H	Climbing Floribunda
'Climbing Josephine Bruce'		deep scarlet	Z5		Climbing Hybrid Tea
'Climbing Lady Hillingdon'	🏆	apricot	Z7	H	Climbing Tea
'Climbing Lady Sylvia'		pink	Z5		Climbing Hybrid Tea
'Climbing Mme Abel Chatenay'		pink	Z6	H	Climbing Hybrid Tea
'Climbing Mme Butterfly'		pale peach	Z5		Climbing Hybrid Tea
'Climbing Mme Caroline Testout'		pink	Z5		Climbing Hybrid Tea
'Climbing McGredy's Yellow'		pale yellow	Z5		Climbing Hybrid Tea
Climbing Mrs Herbert Stevens'		white	Z6	H	Climbing Hybrid Tea
'Climbing Mrs Sam McGredy'	🏆	coppery salmon	Z5		Climbing Hybrid Tea
'Climbing Niphetos'		white	Z7	H	Climbing Tea
'Climbing Ophelia'		pink	Z5		Climbing Hybrid Tea
'Climbing Paul Lédé'		peach-pink	Z7	H	Climbing Tea
'Climbing Pompon de Paris'		deep pink	Z6	H	Climbing China
'Climbing Shot Silk'	🏆	coral pink	Z5		Climbing Hybrid Tea
'Climbing Souvenir de la Malmaison'		pale pink	Z6	H	Climbing Bourbon
'Compassion'	🏆	pink	Z5		Climbing Hybrid Tea
Constance Spry®	🏆	pink	Z5		Climbing/Shrub English rose
'Cooperi'		white	Z7	H	Rambler
'Crépuscule'		apricot	Z7	H	Noisette

'Cupid'		pale peach-pink	Z5		Climbing Hybrid Tea
'Desprez à Fleurs Jaunes'	🏆	soft yellow	Z7	H	Noisette
'Dream Girl'	🏆	salmon pink	Z5		Climbing
Dublin Bay	🏆	scarlet	Z5		Climbing
'Easlea's Golden Rambler'		soft yellow	Z5		Rambler
'Emily Gray'		soft yellow	Z6		Rambler
× *fortuneana*		white	Z7	H	Rambler
'Francis E. Lester'	🏆	pink	Z5		Rambler
'François Juranville'	🏆	salmon	Z5		Rambler
Galway Bay®		cerise-coral	Z5		Climbing Hybrid Tea
'Gardenia'		creamy white	Z7	H	Rambler
'Ghislaine de Féligonde'		pale apricot	Z6		Rambler
gigantea		creamy white	Z7	H	Climber
'Gloire de Dijon'	🏆	apricot-buff	Z7	H	Climbing Tea
Gloriana '97		cerise-pink	Z5		Climbing Miniature
Golden Showers®	🏆	soft yellow	Z5		Climbing
'Grimpant Cramoisi Supérieur'		red	Z7	H	Climbing Tea
'Guinée'		deep red	Z5		Climbing Hybrid Tea
Handel®	🏆	pale pink edged cerise	Z5		Climbing
'Heideröslein'		pink	Z5		Rambler/Shrub
Highfield		yellow	Z5		Climbing Hybrid Tea
'Jean Guichard'		deep pink	Z7	H	Rambler
'Jeanne Lajoie'		pink	Z5	C	Climbing Miniature
'Kew Rambler'		pink	Z5		Rambler
'La Follette'		pink ageing carmine	Z7	H	Climbing
laevigata		white	Z7	H	Rambler
'Lamarque'		white	Z7	H	Noisette
Laura Ford	🏆	yellow ageing peach	Z5		Climbing Miniature
'Laure Davoust'		pink	Z5		Rambler
Lawinia®	🏆	rich pink	Z5		Climbing Hybrid Tea
Leaping Salmon		salmon pink	Z5		Climbing Hybrid Tea
'Léontine Gervais'		apricot-pink blend	Z5		Rambler
'Leverkusen'		pale yellow	Z5		Climbing
Little Rambler		pale pink	Z5		Climbing Miniature
'Mme Alfred Carrière'		white	Z6	H	Noisette
'Mme Driout'		pink striped carmine	Z7	H	Climbing Tea
'Mme Grégoire Staechelin'	🏆	rich pink	Z5		Climbing Hybrid Tea
'Mme Isaac Pereire'	🏆	cerise	Z5		Climbing Bourbon
'Mme Jules Gravereaux'		apricot	Z7	H	Climbing Tea
'Maigold'	🏆	golden yellow	Z5		Pimpinellifolia Hybrid
'Maréchal Niel'		soft yellow	Z7	H	Noisette
'Meg'		peach-pink	Z5		Climbing Hybrid Tea
'Mermaid'	🏆	pale yellow	Z6	H	Climbing
'New Dawn'		pale pink	Z5		Climbing/Rambler
Nice Day		salmon pink	Z5		Climbing Miniature
Night Light®		golden yellow	Z5		Climbing
× *odorata* 'Pseudindica' (Fortune's double yellow)		peach	Z7	H	Climbing China
'Parade'	🏆	cerise	Z5		Climbing
Parure d'Or®		soft yellow, edges suffused deep pink	Z5		Climbing Hybrid Tea
'Paul Transon'	🏆	coppery salmon	Z5		Rambler
'Paul's Lemon Pillar'		pale lemon	Z5		Climbing Hybrid Tea
Penny Lane		blush with pale peach center	Z5		Climbing
'Phyllis Bide	🏆	pale peach blend	Z5		Rambler
'Pink Perpétué'		pink	Z5		Climbing
Polka®		peach	Z5		Climbing (Romantica® series)
'Rêve d'Or'		buff-yellow	Z7	H	Noisette
'Rose-Marie Viaud'		cerise-purple ageing grayish purple	Z5		Rambler
'Rosy Mantle'		deep pink	Z5		Climbing
'Royal Gold'		golden yellow	Z5	H	Climbing
'Sander's White Rambler'	🏆	white	Z5		Rambler
'Schoolgirl'		apricot	Z5		Climbing
'Sombreuil'		white	Z7	H	Climbing Tea
'Souvenir d'Alphonse Lavallée'		deep red	Z5		Climbing Hybrid Perpetual
'Souvenir de Claudius Denoyel'		deep red	Z5		Climbing Hybrid Tea
'Souvenir de Mme Léonie Viennot'		coppery pink	Z7	H	Climbing Tea
'Souvenir du Docteur Jamain'		deep red	Z5		Climbing Hybrid Perpetual
Sparkling Scarlet		scarlet	Z5		Climbing Floribunda
Super Dorothy®		pink	Z5		Rambler
Super Excelsa®		crimson	Z5		Rambler
Super Fairy		pink	Z5		Rambler
Super Sparkle		crimson	Z5		Rambler
'Swan Lake'		pale blush pink	Z5		Climbing
Sympathie®		crimson	Z5		Climbing
'Tausendschön'		peach blend	Z5	H	Rambler
'Tea Rambler'		pink	Z5		Rambler
'Veilchenblau'	🏆	purple	Z5		Rambler
'Violette'		purple	Z5		Rambler
'Vicomtesse Pierre du Fou'		red ageing coral	Z6	H	Climbing Hybrid Tea
Warm Welcome	🏆	vermilion	Z5		Climbing Miniature
White Cockade®	🏆	white	Z5		Climbing
'William Allen Richardson'		apricot-yellow	Z7	H	Noisette

Taller Bush Roses

I have selected this list because I think this size and character of rose exceptionally useful when grouped in the mixed border. Though most are Hybrid Teas or Floribundas, a couple of similar Shrub varieties are included. Many are also suitable for hedges, though some have ugly ankles that need to be hidden.

Alexander®	🏆	vermilion	Z5		Hybrid Tea
Cardinal Song		red	Z5		Hybrid Tea/Grandiflora
Chinatown®		yellow	Z5		Floribunda/Shrub
'Fervid'		scarlet	Z5		Floribunda
'Fred Loads'		vermilion	Z5		Floribunda
Gold Medal®		golden yellow	Z5		Hybrid Tea/Grandiflora
Grand Nord®		ivory white	Z5		Hybrid Tea
Loving Memory		deep red	Z5		Hybrid Tea
'Magenta'		mauve-pink	Z5		Hybrid Tea
'Mister Lincoln'		deep red	Z5		Hybrid Tea
Octavia Hill		pink	Z5		Floribunda/Shrub
Oranges and Lemons™		yellow striped vermilion	Z5		Shrub/Floribunda
Pearl Drift®		pearly white	Z5		Shrub
Prima	🏆	blush pink	Z5		Shrub/Floribunda
Royal Dane®		vermilion	Z5		Hybrid Tea
Solitaire®		yellow flushed pink	Z5		Hybrid Tea
'The Queen Elizabeth'	🏆	pink	Z5		Floribunda/Grandiflora
Tintinara		light red	Z5		Hybrid Tea
Tournament of Roses		pink	Z5		Hybrid Tea/Grandiflora
Uncle Walter		deep red	Z5		Hybrid Tea/Shrub

Some Roses that Should Be More Widely Grown

The following few roses are not widely available around the world, though I think each is excellent and can play a valuable role in the garden, often not duplicated by any other variety. This is therefore a challenge to nurseries to propagate and promote them and an exhortation to gardeners to buy and use them whenever they become available.

'Alexandre Tremouillet'	creamy white with pale yellow center	Z5		Rambler
Awakening	light pink	Z5		Rambler
'Beau Narcisse'	purplish mauve	Z4	C	Gallica
'Blossomtime'	pink	Z5		Climbing
Centenaire de Lourdes®	pink	Z5		Floribunda
'Cymbifolia'	white	Z4	C	Alba
'Declic'	lilac-pink	Z5		Shrub
Douceur Normande®	coral pink	Z4	C	Shrub/Ground Cover
'Edmond Proust'	light pink	Z5		Rambler
'Elisa Robichon'	pale blush	Z5		Rambler
'Geschwinds Nordlandsrose'	pale pink	Z5	C	Rambler
'Geschwinds Orden'	cerise	Z5	C	Rambler
'Heideröslein'	pink	Z5		Rambler/Shrub
Heideschnee®	white	Z5		Ground Cover
'Horstmanns Rosenresli'	white	Z5		Floribunda
'Indigo'	purple	Z5		Damask Portland
International Herald Tribune®	amaranth purple	Z5		Floribunda
'James Veitch'	purple	Z5		Damask Portland Moss
'Laure Davoust'	light pink	Z5		Rambler
'Le Rire Niais'	pink	Z5		Centifolia
'Léon Lecomte'	pink	Z5		Damask
'Menja'	pale blush pink	Z5		Shrub
'Neige d'Avril'	white	Z5		Rambler
Parure d'Or®	soft yellow, edges suffused deep pink	Z5		Climbing Hybrid Tea
'Paul Noël'	coppery pink	Z5		Rambler
Pheasant (syn. Heidekönigin®)	pink	Z5		Climbing Miniature/ Ground Cover
'Sourire d'Orchidée'	pale flesh pink	Z5		Shrub

First Stages in the Evolution of Garden Roses in Europe pre–1800

by Gordon D. Rowley *after* Hurst, 1941 *and* mss.

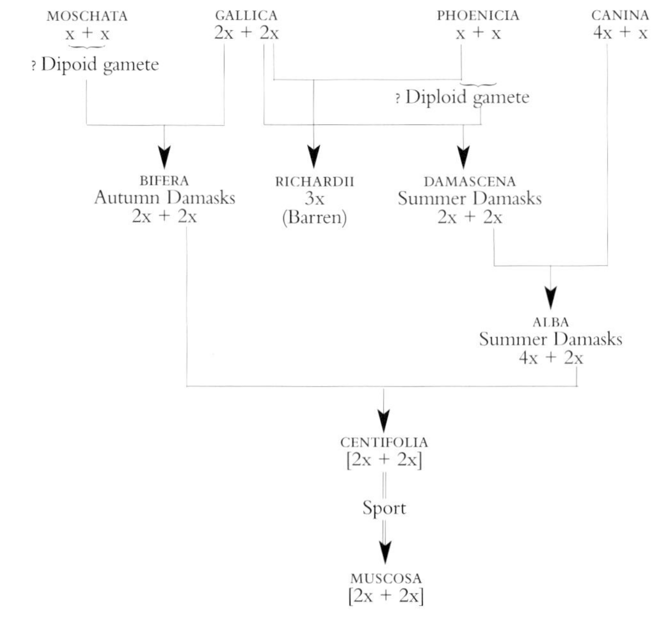

Simplified Genealogy of the Main Groups of Garden Roses

by Gordon D. Rowley *after* Hurst, 1941

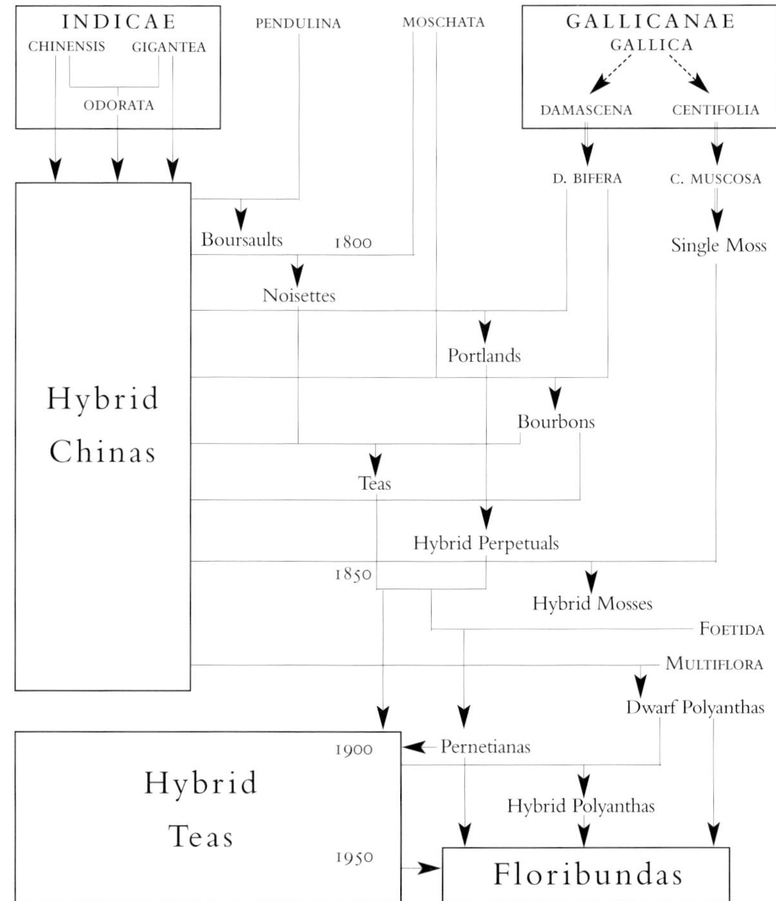

A single line indicates hybridization
A double line indicates sporting
A dotted line indicates possible relationship

Bibliography

The following list of bibliographic sources is by no means exhaustive but lists some of the works used in the preparation of this book. The editions cited are not preferred over others nor are they necessarily the most recent - they just happen to be the ones I own - but in most cases the earliest editions were also checked to assess to what extent rosarians' opinions changed over the years. The *American Rose Annual* is recommended for useful local information on rose growing in almost every one of the United States; the Heritage Rose Group has seven regional groups and publishes a quarterly Rose Letter. In Australia, the *Australian Rose Annual* includes yearly categorized lists of recommended roses from each of the state rose societies and there is a society for those interested in old roses, Heritage Roses in Australia Inc. The Royal National Rose Society issues a quarterly journal, *The Rose*, and has a Historic Roses Group, issuing a six-monthly magazine. The catalogues of local rose nurseries are also a source of much useful information about which roses are most likely to thrive in your own area.

American Rose Annual. (1917 et seq.) American Rose Society.

Austin, D. (1988). *The Heritage of the Rose*. Antique Collectors' Club, Woodbridge, Suffolk.

Austin, D. (2nd ed. 1996). *English Roses*. Conran Octopus, London.

Balmori, D., McGuire, D.K. & McPeck, E.M. (1985). *Beatrix Farrand's American Landscapes*. Sagapress, Sagaponack, New York.

Bates, H.E. (1971). *A Love of Flowers*. Michael Joseph, London.

Beales, P. (1992). *Roses*. Harvill, London.

Beales, P. (1996). *Visions of Roses*. Little, Brown & Co., London.

Beales, P., Cairns, T., Duncan, W. et al. (1998). *Botanica's Roses* (with CD-ROM). Grange Books, Rochester, Kent.

Bean, W.J. (8th ed. Vol. 4 1980, ed. Taylor, G. & Clarke, D.L. & Supp. 1988 ed. Clarke, D.L.). *Trees and Shrubs Hardy in the British Isles*. John Murray, London.

Bowles, E.A. (1914, reprinted 1972). *My Garden in Summer*. David & Charles, Newton Abbot, Devon.

Brickell, C.D. (ed.). (1996). RHS *A-Z Encyclopedia of Garden Plants*. Dorling Kindersley, London.

Buist, R. (1844). *The Rose Manual*. Philadelphia.

Bunyard, E.A. (1937). *Old Garden Roses*. Country Life, London.

Cairns, T. (ed.). (1993). *Modern Roses 10: The Comprehensive List of Roses of Historical and Botanical Importance Including All Modern International Rose Registrations*. American Rose Society, Shreveport, Louisiana.

Cochet-Cochet, P. & Mottet, S. (5th ed. 1925). *Les Rosiers*. Librairie Octave Doin, Paris.

Collins, D. & Sharp, M.L. (2nd ed. 1957). *Roses Illustrated and How to Grow Them*. Portland Rose Society, Oregon.

Dickerson, B.C. (1992). *The Old Rose Advisor*. Timber Press, Portland, Oregon.

Dobson, B.R. & Schneider, P. (Published annually). *The Combined Rose List*. P. Schneider, Mantua, Ohio.

Don, G. (Vol. 2 1832). *A General History of the Dichlamydeous Plants*. Gilbert & Rivington, London.

Eagle, B. & D. (1996). *Growing Miniature and Patio Roses*. Cassell, London.

Edland, H. (1963). *The Pocket Encyclopaedia of Roses*. Blandford Press, London.

Elliott, B. (1986). *Victorian Gardens*. Batsford, London.

Farrer, R. (1909). *In a Yorkshire Garden*. Edward Arnold, London.

Fearnley-Whittingstall, J. (1980). *Rose Gardens*. Chatto & Windus, London.

Foster-Melliar, A. (1910). *The Book of the Rose*. Macmillan, London.

Gault, S.M. & Synge, P.M. (1971). *The Dictionary of Roses in Colour*. Ebury Press & Michael Joseph, London.

Girouard, M. (1983). *Robert Smythson and The Elizabethan Country House*. Yale University Press, London.

Gore, C.F. (1838). *The Book of Roses or the Rose Fancier's Manual*. Henry Colburn, London.

Greuter, W. et al. (ed.). (1994). *International Code of Botanical Nomenclature* (Tokyo Code). Koeltz Scientific Books, Königstein, Germany.

Griffiths, T. (1990). *A Celebration of Old Roses*. Michael Joseph, London.

Groen, J. van der. (1670). *Den Nederlandtsen Hovenier*. Amsterdam.

Groeningen, I. Van. (1996). *The Development of Herbaceous Planting in Britain and Germany from the Nineteenth to Early Twentieth Century*. University of York.

Harkness, J. (1985). *The Makers of Heavenly Roses*. Souvenir Press, London.

Harvey-Cant, F.S. (1951). *Rose Selection and Cultivation*. Macgibbon & Kee, London.

Haw, S.G. (1996). *The New Plantsman*, 3(3): 143-46. Royal Horticultural Society, London.

Hayden, R. (1980). *Mrs Delany: her life and her flowers*. Colonnade Books, London.

Henslow, T.G.W. (1922). *The Rose Encyclopaedia*. Vickery, Kirle & Co., London.

Hessayon, D.G. (1996). *The New Rose Expert*. Expert Books, London.

Hibberd, S. (2nd ed. 1895). *Rustic Adornments for Homes of Taste*. Collingridge, London.

Hillier *Manual of Trees and Shrubs*. (1991). 6th ed. David & Charles, Newton Abbot, Devon.

Hobhouse, P. & Wood, C. (1988). *Painted Gardens: English Watercolours 1850-1914*. Pavilion Books, London.

Hole, S.R. (1892). *A Book about The Garden*. Edward Arnold, London.

Hole, S.R. (1904). *A Book about Roses*. Edward Arnold, London.

Huxley, A. (ed.). (1992). *The New Royal Horticultural Society Dictionary of Gardening*. Macmillan, London.

Index Kewensis on CD-ROM. (Version 2 1997). Oxford University Press.

Jekyll, G. (1896). *Wood and Garden*. Longmans, Green & Co., London.

Jekyll, G. (6th ed. 1925). *Colour Schemes for the Flower Garden*. Country Life, London. (Revised ed. 1988). Frances Lincoln, London.

Jekyll, G. & Mawley, E. (1902). *Roses for English Gardens*. Country Life, London.

Jekyll, G. & Weaver, L. (1912). *Gardens for Small Country Houses*. Country Life, London.

Johnson, A.T. (1938). *The Garden To-day*. My Garden, London.

Johnson, A.T. (1949). *The Mill Garden*. Collingridge, London.

Keays, E.E. (1935). *Old Roses*. Macmillan, New York.

Krüssmann, G. (1981). *The Complete Book of Roses*. Timber Press, Portland, Oregon.

Krüssmann, G. (1986). *Manual of Cultivated Broad-leaved Trees and Shrubs*. Batsford, London.

Lièvre, A. le. (1980). *Miss Willmott of Warley Place*. Faber & Faber, London.

Lindley, J. (1820). *Rosarum Monographia: or a Botanical History of Roses*. James Ridgway, London.

Lloyd, C. (1957). *The Mixed Border*. Collingridge, London.

Lloyd, C. (1983). *The Adventurous Gardener*. Allen Lane, London.

Lord, W.A. (1994). *Best Borders*. Frances Lincoln, London.

Lord, W.A. (1995). *Gardening at Sissinghurst*. Frances Lincoln, London.

Lord, W.A. (ed.). (1998, published annually). *The RHS Plant Finder*. Dorling Kindersley, London.

Loudon, J.C. (1822). *An Encyclopaedia of Gardening*. London.

Ottewill, D. (1989). *The Edwardian Garden*. Yale University Press, London.

McCann, S. (1985). *Miniature Roses*. David & Charles, Newton Abbot, Devon.

McFarland, J.H. (1937). *Roses of the World in Colour*. Cassell, London.

Miller, P. (Vol. 1, 4th ed. 1743). *The Gardeners Dictionary*. London.

Miller, P. (Vol. 2, 2nd ed. 1740). *The Gardeners Dictionary*. London.

Moody, M. (ed.). (1993). *The Illustrated Encyclopedia of Roses*. Headline Book Publishing, London.
Paterson, A. (1983). *The History of the Rose*. Collins, London.
Park, B. (1956). *Collins Guide to Roses*. Collins, London.
Paul, W. (1848). *The Rose Garden. Sherwood*, Gilbert & Piper, London.
Paul, W. (1892). *Contributions to Horticultural Literature* (1843-1892). London.
Pawsey, A. (1998, published annually). *Find That Rose!* British Rose Growers' Association, Colchester, Essex.
Phillips, R. & Rix, M. (1988). *Roses*. Macmillan, London.
Phillips, R. & Rix, M. (1993). *The Quest for the Rose*. BBC Books, London.
Prince, W.R. (1846). *Prince's Manual of Roses*. Prince, New York.
Pronville, A. de. (1818). *Nomenclature Raisonnée des Espèces, Variétés et Sous-variétés du Genre Rosier*. Huzard, Paris.
Redouté's Roses. (1990). *Wordsworth Editions*, Ware, Hertfordshire.
Robinson, W. (4th ed. 1894). *The Wild Garden*. Oxford.
Robinson, W. (6th ed. 1898). *The English Flower Garden*. John Murray, London.
Rohde, E.S. (1934). *Gardens of Delight*. Medici Society, London.
The Rose Annual. (1907-84). National (later Royal National) Rose Society.
Russell, V. (1995). *Monet's Garden*. Frances Lincoln, London.
Sackville-West, V. (1951). *In Your Garden*. Michael Joseph, London.
Sackville-West, V. (1953). *In Your Garden Again*. Michael Joseph, London.
Sackville-West, V. (1955). *More For Your Garden*. Michael Joseph, London.
Sackville-West, V. (1958). *Even More For Your Garden*. Michael Joseph, London.
Scaniello, S. (1995). *Easy-care Roses*. Brooklyn Botanic Garden, New York.
Scarman, J. (1996). *Gardening with Old Roses*. HarperCollins, London.
Sinclair, A. & Thodey, R. (1993). *Gardening with Old Roses*. Cassell, London.
Shepherd, R.E. (1954). *History of the Rose*. Macmillan, New York.
Steen, N. (1967). *The Charm of Old Roses*. Herbert Jenkins, London.
Thomas, G.S. (1987). *A Garden of Roses*. Pavilion Books, London.
Thomas, G.S. (1995). *The Graham Stuart Thomas Rose Book*. John Murray, London.
Thomas, G.S. (1997). *Cuttings from My Garden Notebooks*. John Murray, London.
Thomas, H.H. (2nd ed. 1920). *The Rose Book*. Cassell, London.
Trehane, R.P. (1995). *International Code of Nomenclature for Cultivated Plants - 1995*. Quarterjack Publishing, Wimborne, Dorset.
Tutin, T.G. et al. (1968). *Flora Europaea* (Vol. 2 - Rosaceae to Umbelliferae). Cambridge University Press.
Verrier, S. (1996). *Rosa gallica*. Florilegium, Balmain, NSW, Australia.
Warner, C. (1987). *Climbing Roses*. Century Hutchinson, London.
Weston, R. (1775). *The English Flora: or a Catalogue of Trees, Shrubs, Plants and Fruits*. London.
Willson, E.J. (1982). *West London Nursery Gardens*. Fulham and Hammersmith Historical Society, London.

Rose Nurseries

Much the most useful guide to availability of rose varieties world-wide is *The Combined Rose List* by Bev Dobson and Peter Schneider, published annually and available form Peter Schneider, P.O. Box 677, Mantua, Ohio, USA. Many countries have their own plant finders covering more or less all garden plants including roses. For the British Isles, *Find That Rose!* and *The RHS Plant Finder* are published annually, as is PPP Index (European sources including British Isles). The Andersen List gives sources in the United States and is published every few years. Your local rose nursery is likely to be a helpful source of advice about the best roses for your own area and climate.

Australia

Golden Vale Nursery, Golden Vale Rd, P.O. Box 66, Benalla, Victoria 3672.
Tel. & Fax (61) 03 5762 1520 Export: Interstate

Reliable Roses, George Road, Silvan, Victoria 3795.
Tel. (61) 03 9737 9313 Export: Interstate

Swane Bros Pty Ltd, 490 Galston Rd, (P.O. Box 29), Dural, NSW 2158
Tel. (61) 02 651 1322 Fax (61) 02 651 2146 Export: Interstate

Belgium

Pépinières Louis Lens s.a., Rudy Velle, Redinnestraat 11, 8460 Oudenburg
Tel. (32) 059 267 830 Fax (32) 059 265 614 Export: Yes

Canada

Carl Pallek & Son Nurseries, Box 137, Highway #55, Virgil, Ontario L0S 170
Tel. (1) 905 468 7262 Fax 905 468 5246 Export: Canada only

Pickering Nurseries Inc., 670 Kingston Road, Pickering, Ontario L1V 1A6
Tel. (1) 905 839 2111 Fax 905 839 4807 Export: USA & Canada only

Denmark

Rosenplanteskolen i Løve, Plantevej 3, 4270 Høng
Tel. (45) 5356 9313 Fax (45) 5359 9019 Export: Yes

France

SA Meilland Richardier, 50, rue Professeur Depéret, 69160 Tassin-la-demi-Lune
Tel. (33) 04 78 34 00 34 Fax (33) 04 72 38 09 97 Export: Yes

Roseraie de Berty, 07110 Largentière
Tel. (33) 04 75 88 30 56 Fax (33) 04 75 88 36 93 Export: Yes

Roseraie Guillot, Domaine de la Plaine, Chamagnieu, 38460 Crémieu
Tel. (33) 04 74 90 27 55 Fax (33) 04 74 90 27 17 Export: Yes

Les Roses Anciennes de André Eve, B.P. 206, 28, Morailles, Pithiviers-le-Viel, 45300 Pithiviers
Tel. (33) 16 38 30 01 30 Fax (33) 16 38 30 71 65 Export: Yes

Rosiers Anciens Bernard Boureau, 28 bis, rue du Maréchal Galliéni, 77166 Grisy Suisnes
Tel. (33) 64 05 91 83 Fax (33) 64 05 97 66 Export: No

Germany
Rosen von Schultheis, Bad Nauheimer Str. 3-7, 61231 Bad Nauheim-Steinfurth
Tel. (49) 06032 81013 Fax (49) 06032 85890 Export: Yes

Rosenschulen W. Kordes' Söhne GmbH & Co KG, Rosenstrasse 54, 25365 Klein Offenseth - Sparrieshoop
Tel. (49) 04121 48700 Fax (49) 04121 84745 Export: Yes

Italy
Walter Branchi, Le Rose, Corbara 55, 1-005019 Orvieto (Terni)
Tel. & Fax (39) 0763 304154 Export: Yes

Rose & Rose Emporium, Contrado Fossalto 9, 05015 Fabro (Terni)
Tel. (39) 0763 82812 Fax (39) 0763 82828 Export: Yes

Netherlands
Belle Epoque Rosenkwekerij, J.D. Maarse en Zonen B.D., Oosteinderweg 489, 1432 BJ Aalsmeer
Tel. (31) 02977 42546 Fax (31) 02977 40597 Export: Yes

New Zealand
Camp Hill Roses, Wharetoa 4RD, Balclutha.
Tel. & Fax (64) 03 415 9039 e-mail camphill.roses@xtra.co.nz
Export: No

Southern Cross Nurseries, Prebbleton, Christchurch.
Tel. (64) 03 349 3051 Fax (64) 03 349 9460 Export: Yes

South Africa
Eden Rose Nursery c.c., P.O. Box 719, Noorder Paarl 7623
Tel. (27) 021 868 3194 Fax (27) 021 868 3105 Export: No

Ludwigs Rose Farm c.c., P.O. Box 28165, 0132 Sunnyside, Pretoria
Tel. (27) 012 5440144 Fax (27) 012 5440813
e-mail ludroses@smartnet.co.za Export: No

United Kingdom
David Austin Roses, Bowling Green Lane, Albrighton, Wolverhampton, WV7 3HB
Tel. (44) 01902 373931 Fax (44) 01902 372142 Export: Yes

Peter Beales Roses, London Road, Attleborough, Norfolk, NR17 1AX
Tel. (44) 01953 454707 Fax (44) 01953 456845
e-mail sales@classicroses.co.uk Export: Yes

James Cocker & Sons, Whitemyres, Lang Stracht, Aberdeen AB9 2XH, Scotland
Tel. (44) 01224 313261 Fax (44) 01224 312531 Export: Yes

R. Harkness & Co. Ltd, The Rose gardens, Hitchin, Herts. SG4 0JT
Tel. (44) 0462 420402 Fax (44) 0462 422170 Export: Yes

Mattock's Roses, The Rose Nurseries, Nuneham Courtenay, Oxford OX44 9PY
Tel. (44) 01865 343265 Fax (44) 01865 343267 Export: Yes

United States
Lowe's Own-Root Roses, 6 Sheffield Road, Nashua, NH 03062-3028
Tel. (1) 603 888 2214 Export: Yes

The Mini-Rose Garden, P.O. Box 203, Cross Hill, SC 29332
Tel. (1) 864 998 4331 Export: USA only

Nor'East Miniature Roses, Inc., P.O. Box 307, Rowley, MA 01969
Tel. (1) 508 948 7964 Export: USA only

Royall River Roses, 70 New Gloucester Road, North Yarmouth, Maine 04097
Tel. (1) 207 829 5830 Fax (1) 207 829 6512 Export: USA & Canada only

Spring Valley Roses, P.O. Box 7, N7637 330th Street, Spring Valley, WI 54767
Tel. (1) 715 778 4481 e-mail svroses@win.bright.net
Export: USA only

Wayside Gardens, 1 Garden Lane, Hodges, SC 29695-0001
Tel. (1) 1 800 845 1124 Export: USA only

Hardiness Zones

The hardiness zone ratings given for each plant – indicated in the index by the letter "Z" and the relevant zone number – suggest the appropriate minimum temperature a plant will tolerate in winter. However, this can only be a rough guide. The hardiness depends on a great many factors, including the depth of a plant's roots, its water content at the onset of frost, the duration of cold weather, the force of the wind, and the length of, and the temperatures encountered during, the preceding summer. The zone ratings are those devised by the United States Department of Agriculture.

Celsius	Zones	°Fahrenheit
below -45	1	below -50
-45 to -40	2	-50 to -40
-40 to -34	3	-40 to -30
-34 to -29	4	-30 to -20
-29 to -23	5	-20 to -10
-23 to -18	6	-10 to 0
-18 to -12	7	0 to 10
-12 to -7	8	10 to 20
-7 to -1	9	20 to 30
-1 to 4	10	30 to 40
above 4	11	above 40

Index

Page nos in **bold** refer to principal references. Page nos in *italics* refer to illustration captions. For an explanation of hardiness zones (not given for annuals), e.g. Z7, see p 185.

Author's Acknowledgments

I am particularly grateful to all at Frances Lincoln who have helped to produce this book, especially Jo Christian, Penelope Miller, Trish Going, Sarah Mitchell, Serena Dilnot, Ginny Surtees, Jo Grey, Sarah Pickering, Simon Towler and Erica Hunningher. John Elsley has provided most useful advice about roses in North America and Brent Elliott and Jan Woudstra on matters of garden history. My thanks go also to owners, managers and gardeners of all the rose gardens I photographed who went out of their way to help and allowed me to visit at antisocial hours; I am especially grateful to those at Bagatelle, Elsing Hall, Giverny, Helmingham Hall, Mottisfont Abbey, the Roseraie Départementale du Val-de-Marne and Sudeley Castle for their kindness and co-operation.

T.L.

Publisher's Acknowledgments

Project Editor Jo Christian
Editor Penelope Miller
Editorial Assistance Tom Armstrong
Tom Windross

Art Editor Trish Going
Picture Research Sue Gladstone
Production Stephen Stuart

Horticultural Consultant John Elsley
Art Director Caroline Hillier
Head of Pictures Anne Fraser

Photographic Acknowledgments
All photographs copyright © Tony Lord, except for the following:

Jonathan Buckley 68 (Helen Yemm's garden, London), 126 (Chenies Manor, Buckinghamshire), 160 (Hollington Nurseries, Buckinghamshire)

John Fielding 131

Jerry Harpur 31 (Cellars Hotel, Constantia, Cape, South Africa), 64-65 (Stellenberg, Cape Town, South Africa), 85 (Stellenberg, Cape Town, South Africa), 104 (Cottage Garden Roses, Stretton, Staffordshire)

Andrew Lawson 1, 23, 44, 77, 80 (RHS Chelsea Flower Show, 1994), 91 (Briar Rose Cottage, Orinoco, New Zealand), 111, 122 (Kiftsgate Court, Chipping Campden, Gloucestershire)

Georges Lévêque 109 (Barnsley House, Gloucestershire), 123 (Mrs Louise Warne, Frith Hill, Near Petworth, West Sussex)

S & O Mathews 62

The National Gallery, London 19 (*Flowers in a Terracotta Vase* 1736, Jan van Huysum)

Clive Nichols /Meadow Plants, Berkshire 112-113

Clay Perry 4-5, 38-39 (David Austin Roses, Albrighton, Shropshire), 52-53 (Lord & Lady Ashcombe, Sudeley Castle Gardens, Winchcombe, Gloucestershire)

Stephen Robson 2-3 (Trostrey Lodge), 56-57 (Trostrey Lodge), 86-87 (Heale House, Wiltshire), 92-93 (Hailsham Grange), 94-95 (Trostrey Lodge), 143 (Trostrey Lodge)

Royal Horticultural Society, Lindley Library 20

Vivian Russell 132, 147, 149 (Mirabel Osler), 166-167 (Mirabel Osler)

Juliette Wade 74-75 (Mr & Mrs Owen, The Old Chapel, Chalford, Gloucestershire), 82 (Gwen Bishop, Combe, Oxfordshire)

Steve Wooster © FLL 133 (Beth Chatto)